IMS CRASH COURSE

IMS Crash Course

Steven Shepard

McGraw-Hill

New York   Chicago   San Francisco   Lisbon
London   Madrid   Mexico City   Milan
New Delhi   San Juan   Seoul   Singapore
Sydney   Toronto

The **McGraw·Hill** Companies

Library of Congress Cataloging-in-Publication Data is on file.

2 3 4 5 6 7 8 9 0   FGR/FGR   0 1 9 8 7 6

ISBN 0-07-226306-7

The sponsoring editor for this book was Jane Brownlow and the production
supervisor was David Zielonka. It was set in New Century Schoolbook by Patricia
Wallenburg.

Printed and bound by Quebecor Fairfield

This book is for my son, Steven Junior.
How wonderful to have a son that I can look up to—
And I don't mean physically.
I love you.

CONTENTS

Contents

Contents

ACKNOWLEDGMENTS

I'd like to begin with very special thanks to my old friend Kenn Sato for his usual high degree of editing skill and literary pushback. Kenn, thanks also for your engaging e-mail messages. Few things give me as much enjoyment as one of your so-wonderful-to-read missives in my in-box after a long and exhausting airplane ride to who knows where. As I write this, I am sitting at the dining room table in my apartment in Johannesburg, having just read your most recent message about the novel we're writing together. Thanks for the energy.

For their generous contributions and counsel and for the honor of call-ing you all friends, I also thank Phil Asmundson, Kim Barker, Paul Bedell, Jane Brownlow, Peter Carbone, Phil Cashia, Steve Chapman, Anthony Contino, Jonathan Dunne, Andy Harrs, Dave Heckman, Issac-Aaron Jayaraj, Tony Kern, Charles Krempa, Dee Marcus, Roy Marcus, Gary Martin, Dennis McCooey, Paul McDonagh-Smith, Tom McNulty, Jim Nason, Alan Nurick, Chris O'Gorman, Dick Pecor, Kenn Sato, Karen Schopp, Dave Schultz, Mary Slaughter, Fernando Toledo, Calvin Tong, Craig Wigginton, and Morley Winograd.

Sabine, Steve, Cristina, Mom, and Dad, thank you for being my fam-ily. What a wonderful life you have given me.

■ **FOREWORD** ■ ■ ■

As many of you know, I have written quite a few books—31 of them if my count is accurate. As an author I am about as professionally schizophrenic as a person can get without needing medication. On the non-telecom side of the bookshelf I've written about scuba diving (*Commotion in the Ocean: A Technical Diving Manual*), California history (*A Matter of Last Resort: The Story of Byron Hot Springs*), and the difficulties of cultural reentry (*Managing Cross-Cultural Transition: A Handbook for Corporations, Employees and Their Families*). On the more technical end of things I have written about convergence (*Telecommunications Convergence*, first and second editions), basic telecom (*Telecom Crash Course*, first and second editions), SONET and SDH (*SONET and SDH Demystified*), videoconferencing (*Videoconferencing Demystified*), VoIP (*VoIP Crash Course*), metro networks (*Metro Networks Demystified*), optical networking (*Optical Networking Crash Course*), and RFID. Somewhere along the way, just for fun, I wrote a Spanish-English telecom dictionary.

All those titles, especially the technology-related books, have one common characteristic: They are all about reasonably well defined and mature topics. In each case I chose to write about the topic because of a desire to link a technical and often difficult-to-understand technology to the market it addresses, thus increasing its relevance in the hearts and minds of readers. Never have I tried to supplant the relevance or effectiveness of other more technical titles; my only goal has been to provide social, economic, cultural, and business relevance.

This one is a bit different, and I owe it to my readers to preface the book with an explanation. This book is about the IP Multimedia Subsystem, commonly known as IMS. IMS is a much talked about, much anticipated, extraordinarily interesting enigma. Enigma? Yes, indeed. I choose that word very carefully. An enigma is defined as something that is "puzzling, ambiguous, inexplicable." It comes from the Greek word *ainigma*, which means "to speak in riddles." The *reason* I choose that word is that the more I studied IMS in preparation for writing this book, the more I realized that I'm writing about (and this is being generous) a technology that is still very much in its infancy. *Embryonic* may be a more accurate characterization of its state of development and deployment, but I'll be generous and stick with *infancy*.

That said, let me add this: After studying IMS for many months and conducting interviews with people in the industry who are far more technical than I am, I came to several relevant conclusions. First and foremost, IMS is a new, well-defined, but hazily understood technology family. It is awash in standards, but as the old joke goes, the nice thing about standards is that there are so many to choose from. Standards are designed to be interpreted by implementers, and IMS has been interpreted 20 ways from Sunday by the many industry players who are jockeying for position to benefit from it.

Second, there are as many opinions about what IMS is as there are people who care. When people ask me what IMS stands for, I get a kick out of their deer-in-the-headlights reaction when my response "IP Multimedia Subsystem" leaves them no better off than they were when "IMS" was all they knew. Manufacturers and service providers be warned: IP Multimedia Subsystem is meaningless to the market. If your goal is market penetration and sticky customers, you must give them more to cling to than a catchy acronym. More on this later.

Third, and perhaps most important, in my opinion IMS represents the most powerful and defining telecommunications innovation to come along in the last 50 years. I believe this, ironically, because of the fact that it is not a technological innovation—not really. More than that, it is a social innovation on the part of manufacturers and service providers, the result of a fundamental realization on their part *that the network becomes infinitely more powerful, relevant, and revenue-centric when it adapts to the user rather than when the user is forced to adapt to the network*. Of course, this change is so fundamental that it will not come quickly or easily, but mark my words: The first manufacturer-service provider combination to get it right and roll out a service with this fundamental characteristic will win the game hands down.

Consider the following example: I hop in my car in the morning to drive to the office, briefcase in one hand and cup of coffee in the other. Driving to work, I stop at a light, and while I'm sitting there waiting for the green, my PDA beeps at me. Puzzled, I pull it from my pocket, and on the screen I see the following message:

Pay attention to what just happened. My friend Dennis called me on my home number, but the network determined that I wasn't home. Rather than send the call to voice mail, *it found me* and then offered me the option to receive the call on my PDA, since I have PocketSkype on the device and was apparently within some wireless network domain where I could be reached. In the traditional world of network services, the network would have allowed the call to ring until it went to voice mail. It would not have attempted to forward the call unless I specifically had told it to do so by call-forwarding the number and even then I'd have to decide whether to call-forward to my mobile number, or to my SkypeIn number. And even if I *had* call-forwarded my home number to my mobile, I would have missed the call because I forgot to turn the device on.

In the current scenario, the network *knew* I wasn't in the house because of the always-on GPS feature in the mobile phone. Detecting that the mobile was not powered up, the system went to a database and learned that I have Skype on my PDA and that forwarding the call to the PDA was a viable option.

See what happened? Instead of me having to think ahead and adapt to the limited capabilities of the network, the network adapted to the limited capabilities of my barely functioning early-morning brain.

Here's another scenario. Returning home from dinner one evening, my wife, Sabine, suddenly says, "Oh, I forgot. I need to run into Williams-Sonoma for just a second to pick something up. Would you mind stopping for me? I'll just be a second, and you can wait in the car."

There are several messages in that quote. The first is that "I'll just be a second" is relative. My wife in Williams-Sonoma is like me in a book-store: We operate on what I like to call Michener seconds. Ever read a James Michener novel? Why say in a paragraph what you can write (beautifully, by the way) in 170 pages? So I know that she'll be longer than she thinks. The fact that I can wait in the car is a good thing because I can't even *name* most of the things they sell in Williams-Sonoma. But I won't be bored.

We park in the parking lot, and Sabine hops out. I pull out my PDA, turn it on, press a few buttons, and voilà, a rerun of *Law and Order* appears on the screen. Perfect. Somewhere down the line I'll be billed for whatever I watch. By the way, during the commercials I flip over to the e-mail application and check messages. I don't get a welcome screen asking me which wireless provider I want to use or how much time I want to buy because the network already knows my personal preferences and sets up the session accordingly. Again, access to *my stuff* on *my terms*, not the network's.

Here's another example. Driving to work, talking on your CDMA phone, you pull into the parking lot, hop out, and walk into the lobby. Unfortunately, the steel in the structure disrupts the cellular signal, and the call begins to fade. No problem: The phone recognizes that you are standing in a WiFi hot spot and transfers the call over to the corporate LAN. You continue to talk as you walk to your office and, when you enter it and sit down, the network and your mobile phone recognize that the Bluetooth signal emanating from your desktop computer is stronger than the WiFi signal, and the call is transferred once again. No interruption in service and no decision required on your part because the network knows what you want to do and adapts accordingly.

In 2000 I wrote a book called *Telecommunications Convergence: How to Profit from the Convergence of Technologies, Companies, and Services.* In that book I described the nascent convergence phenomenon as being made up of three separate but highly related processes: the convergence of technologies, which described the inexorable movement of all networking processes toward IP; the convergence of companies, which described the feeding frenzy that characterized the height of the bubble during which companies were gobbling one another up at a frenetic pace; and the convergence of services, which described the ultimate end state, the idea that multiple mutually interactive service types could be delivered to the user, on the user's terms, via a single network interface.

Unfortunately, in 2000 this concept was ahead of its time and, when the telecom bubble collapsed under the weight of its own ridiculousness, it took convergence with it. Now, however, convergence is back, and this time it's real and it's timely. Technology convergence has picked up speed, helped along by regulatory decisions that have empowered the ILECs with recognition of the fact that the local loop is a natural monopoly while simultaneously opening the door to facilities-based competition, an opportunity that flies in the face of ILEC hegemony. Company convergence is accelerating largely because of a grudging recognition of the fact that in today's service-driven economy, companies in the telecom game have two choices: They can have some of the money or *none of the money.* Gone are the days when a single company could do it all. Alliances and partnerships are the way of the new telecom world; companies hard-pressed to learn or unwilling to engage will not last.

Finally, services convergence is the ultimate goal. Not only is it now feasible to deliver multiple service modalities over a single form of network access, multiple services can be delivered to any number of devices whenever and wherever the user wants them. Instead of the user having to adjust his or her behavior to match the limitations of the network, the network will adjust its behavior to match the increasing capabilities of the mobile user. If it fails to do so, money will not change hands. It's as simple as that.

Ultimately, IMS and convergence are one and the same thing. IMS is all about delivering the right service, to the right device, over the right access infrastructure, at the right time, for the right price. Sound complex? Perhaps. How in the world can we get the right content to the user when the user is out roaming, using who knows what device? How can we possibly find the user, and how can we possibly know what his or her service delivery preferences are? Finally, how in the world would we bill for such a thing?

Difficult questions to answer, I'll admit. However, a bit of perspective. As I write this, I am sitting at the dining room table in the little condo where I'm staying for a few weeks in Johannesburg, South Africa, while working down here. All morning long my mobile phone has been ringing with calls from the States and Europe. The callers dialed the same number they dial when I'm in the States; in fact, most of them are surprised to learn that I'm in Africa, given the quality of the connection. To make this happen, to make my phone work in Africa, *all I had to do was turn it on.* No special procedures, no special number, no outgoing message to callers telling them, "Sorry, I'm out of the country; please dial this 37-digit number to reach me." Furthermore, all the features I enjoy in the States are available to me here. Caller ID, ring tones, three-way calling, and so on, all work here as well as they do in the States.

Why is this? What makes it possible? The same technologies that make it work at home: Home Location Registers (HLRs) and Visitor Location Registers (VLRs) in the local wireless network and Signaling System Seven (SS7) in the wireline infrastructure. No magic—just a solid relationship between telephony and information technology (IT). Telephony makes the phone network operate well; IT operates the databases and access computers that give the telephone network the ability to discover my calling preferences and deliver them to me wherever and whenever I like.

This is not new: We've been doing this for years. The difference is that in the IMS world, the line between *wireline* and *wireless* disappears and the service becomes simply access. Furthermore, access takes on a whole new meaning. In the traditional telephony world, access means *access to the network.* In the IMS world, it means *access to my stuff.* Service providers must learn this and learn it fast if they are to survive the onslaught.

This book is about a set of technologies that will revolutionize service delivery and open up a broad swath of revenue opportunities for forward-thinking and fast-moving service providers. However, this is not for the faint of heart: There's risk involved, but it's prudent risk. Years ago I found this quote thumbtacked to the wall of a cubicle:

> Recognize that every out-front maneuver you make is going to be lonely and a little bit frightening. If you feel entirely comfortable, then you're not far enough ahead to do any good. That warm sense of everything going well is usually the body temperature at the center of the herd.

In today's telecom environment being at the center of the herd is not an option. Leadership is an absolute must, but having a clear understanding of exactly what leadership is before jumping into the fray is critical as well. Within the context of our industry I define leadership as an art form. It is the art of creating a vision of the future that is so powerful and so compelling that everyone around you—your peers, your subordinates, your bosses, your suppliers, and even your competitors—feels compelled to enroll in the vision to help you achieve it. Walking into a customer meeting with a technical specification, a network diagram, and a price sheet will not go far in today's increasingly competitive environment. Walking into that meeting with a vision of a user-aware network, however, will open the right doors and create the beginnings of a long-term and sticky relationship.

With all that being said and with an understanding that IMS is still in diapers, what can you expect to find in this book? First of all, you will find a great deal of justification for IMS written in business terms. We begin with a timeline that explains how we got where we are today, where we're going next, and how we're going to get there. We then dive into the specific history of IMS before explaining how it works and where it fits into the services pantheon. Next we talk about the inner workings of IMS before examining regulatory considerations that might affect its deployment. Finally, we look at the players in the IMS game: what you can expect from them, how they're positioning themselves, and what questions you should ask of them before buying.

As with all my books and by popular demand, this title includes a comprehensive acronym list and a glossary of terms. One word of warning and an apology of sorts: Because IMS is so new and so volatile, a great deal will change over the coming months and years, if for no other reason than the fact that all the players in the game recognize that there is no "end state" for IMS. It is a progression of events toward a massively evolved network and, although the bulk of those tectonic defining moments will not happen soon, they are already under way and their effects are being felt globally. Certain elements of this book therefore will be out of date as the technology changes. To this end I have written the book at a level where large-scale change will affect it only minimally and also have flagged areas where the reader should watch for updates and changes. As many of you know, I keep a constantly updated library of white papers on my website (www.ShepardComm.com) and will be posting IMS papers there very soon that will supplement this book as things evolve. That's my promise to you.

As always, thanks for lending your eyes and, in advance, thanks for the error detection. As an author, it's great when your reader is your own personal data link layer as well. Please send comments, questions, and discussion items to me at Steve@ShepardComm.com. I look forward to hearing from you. All the best!

Steven Shepard
Johannesburg, Whitefish, Ottawa, Chateaufort,
Atlanta, Raleigh, Annapolis, Williston
November 2005

ABOUT THE AUTHOR

Steven Shepard is the president of the Shepard Communications Group in Williston, Vermont. A professional author and educator with 24 years of varied experience in the telecommunications industry, he has written books and magazine articles on a wide variety of topics. His books include:

- *Telecommunications Convergence: How to Profit from the Convergence of Technologies, Services and Companie*s (McGraw-Hill, New York, 2000)
- *A Spanish-English Telecommunications Dictionary* (Shepard Communications Group, Williston, Vermont, 2001)
- *Managing Cross-Cultural Transition: A Handbook for Corporations, Employees and Their Families* (Aletheia Publications, New York, 1997)
- *An Optical Networking Crash Course* (McGraw-Hill, New York, February 2001)
- *SONET and SDH Demystified* (McGraw-Hill, 2001), *Telecom Crash Course* (McGraw-Hill, New York, October 2001)
- *Telecommunications Convergence, Second Edition* (McGraw-Hill, New York, February 2002)
- *Videoconferencing Demystified* (April 2002, McGraw-Hill)
- *Metro Networking Demystified* (McGraw-Hill, New York, October 2002)
- *RFID Demystified* (McGraw-Hill, New York, July 2004)

- *Managing Supply Chain Technology* (with Jack Garrett; in progress)
- *Telecom Crash Course, Second Edition* (McGraw-Hill, New York, June 2005); and
- *VoIP Crash Course* (McGraw-Hill, New York, July 2005)

WiMAX Crash Course and *How to Do Everything with VoIP* will be published by McGraw-Hill in early 2006.

Steve is also the Series Advisor of the McGraw-Hill *Portable Consultant* book series.

Mr. Shepard received his undergraduate degree in Spanish and Romance Philology from the University of California at Berkeley and his Masters Degree in International Business from St. Mary's College. He spent eleven years with Pacific Bell in San Francisco in a variety of capacities including network analysis, computer operations, systems standards development, and advanced technical training, followed by nine years with Hill Associates, a world-renowned telecommunications education company, before forming the Shepard Communications Group. He is a fellow of the Da Vinci Institute for Technology Management of South Africa, a member of the Board of Directors of Champlain Community Television, a Founding Director of the African Telecoms Institute, and a member of the Board of Trustees of Champlain College in Burlington, Vermont. He is also the Resident Director of the University of Southern California's Executive Leadership and Advanced Management Programs in Telecommunications, and adjunct faculty member at the University of Southern California, The Garvin School of International Management (Thunderbird University), the University of Vermont, Champlain College and St. Michael's College. He and his wife Sabine have two children.

Mr. Shepard specializes in international issues in telecommunications with an emphasis on strategic technical sales; services convergence; the social implications of technological change; the development of multilingual educational materials; and the effective use of multiple delivery media. He has written and directed more than 40 videos and films and written technical presentations on a broad range of topics for more than 70 companies and organizations worldwide. He is fluent in Spanish and routinely publishes and delivers presentations in that language. Global clients include major telecommunications manufacturers, service providers, software development firms, multinational corporations, universities, professional services firms, advertising firms, venture capital firms, and regulatory bodies.

The History and Background of IMS

The Chinese character "Wei" (top) means "danger" or "to encircle," and the character "Ji" (bottom) means "opportunity." Together they mean "crisis."

The Early History of IMS

To understand the origins of the IP Multimedia Subsystem (IMS) one must go back into the dark history of telecommunications: the 1970s, when telecom was an arcane art practiced solely by the druids and technomancers at the telephone company. More than anything else, it is necessary to examine the forces leading up to the emergence of IMS because those early forces coalesced into the driving momentum behind IMS as a technological reality. We also must examine those forces to ensure that we understand that IMS is purely a services-driven play, one of the first. Beginning in the 1970s, as information technology (IT) came into the modern corporation in a big way and soon mated itself to telecom, the promises of a services-driven technology infrastructure began to take shape.

In the 1970s, corporations were monolithic entities that were managed from the top down. The people at the top of the company held all the decision-making power, and lower-level personnel were responsible for carrying out the dictates of senior management. True to form, networks in those days were top-down entities, with all the processing power concentrated in the mainframe and all the lower-level nodes designed to carry out the whims of the central processor (there's a reason they call them dumb terminals; see Figure 1-1).

That model worked well in the days when corporations wielded all the power, as they did in the largely monopolistic environment of the telephony industry before the divestiture of AT&T in 1984. Competition, such as it was, proceeded at a stately pace, and there was no need for haste. That changed, however, after divestiture and the introduction of full-blown competition into the game. Consider the following:

A greater vulnerability than legacy assets is a legacy mindset. It may be easy to grasp this point intellectually, but it is profoundly difficult to practice. Managers must put aside the presuppositions of the old competitive world and compete according to totally new rules of engagement. They

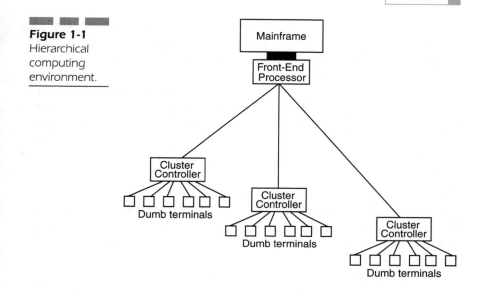

Figure 1-1
Hierarchical computing environment.

must make decisions at a different speed, long before the numbers are in place and the plans formalized. They must acquire totally new technical and entrepreneurial skills, quite different from what made their organizations (and them personally) so successful. They must manage for maximal opportunity, not minimum risk. They must devolve decision-making, install different reward structures, and perhaps even devise different ownership structures. They have little choice. If they don't deconstruct their own businesses, somebody else will do it to them.

This quote is from the remarkable book *Blown to Bits: How the New Economics of Information Transforms Strategy* by Philip Evans and Thomas S. Wurster.[1] Three points jump out from the quote. The first is in the first line, which observes that old thinking is far more harmful than old hardware. The second comes halfway through the paragraph when the authors observe that managers must manage for the achievement of maximum opportunity rather than for the minimization of risk. Finally, a bit later, the authors observe that managers must devolve decision making, moving it as far down into the corporation as they can, because they have little choice: They can do it themselves, or they can wait for a competitor to do it to them.

In response to this situation, most corporations moved to a flatter, leaner, more responsive structure, and with them evolved their IT

---

[1] Philip Evans and Thomas S. Wurster, *Blown to Bits: How the New Economics of Information Transforms Strategy*. Boston: Harvard Business School Press, 1999.

domains. The mainframe computer, instead of sitting at the center of the Ptolemaic technology universe, moved to the edge and became a giant server attached to the same network as the terminals. At the same time, the dumb terminals were replaced by far more intelligent personal computers (PCs) capable of independent decision making. For the first time, users had a modicum of control over the applications they depended on in the workplace, and the pace of business was changed forever. Instead of having to respond to the whims of the IT infrastructure, IT suddenly was forced to adapt to the demands of the individual user.

This also resulted in a fundamental change in the network. Instead of the hierarchical topology depicted in Figure 1-1, the network flattened as proletarian forces drove demand for peer-to-peer networking. Instead of all services being delivered to the user from a small number of core devices, as shown in Figure 1-2, processing capability moved from the core to the edge, resulting in service delivery from a large number of edge devices (Figure 1-3). The key result of this capability migration was far more targeted and granular service delivery on a user-by-user basis. As this evolution progressed and quality of service (QoS) advanced, users became far more demanding. They wanted more out of their network connections simply because the network was capable of giving it to them.

Somewhere along the way, though, things took a funny twist: A love affair began to grow between the users of the service, the service providers, and the underlying technologies. Technology, rather than the service, became the digital equivalent of a pheromone, the siren song that attracted the users to the network. That relationship continued for quite a few years, helped along by new applications and technologies that fed the fires of technopassion. To understand how that happened

Figure 1-2
Network-
centric service
delivery
environment.

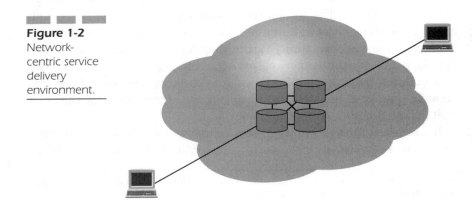

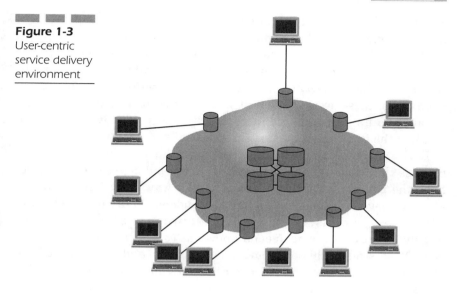

Figure 1-3
User-centric
service delivery
environment

and why, it is useful to go back and look at that remarkable—and ultimately painful—period known as the telecom bubble.

The Telecom Bubble

There are as many explanations for the speculative dot-com bubble as there are people willing to come up with them. There is also a great deal of speculation about its actual starting date. Some trace it to August 1995, when Netscape issued its initial public offering (IPO); others place it in 1973, when Vinton Cerf and Robert Kahn created Transmission Control Protocol/Internet Protocol (TCP/IP), the seminal protocol suite that underlies the Internet's remarkable functionality. Some trace it to that fateful year when Al Gore invented the Internet (sorry; couldn't resist).

I tend to place it in 1974, but for a largely nontechnical reason, as we'll see.

The Phases of Mania

Speculative bubbles typically pass through four distinct evolutionary stages as they move from inception to crash. The first stage is a shift in collective expectations, generally as a result of a widely heralded technological innovation. The eighteenth-century canal-building frenzy in the United Kingdom is one example, as are the buildups after the steam engine and railroads in the United States in the nineteenth century. In the case of the turn-of-the-century (*twenty-first* century) bubble, there were two of these events. The first was the creation of the Internet; the second was its dramatic rise in popularity and public awareness as a result of the first browsers (Mosaic, specifically).

Early adopters play an important role during this initial phase because they dispel the fear of change as the public begins to comprehend the potential of the shift that is under way. They cannot carry it alone, however. Markets have a natural tendency to resist the introduction of new products and the resulting disruption of the status quo, largely because of a phenomenon known as *equilibrium theory*. Doctor John Nash studied this phenomenon extensively and was awarded the Nobel Prize in Economics in 1994 for his work on the theory.

Basically, equilibrium theory states that markets go into equilibrium when (1) all individuals in the market believe they are making the best possible choice for themselves and (2) they believe everybody else is doing that as well. As long as everybody makes the same decisions, the market is happy and all user expectations are validated. As soon as an innovation is introduced, however, the equilibrium is disturbed as users begin to question whether they have made the best decision for themselves, since there now appears to be a viable option. Typically, markets reject a high percentage of such innovations before they achieve critical market mass because to accept them would be to admit having made a wrong decision earlier.

Nevertheless, some innovations make their way through the market's gauntlet for a variety of reasons, one of which is the need to sell beyond the earlier adopters. Although the early adopters are important members of a market community, there are typically not enough of them to overcome the market's tendency to backslide. Innovators must sell beyond the early adopters to channels, corollary product manufacturers, and even competitors if they are to succeed with their innovations. This brings on the second phase of the bubble.

The second phase is the gold rush phase, during which the technology achieves mass-market penetration, sometimes called critical mass. By this point early adopters have proved that the new innovation is safe and other members of the community have begun to use it. At this stage it achieves widespread appeal with strong growth, and a buzz begins to grow around the product or service. Think back to the late 1990s, when optical networking was the hot topic and optical start-up growth was downright viral. Or think about the early introductory stage of the iPod, the Macintosh, the Palm Pilot, or, more recently, wireless fidelity (WiFi).

The third stage is market mania, a period of unbridled euphoric overinvestment that seems to occur with very little thought about why it is happening. Stock prices rise to ridiculous levels as investment flows in, driving demand higher and higher. George Soros described this "reflexivity" phenomenon as a cycle in which the market becomes its own fuel, the economic equivalent of a perpetual motion machine. As stock prices climb, the excitement grows, causing more money to flow in, driving prices even higher. A cycle is created in which the market feeds on its own frenzied behavior. Unfortunately, this also works in the opposite direction.

Then, in phase 4, the bubble bursts. Like the little boy who had the audacity to declare the emperor naked, the harsh light of marketplace reality sooner or later reveals the flaws of overinvestment and, in a rash of sell-offs, the market declares its sanity once again and sets itself aright. During this phase companies go broke, corporate executives are accused of malfeasance, economies shrink, and balance returns. As painful as this phase may be, it is a sign that sanity never left; it just went dormant for a while.

In this section we look to the future, but to understand it we must first look back. As Alan Kay (Figure 1-4), one of the founders of modern personal computing (he cocreated Smalltalk, object-oriented programming, and the laptop computer), once observed, "The best way to predict the future is to invent it." A corollary to that is the belief that those who fail

Figure 1-4
Alan Kay.
Photo courtesy
National
Academy of
Engineering.

to heed the lessons of history are doomed to repeat it. An understanding of the future requires an appreciation of the past; let's chart the track of the perfect financial storm that ravaged the technology sector at the dawn of the twenty-first century and set the stage for the market-driven introduction of IMS.

██ Countdown

The bubble initially began to build in 1968 when Doug Engelbart (Figure 1-5), a researcher at Stanford University, demonstrated ONLine. Best known for creating the first mouse, Engelbart also is credited with the invention of the first hypertext system that allowed crude graphics to be drawn on the screen by using the mouse. ONLine was riveting, a sign of what was yet to come. It could only draw straight lines up and down and side to side, and that was enough to whet the appetites and fire the imaginations of technologists. But ONline was a stand-alone application: It needed a network to help it and systems like it achieve their full promise.

In 1969, the federal government's Advanced Research Projects Agency (ARPA) put its ARPANET online for the first time. The predecessor to the public Internet, ARPANET was the first packet-based network of its kind. It would become the connective tissue that ultimately would create the complex organism known as the Internet.

The early 1970s were years of remarkable scientific advancement in computing and networking. In 1971, Ted Hoff (Figure 1-6) at Intel cre-

Figure 1-5
Doug
Engelbart.
Photo courtesy
Stanford
University.

Figure 1-6
Ted Hoff.
Photo
courtesy Intel
Corporation.

ated the first functional microprocessor, one of the most seminal technological advancements of all time. It would go on to revolutionize all
industries, making low-cost and immensely powerful computers and networks accessible to all.

In 1973, Vinton Cerf (Figure 1-7; Cerf is on the left) and Robert Kahn
wrote the Transmission Control Protocol (TCP) and the Internet Protocol (IP), facilitating the evolution of the ARPANET from an X.25-based
packet network to TCP/IP, which was simpler and significantly more
powerful. Soon ARPANET would break free of its U.S. Department of
Defense constraints, undergoing a form of technological mitosis to create
its public Internet progeny.

The 1960s and 1970s were periods of tinkering and inventiveness in
electronics; companies such as Heathkit sold build-it-yourself packages for everything from the first color televisions to ham radio sta-

Figure 1-7
Vinton Cerf
(right) and Bob
Kahn (left).
Photos
courtesy of
Google Press
Images.

tions, and magazines such as *Popular Electronics* were, well, popular. In 1975, U.S. Air Force officer Ed Roberts, the founder of Micro Instrumentation and Telemetry Systems (MITS), built the Altair (Figures 1-8 and 1-9), in today's terms a laughably simple 2-MHz computer but one that would catalyze the industry two years later, although it would be longer before anyone realized its true impact. In 1976, Steve Wozniak and Steve Jobs, using components and concepts created largely at Xerox PARC, built the Apple I and, in 1977, came the catalytic event that would turn the industry on its ear. Two brilliant computer science buffs wrote software for Roberts's Altair. They called their company Microsoft, and their names were Bill Gates and Paul Allen. Four years later a greatly improved version of that software was licensed to IBM for use in the first personal computer. This was the beginning of history: IBM would lend an air of stability to the business of personal computing.

Time passed. The industry waxed and waned, never leaving the public consciousness for very long. The year 1984 began with a remarkable Super Bowl commercial. Dark and foreboding in the Ridley Scott style, it featured a room full of monochromatic drones mindlessly watching Big Brother (IBM) on a huge screen until a woman in red running shorts and a white tank top entered the room chased by soldiers. Before they could catch her, she heaved a sledgehammer at the screen, causing a powerful explosion and precipitating a computing evolution. The advertiser was Apple; the product ("Now you'll see why 1984 won't be like 1984!") was the Macintosh. Few people watching had ever heard of a Mac; within months they would never forget it.

Figure 1-8
The Altair.

Figure 1-9
Popular
Electronics
Magazine
featuring the
Altair.

That was also the year Cisco Systems was founded. The company did not go public until 1990, but when it did, it went public with a vengeance of acquisition. During the six-month period that ended in January 1999 the firm's revenues were a staggering $5 billion, with profits of more than $800 million.

Other Forces

The revolutionary change that was transforming the landscape was not purely technological. In 1974, just before Roberts's creation of the Altair, the federal government smoothed out a wrinkle in the fabric of the tax code. Amendment 401(K) gave ordinary people the ability to place certain kinds of income (bonuses, for example) into special tax-deferred accounts so that they could bolster their retirement funds. This may seem like a charitable act on the part of the government, but it had an ulterior motive. Personal savings in the United States had fallen to low levels, and the government wanted cash infused back into the system. The 401(k) was an elegant way to provide that incentive. In 1980, the amendment was changed again, this time allowing a certain percentage of regular income (as opposed to just bonuses) to be sheltered in the same way. This tax law change had the desired effect: People began to save. The changes, however, were twofold. The first provided an incentive to save, a move that briefly (but, alas, only temporarily) reinvigorated the banking world. The second introduced the ordinary citizen to the stock market through a new investment instrument called the mutual fund. Between 1981 and 1985 these "baskets of stocks," designed to protect the buyer from the vagaries of any single company's poor financial performance, grew from just over 600 to over 1500. In 1985, the amount of cash in mutual funds surpassed that held in the money market. And for the next 10 years, they multiplied like rabbits.

By 1995, over $100 billion had been invested in mutual funds. Those were heady times and, in August, Marc Andreéssen and Jim Clarke started Netscape Corporation, issuing an IPO that surprised everyone in

Measuring the Dow and NASDAQ

The Dow Jones Industrial Average (as well as a number of other measures) is monitored closely by the financial staff of the *Wall Street Journal*. The average is calculated by using the stock prices of 30 selected companies. At the time of this writing, the 30 companies, which are subject to change, are 3M, Alcoa, Altria Group, American Express, AT&T, Boeing, Caterpillar, Citigroup, Coca-Cola, DuPont, Eastman Kodak, ExxonMobile, GE, HP, Home Depot, Honeywell International, Intel, IBM, International Paper, J.P. Morgan Chase, Johnson & Johnson, McDonald's, Merck, Microsoft, Proctor & Gamble, SBC, United Technologies, Wal-Mart, and Disney. The calculation of the average involves a system of weighted averages based on size and influence: The larger, more influential companies carry more weight in the calculation. Furthermore, the stock prices are adjusted for splits.

The NASDAQ composite index includes all the stocks listed on the NASDAQ—around 5000 companies—weighted according to their market value based on the last sale price multiplied by the total shares outstanding. Because of the weighting factor, a price change in the larger companies, such as Microsoft, Cisco, Intel, and Dell, will have a larger impact on the composite than will a similar price change in a smaller company.

terms of the ferocity of the stock price run-up. Andreéssen was a 21-year-old computer scientist at the University of Illinois at Urbana-Champaign; Clarke was the founder and onetime chairman of Silicon Graphics. A few years earlier the National Center for Supercomputer Applications (NCSA) had made its Mosaic browser publicly available (Andreéssen was intimately involved with Mosaic), converting the Internet from being the exclusive domain of technodweebs and cybergeeks to a click-drag-drop environment in which *anyone* could play. Netscape built on the excitement and promised a simple interface and expanded access to information, and it rode high on the investment wave that buoyed it. The investments just kept coming: Between 1996 and 1999, investors buried mutual funds in an almost unimaginable $170 billion per year. The bubble was alive and expanding fast.

The period 1995–1996 was a gateway, the handoff between gold rush and mania. The manic phase was kicked off with the spin-off of Lucent Technologies from AT&T in April 1996. Within days of its independence, Lucent's market cap exceeded that of its former parent, a phenomenon that never had occurred before. By 1998, the firm's net income exceeded $1 billion per year, and it was the most widely held stock in the United States.

Needless to say, the stock market was on fire in this period. Between the beginning of 1995 and the middle of 1996, the Dow Jones Industrial Average climbed from 3800 to over 5600, a rise of 45%, and the NASDAQ soared 65% from 750 to 1250. By February 1997 the Dow had roared past the 7000 mark. In the first four months of 1996, mutual funds took in an additional $100 billion in investments. For the sake of comparison, note that in 1990 the sector accumulated $12 billion *in an entire year*.

The press was going wild over this strange new Midas-driven world. In 1995, the bellwether magazine *Fast Company* came to light, followed by *TheStreet.com* (1996), *The Industry Standard, Business 2.0, Upside*, and *Red Herring* (1998). Those magazines would stoke the fires of the investment mania by proclaiming that Moore's law would never plateau and that the buildout would go on forever. Encouraged by each other's enthusiastic reporting, these sources of "accurate information" fed on each other and contributed to the market enthusiasm on which the bubble's expansion fed. Even the most stalwart publications were not immune: *The Atlantic Monthly* published an issue bearing a cover story titled "Dow 40,000?"

In fairness, there was a lot for these publications to crow about. In 1998, AOL's stock climbed 593%, Yahoo's 584%, and Amazon's an amazing 970%. In April of that year, the Dow hit 9000 and Yahoo! had its first profitable quarter. In Jul, Broadcast.com issued its IPO and watched its stock climb 250% in the first day of trading. In November AOL surprised the world when it bought Netscape for $4.2 billion in stock.

The period between October 1998 and April 2000 was the pinnacle of the bubble's growth. The venture capitalists (VCs) were on a spending rampage, and few business plans were turned away by the money machine. During that time more than 300 Internet companies (dot-coms) issued IPOs. Some of them bordered on the ridiculous yet still got money; most were gone within a year of being funded.

Technologically, there were equally exciting activities under way. Between 1998 and 2000, the amount of optical fiber installed around the world increased by a factor of 5 in anticipation of the burgeoning and never-ending demand for optical bandwidth. In those days there were no fewer than 15 national fiber networks in place, all competing (supposedly) for customer traffic. Each had more bandwidth than global demand merited (any one of them could have handled all global traffic with ease), a model apparently based on the "mutually assured destruction" model of the Cold War, but they believed that demand would grow to meet and exceed the in-ground capacity they had created. Of course, we now know that many of them were selling bandwidth to each other, creating the illusion of sales and at the same time creating a similar illusion of deductible expenses.

There were, of course, some concerns during that time, although many were not voiced publicly. The Fed chairman, Alan Greenspan, was worried about the extent of the speculative bubble, noting that central bankers find it inordinately difficult to detect the presence of a bubble phenomenon while it is happening. It was his own uncertainty that worried him, his fear of not knowing. During that time he considered raising interest rates but was worried about the impact that move would have on the deepening financial crisis in Asia. So he watched, he worried, and he waited.

By the time 1999 rolled around, there did not appear to be an obvious reason for concern. On March 29, the Dow closed above 10,000 for the first time, and on December 29, nine months later, it closed just shy of 11,500, with the NASDAQ showing an equally impressive level of 4070. Then, on January 10, 2000, in a move that shook the world, AOL announced that it would acquire the venerable Time-Warner for a staggering $165 billion, the largest business transaction of all time. This was a match that appeared perfect in every respect. The brash, bold personality of AOL, led by the charismatic Steve Case, combined with steady, staid Time-Warner, led by the comparatively invisible Gerald Levin, seemed flawless. The market agreed; the stock price and AOL subscribership ballooned in the months that followed.

By the end of 2000, mutual funds contained more money than the banking system: $7 trillion, of which $4 trillion was in stock funds. In 2001, there were more than 8,000 mutual funds in existence, a number that is meaningful only when one considers that the New York Stock Exchange and NASDAQ combined had fewer than 8,000 represented companies on their membership charts. The market had become a household commodity, and the latest phenomenon to appear was the amateur investor: the investment club and day trader. And why not? Who could lose in such an ebullient market?

The Bubble Bursts

What precipitated the financial train wreck that followed such a remarkable ride? We have discussed some of the contributing factors, but others came down to simple questions of responsible financial oversight and the need for a healthy dose of managerial skepticism. These companies were betting on the promise of returns, and the VCs were right there with them, providing the financial wherewithal to get them off the ground. The fact that they had questionable business plans, few customers, no revenues, and little in the way of plans for change had no bearing. Most of them would disappear abruptly and painfully; a few would survive after a prolonged rocky start. Consider Amazon, for example. On average, Amazon paid its suppliers $16 per book, including shipping. They then paid an average of $8 per book for advertising and $1 for overhead, yet the average customer paid $20 per book. You do the math.

I don't mean to pick on Amazon; it has survived, after all, is immensely popular, and is performing reasonably well. Similar financial behavior models applied to other major companies, however. Sustained losses of hundreds of millions of dollars year after year, coupled with revenues of less than a $100 million and small numbers of customers, should have provided minimal environmental clues to those at the corporate helm. The little boy had not yet arrived, however, and the emperor continued unfazed, marching regally along in his digital underwear.

Ultimately, much of the carnage could have been prevented if corporate leaders had asked three simple questions. The first was, "It's cool, but what's it for?" Consider the case of Third-Generation Wireless

(3G). I still have in my archives a sheaf of advertisements from late 1990s trade journals that say things like "We can deliver 2 Mbps to your cell phone!" For what? No applications existed at the time to take advantage of broadband wireless. What were users supposed to do, talk faster? If executives simply had asked that first question, there might have been far fewer companies sitting on spectrum investments they were unable to use due to a dearth of available—and functional—applications.

The second question was, "Are you sure?" During the turn of the twenty-first century the observation was made that the Internet was doubling in size every 50 days. Remarkable! The result was that manufacturers such as Cisco began to manufacture at a frantic pace, and optical companies began to dump fiber into the ground at a furious rate. In fact, the Internet was doubling in size *every 400 days*. This is a remarkable growth rate—it basically means that the Internet was doubling in size every year—but it's a far cry from 50 days. The end result was massive inventory overhangs—read "stranded capital"—and an in-place optical network of which we currently are using approximately 7%.

▉ The Beginning of the End

On March 10, 2000, the NASDAQ closed above 5000. The market had become top-heavy, and analysts had begun to write about a possible major correction looming on the horizon. But investors were not to be deterred: They continued to push for growth. In their minds 5000 was just a step along the way.

On March 13, the NASDAQ hiccuped and fell 500 points, a jarring correction that didn't last. All the markets had become highly volatile, going up and down like a sine wave. Meanwhile, in the shadows, financial researchers were studying the performance of dot-com companies, looking at time horizons and cash burn velocities. They concluded that a serious correction was imminent and that many of the companies would not survive it, but they were largely ignored. Mania, it seems, is a powerful distracter.

On March 21, the Federal Reserve met and decided to raise interest rates again in an attempt to cool things down. Investors, however, were not to be deterred and, once again, the markets surged ahead. In the third week of March, Cisco passed Microsoft as the world's most valuable corporation when its market cap exceeded $555 billion. Not bad for a company that had been public for only a decade.

Meanwhile, public skepticism about the longevity of the bubble was beginning to grow. Journalists, having read the reports issued by the financial analysts, heard the concerns of the Fed, and seen the fantasy that was so much a part of the run-up of the market, began to write cautiously about the continuing climb and about real versus perceived value. The markets experienced a few stumbles and hiccups but always recovered and climbed. Nevertheless, the writing was on the wall. The financial markets were poised like a great Jenga game, waiting for the right person to pull the keystone.

(Jenga is a game in which players stack up wooden blocks and then slowly remove them. Whoever pulls the piece that causes the tower to fall loses the game.)

Then, on April 3, the NASDAQ fell 349 points. There were a number of contributing factors, not the least of which was an announcement that initial attempts to mediate the ongoing Microsoft antitrust case had failed. Microsoft's stock fell and dragged many others along with it. At midday on April 4, the NASDAQ was down 575 points and the Dow was down 504. By the end of the day both had bounced back to levels that were close to where they had started, but the message was clear. The bubble had burst, and the money in it, like pent-up water, was starting to seek a new and much lower level.

Sell-Off

On April 10, one month after the NASDAQ peak, the sell-off started. It continued through April 11 and into April 12. The NASDAQ had been hovering around 4500; on April 12 it closed at 3769, down over 40% from its March peak. On April 13 the NASDAQ closed at 3677, and the Dow at 10,924. The sell-off, which many had hoped would be nothing more than a speed bump, was accelerating.

On April 14 the Dow fell 618 points, its biggest one-day decline in history, to 10,306, and the NASDAQ fell 355 points to 3321. The NASDAQ was bleeding profusely from the death of a thousand cuts: In one week it had fallen over 1100 points, losing more than 25% of its value. Between its peak in March and its decline point in April, the NASDAQ lost 1727 points: roughly 34% of its overall value. Just under $2 trillion in company value had vaporized. The table below illustrates some of the most visible losses.

Company	March 2000	April 2000	% Decline
Amazon.com	66 7/8	46 7/8	29.9
AOL	58 5/8	55	6.2
Ariba	305 3/8	62 1/4	79.6
Ebay	193 1/4	139 5/16	27.9
Inktomi	169 5/16	100 13/16	40.5
Internet Capital Group	143 9/16	40	72.1
Priceline.com	94 1/2	58 9/16	38
Verisign	239 15/16	97 13/16	59.2
Yahoo!	178 1/16	116	34.8

In August, the NASDAQ fell below 3000, and companies that had become household names and on which people had bet their entire fortunes and retirement accounts began to fail by the dozens. Their financial statements, largely ignored in the mania that preceded the bursting of the bubble, were painfully embarrassing: "The firm had losses of $66 million for the year on revenues of $747,000." The story was repeated over and over.

In December, the Federal Reserve met once again but decided to leave interest rates alone for the time being. The NASDAQ fell more than 80 points shortly thereafter to 2471, and the Dow dropped 82 points to 10,787. The year 2000, which was thankfully over, had seen the greatest financial decline in history: The NASDAQ lost 39% of its value, and the Dow lost 6%. It was nothing more than a badly needed correction, but the fall from grace was enormously painful.

■■■ Aftermath

"He's gone from Internet poster boy to Internet piñata."
—Venture capitalist John Doerr of Kleiner Perkins
Caufield & Byers on Jeff Bezos and the Amazon roller coaster.

It had to happen sooner or later, and it finally did: The market corrected itself the way it was designed to do, washing itself clean of the insanity of the previous five years. And when the water was gone and the riverbed lay bare, something else became painfully visible: the questionable accounting practices of some of the most revered names in the industry and the support infrastructure around it. Enron, WorldCom, Adelphia, Arthur Andersen, and dozens of other seemingly circumspect companies were caught with their hands in the proverbial cookie jar, helping themselves to the money of others. It isn't over yet and probably won't be for years.

What we *do* know is that in spite of the huge financial losses (even though many of them were on paper only) that took place during the bubble, a great deal of good came out of the period 1996–2001. The level of technological evolution that resulted from the money that flowed into the industry could not have occurred otherwise. "The magnetism of money and minds" worked, and look what resulted: the personal digital assistant (PDA), multigigabit long-haul optical transport, high-speed wireless solutions such as WiFi and Bluetooth, universally available DSL and cable modem technology, everything-over-IP service, multiservice switching and routing platforms, a more realistic (although not perfect) regulatory environment and enhanced awareness of its importance, staggeringly fast and capable semiconductors, film-quality digital photography, high-quality low-cost laser and ink-jet printers, data-mining and knowledge management applications, movies on DVD, and manufacturers and service providers that really understand that *service* is the key word today, not technology.

State of the Industry after the Bubble

The crash of the technology industry left its ugly mark all over the world. By many accounts, $7 trillion in market value evaporated and blew away, carrying with it retirement accounts, thousands of jobs, stock options, and trust in the marketplace. For some it meant a new career; for others, a jail cell.

Today the industry has recovered to a place of tenuous respect. Hundreds of companies disappeared during the crash, but many remained. Often mortally wounded, they were able to perform enough economic triage to survive until they healed and are beginning to show a respectable face to the world. The industry, however, has changed. It is humbled and a bit meeker and has endured a series of fundamental shifts (see below). Some of those shifts may be disturbing, but all of them are undeniable.

1: The Service Provider Is Dead

Disturbing, isn't it? Yet it's true in one very significant sense. *The service provider as we know it* is certainly dead. Gone are the days when "service" translated into "access and transport" or "dial tone." Today service is defined by the customer and *only* by the customer. Because of technological, regulatory, economic, and competitive forces, it simply no longer is enough to offer network access as a prime differentiator. Consider the impact of emerging technologies. Voice over Internet Protocol (VoIP) has become so widespread and so widely used that it has been adopted by corporations as their preferred communications technology, and manufacturers have scrambled to create and sell next-generation private branch exchanges (PBXs) that are IP-enabled. Cable companies, long the laughingstock of the telecom services industry, are enjoying the last laugh as they become the first sector to offer the triple play of voice, video, and data and in some cases the first to offer a quadruple play by bundling wireless into the mix. By doing this they make the customer inextricably sticky, thus ensuring a long-term relationship with them. Considering the fact that it costs approximately $400 to get a customer back once the customer has been lost to churn, keeping customers close in the first place is a winning strategy and offering them what they want is better still.

New technologies also are serving as disruptive forces. Worldwide Interoperability for Microwave Access (WiMAX), with its 100-Mbps-access bandwidth, 30-mile-diameter cells, and non-line-of-sight OFDM[2] technology, offers an enticing local loop alternative for competitors that want to penetrate incumbent local exchange carrier (ILEC) territories without having to build capital expenditure (CAPEX)-rich access networks.

Consider this example. Power companies have been in the broadband transport business for years. The transmission cable that hangs in great catenaries from pylon to pylon across the landscape may be made of aluminum, but it is still monstrously heavy. To reduce weight the cable is hollow, which is not a problem since the charge travels along the surface

---

[2] Orthogonal frequency division multiplexing, a technique in which the same signal is transmitted multiple times in separate narrow carriers to ensure that fade doesn't overcome the ability of the transmitted signal to reach its destination.

of the conductor anyway thanks to a curious phenomenon known as the skin effect. Since the cable is hollow, it occurred to cable manufacturers long ago that they could increase the value (and price) of the cable by inserting ribbons of optical fiber into the hollow center of the strand without adding appreciably to the span's overall weight. That gave power companies an in-house optical network over which they could transport their own data: power consumption, load sharing, e-mail between substations, and so forth. Unfortunately, they never had a local loop, and so they could never compete with the incumbent telcos. Enter WiMAX. Place a WiMAX node adjacent to a substation, attach it to the optical transport network, power it on, and voilà, instant broadband local loop. Sounds far-fetched? It's already happening around the world.

2: Sorry, There Is No New Killer App

Countless researchers and marketers are out there looking for the next great killer application that will enable and justify the massive investment made to date in telecom infrastructure. I think they're barking up the wrong tree. I don't believe that the market is looking for the next great killer app; I think it is looking for the next great killer way to access the applications it already has. In fact, when I talk with customers (both enterprise workers and residence customers) and ask them what they want from their network, the answer is typically the same: voice, Short Management System (SMS) or Instant Messenger (IM), e-mail, and an occasional Web search. A few people like the idea of being able to download and listen to music on a mobile phone; even fewer want to watch television on a PDA.

Thus, no killer app. But perhaps I speak too soon. In reality there *is* a killer app, but it isn't new. It's the same killer app we've always had. It's called voice. Think about it: We've spent countless billions of dollars, employed millions of people, and created the most complex machine ever built just to allow us to do what we do every day, although in a slightly inferior way. The difference is that today we have delivery options. Not only do we have Public Switched Telephone Network (PSTN)-based voice, we also have voice delivered via Global System for Mobile Communications (GSM), Time Division Multiple Access (TDMA) and Code Division Multiple Access (CDMA) cellular wireless, WiFi, WiMAX, cable, and IP. The introduction of these technology options, particularly the introduction of IP-based voice, has created massive economic disruption in the sector.

Consider the case of Skype (www.skype.com). Created by the same two young programmers who created KaZaA, Niklas Zennström and Janus Friis (Figure 1-10), Skype now boasts close to 200 million downloads of its popular (and free) VoIP client. As Michael Powell, former chairman of the Federal Communications Commission (FCC) observed, "I knew it was over when I downloaded Skype. When the inventors of KaZaA are distributing for free a little program that you can use to talk to anybody else, and the quality is fantastic, and it's free—it's over. The world will change now inevitably." Founder Zennström agrees: "The idea of charging for calls belongs to the last century. Skype software gives people new power to affordably stay in touch with their friends and family by taking advantage of their technology and connectivity investments."

When Skype, Napster, and other peer-to-peer music-sharing programs were shut down after the rock band Metallica's threat of a lawsuit against file sharers, Zennström and Friis went in search of another

Figure 1-10
Niklas
Zennström and
Janus Friis, the
founders of
Skype.

application they could distribute free of charge—and quickly thought about voice. To date more than 180 million people have downloaded the free Skype installer (www.skype.com/download), and as I write this, I'm looking at the Skype welcome screen, which shows me that 3.4 million people are logged into the Skype system (Figure 1-11). I have used Skype for almost two years now, and I find the service excellent. The only downside is that the free version of Skype is a "walled garden" technology: Users can talk only with other Skype users. But with over 3 million people online at any time and with the application's ability to search for other users by city and country, *you'll find someone to talk with*. Skype also supports messaging, voice mail, and videoconferencing.

Of course, the walled garden concept is limiting and so, in early 2004, Skype announced SkypeOut, a paid service that allows Skype users to place calls to regular telephones in many countries for about 2 cents per minute. Skype adds approximately 150,000 downloads every day; by comparison, North American ILECs lose approximately 10,000 access lines per day to competing technologies.

A new twist in the Skype story is its recent acquisition by eBay, and that acquisition is illustrative of what is yet to come in this evolving industry. To the public at large, eBay is the world's garage sale. Want to

Figure 1-11
The Skype user interface. Note the number of users online (bottom right corner).

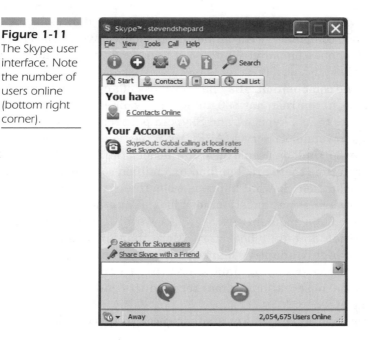

buy a used computer? A rare car? A stuffed ocelot? Baseball cards? Civil War enlistment documents? eBay is the place. The stories, apocryphal though they are, are intriguing and legion. Contrary to popular belief, you can't buy a replacement kidney on eBay.

eBay excels at the fine art of the agora: the public marketplace. It provides a forum where buyers and sellers can interact in a safe, controlled way, and although eBay does not actually enter into the transactions, it facilitates them. A few years ago I became fascinated by the fact that drive-in movies had begun to host flea markets on weekend mornings. I assumed, incorrectly as it turned out, that the drive-ins were hosting the flea markets, giving them a place to conduct their little transactions. In fact, the flea markets had purchased the drive-in movie theaters and the movie business was incidental (in terms of revenue) to what those firms made in flea market facilitation fees. This is eBay: the world's largest online flea market and auction house. It is extraordinarily successful at what it does.

When I think of eBay, I tend to think beyond the immediate and obvious. It is indeed an online auction house, but far more important, it represents perhaps the most successful and effective supply chain implementation in history. It is not constrained the way linear supply chains are but is rather a "hyperchain," a many-to-many model that accelerates commerce, creates arbitrage, and aggressively moves products and services. It is the facilitative catalyst, and now it owns Skype.

What an odd combination. An online auction house buys a free-service Internet telephone company. Why? So it can conduct voice auctions online? Hardly.

Consider the combination. eBay has revenues of approximately $650 million. Skype, in contrast, has $60 million in revenues from the 60 million subscribers to its SkypeOut and SkypeIn paid services [amounting to an average revenue per server (ARPU) of $1 per subscriber per year]. However, over 170 million people have downloaded the free installer, and at any point in time there are 3 million to 5 million computers running the Skype application. So what happens when these two merge?

Before answering that question, let's look at another phenomenon of a company for a moment: Amazon. As we all know, Amazon is much more than an online bookstore. More than anything else, the company is a highly adaptive market analysis engine, aggressively monitoring customer buying habits, creating trend data, and then using statistical observations to market products and services to customers accurately.

Most of us have, at one time or another, received this e-mail:

Dear Amazon.com Customer,

We've noticed that customers who have purchased "Telecom Crash Course" by Steven Shepard also purchased books by Clint Smith. For this reason, you might like to know that Clint Smith's "3G Wireless with 802.16 and 802.11" is now available . You can order your copy by following the link below.

3G Wireless with 802.16 and 802.1

Clint Smith, John Meyer

List Price: $99.95

Price: $99.95

To learn more about 3G Wireless with 802.16 and 802.11, please visit the following page at Amazon.com:

http://www.amazon.com/o/ASIN/0071440828/ref=pe_snp_828

More to explore...

Sincerely,

Amazon.com

Amazon is remarkably adroit at collecting customer data, refining it into tactical information, and then further refining it into strategically targeted behavioral knowledge. When a customer buys a book, Amazon enters that scintilla of data into a database of *related* data, massages the data, and creates, through reliance on the law of large numbers, statistically dependable conclusions about group buying patterns. If it sees that large numbers of customers from a particular demographic sector are buying Dan Brown's *Da Vinci Code*, it can conclude that others in that social stratum also would enjoy the book or a related title. By "smart-bombing" its customer base rather than using a more diffuse shotgun approach, Amazon maximizes sales without annoying customers.

When we apply this concept to the eBay-Skype combination, magic happens. By any argument, eBay is the perfect market model, seamlessly and effortlessly putting buyers and sellers together in a frictionless, anonymous (yet highly personal) environment that accelerates the movement of goods across the supply chain.

Skype, in this context, is in many ways an ideal acquisition. First, the customer who most commonly uses the Internet-based eBay also falls into the social cross section that uses applications such as Skype. Thus, not only does eBay buy an extensive potential customer list, it also buys access to statistically relevant behavioral data derived from a very large (and growing) population it then can use to make product-positioning decisions.

There is a dictum in the technical world known as *Metcalfe's law*. Coined by Ethernet pioneer and 3Com Corporation founder Bob Metcalfe, the law observes that *the value of a connected network is a function of the square of the number of nodes in the connected network*. In other words, the more nodes there are in the network and the more connected (meshed) those nodes are, the greater is the inherent value of the entire network. Consider the World Wide Web. If the entire Web consisted of no more than 20 devices, its value would be hindered severely by the limited quantity of data (information? knowledge?) available from those 20 sites. The Web, however, has approximately *400 million* interconnected hosts and thus has the ability to create uncountable relationships through its fully meshed topology.

Think about the value of the combination of eBay's marketplace hyperchain and Skype's 170 million customers. Now overlay Amazon's customer management function and incorporate the ability to create a voice conversation between a buyer and a seller over Skype's network. Could this be more powerful? Yes, it could.

Consider the value of arbitrage. *Arbitrage* is the practice of buying a product or service in one market and selling it in another to take advantage of a price discrepancy. Arbitrage networks lead to normalized pricing, driving pricing to its optimum point among all rational providers. The competitive playing field is leveled, forcing marketplace participants to compete at the level at which they are most differentiated. This is the value that eBay brings. Because it accelerates the coming together of buyers and sellers, the pricing of products and services is controlled by market behavior.

What would happen if a large corporation used eBay—or the eBay model—as its supply chain? What kinds of products and services would be served by this distribution technique? Does it not make sense that eBay is maneuvering itself to become the world's supply chain brokerage? What would happen if service providers began to sell bandwidth on eBay? Could this not create an accelerated marketplace for the creation of large Mobile Virtual Network Operators (MVNOs)? If one then adds the power of the customer analysis tool to the transaction, an even more powerful combination is created.

Let's add one final piece. In addition to the level market provided by eBay, the seamless and effortless buyer-to-seller communications provided by Skype, and the knowledge management capabilities provided by Amazon-like customer relationship management (CRM) software, we could incorporate a physical distribution mechanism along the lines of an alliance with FedEx. The result would be a powerful, complete end-to-end services chain. This evolving business model is reminiscent of the Japanese *keiretsu* or the Korean *chaebol*: connected corporations that function as a single organism. The difference is that these are physical *and* virtual entities that operate with global scope and therefore have global influence. Their influence grows daily and, because they are global and have minimal cost overhead, they are formidable competitors. The end result is that in the future marketplace competition will occur between fast-moving corporate clusters, not between individual companies. Rewards will accrue to corporations that embrace the fact that they have two choices: They can have *some* of the money or *none* of the money—they no longer can have it all.

The message here is a simple one. This market is evolving in strange and wonderful ways, and the business of telecom is finding itself intertwined in a wide range of newly defined industries. Far more important, the services defined within the scope of telecommunications, particularly VoIP, are changing the competitive landscape. The new entrants—pure VoIP providers, cable, and competitive local exchange carriers (CLECs)—are offering a set of services in the form of the triple play (voice, video, and data) and in some cases the quadruple play (as I like to call it, the fourple play). By offering customers a complete bouquet of communications services, they make the customer far stickier than would be the case if the customer bought a single service. After all, if customers buy the triple-play package and then decide they aren't happy with one component of it, will they exit the entire package just because they are disenchanted with one component? Probably not. Furthermore, it gives the service provider more time to satisfy the customer. The average cost to reacquire a customer after losing him or her to churn (the term for customer turnover) is $400. Since ARPU in the cellular market is between $50 and $70, any opportunity to reduce churn—and therefore the cost of customer acquisition—is a strategically important move.

3: The Local Loop Is a Natural Monopoly: Get Over It

The regulatory environment that has been in place since the signing of the U.S. Telecommunications Act of 1996 fails to address a serious disparity between incumbent providers and would-be competitors. Recent rulings have resulted in a series of decisions designed to bolster competition at the local loop level. Unfortunately, by most players' estimation, they have had the opposite effect. In fact, competition, though important in a healthy economy, should not be the primary goal of a regulatory body. The primary responsibility of a regulator is twofold: to ensure that territory service gaps are identified and filled by the responsible regulated carrier and to ensure that customers using the regulated service have the best possible experience doing so. *A regulator can mandate competition as a way to achieve those goals, but competition is a means to an end, not the end itself.*

The introduction of new technologies always conveys a temporary advantage to the first mover. Innovation involves significant risk; the temporary first-mover advantage allows those movers to extract profits as a reward for taking the initial risk, allowing them to recover the cost of innovation. As technology advances, the first-mover position usually erodes, and so the advantage is fleeting. The relationship, however, fosters zeal for ongoing entrepreneurial development.

Recent regulatory law has required that incumbent providers open their networks to alternative carriers via element unbundling. Although this creates a competitive marketplace, it is artificial. In fact, the opposite often happens. Consider this scenario: Market research indicates to the incumbent telco that demand for residential and small-office, home-office (SOHO) broadband is high enough to merit the substantial investment required to equip the network to deliver it: Digital Subscriber Live Access Multiplexers (DSLAMs) in the central office, an upgraded loop plant, remote terminal upgrades, and so on. However, they know that the instant they bring the service online, they will be required to make those resources available to competitors via local loop unbundling. Consequently, incumbents lose the incentive to invest in new technology. Predictably, they choose to not make the investment, knowing that competitive carriers have neither the financial wherewithal nor the incentive to build their own parallel networks. As a result, broadband deployment is retarded seriously. This is one reason why the United States has one of the lowest broadband penetration rates among First World countries. After all, it is argued, why should incumbents invest tens of millions of dollars and take substantial economic risks when they are required by law to share the rewards of that investment and risk immediately with competitors?

Naturally, the industry's legal machinery kicked in and took local loop unbundling rules to task. In March 2004, the U.S. Court of Appeals struck down FCC rules for how regional telephone companies must open their networks to competitors. Federal law originally required regional phone companies to lease parts of their networks (the UNE-P mandates) to competitors at reasonable rates set by the states. The ILECs long have contended that they have been forced to give competitors rates that are below their actual cost.

In its decision, the court found that the FCC wrongly gave power to state regulators to decide which parts of the telephone network had to be unbundled. The court also upheld an earlier FCC decision that the ILECs are not required to lease their high-speed facilities to competitors at discount rates the way they do with their standard phone lines.

In April 2004, regulators rejected AT&T's petition to eliminate the requirement that it pay long-distance fees on calls transported partially over the Internet. That decision meant that AT&T would be required to pay hundreds of millions of dollars in unpaid retroactive fees to the ILECs.

Earlier in 2004, the FCC had ruled that calls that originated and terminated on the Internet, such as those made using Skype, Vonage, and other voice-over-Internet service providers, are free from the fees and taxes that traditional phone companies are required to pay, such as support for E911, the Universal Service Fund, and the like. In support of that decision the FCC observed that, because calls that travel over the Internet don't provide enhanced features, standard rules apply. Furthermore, in a recent decision, the FCC consolidated all regulatory power over VoIP service at the federal level, wresting it from the states.

Finally, in mid-2005, a couple of major decisions were handed down. In June, the Supreme Court ruled that cable systems are not legally required to lease access to competing providers of high-speed Internet services. The decision concluded the cable industry's open-access battle that started when Steve Case, then the chairman of AOL, petitioned FCC chairman William Kennard to place a condition on AT&T's merger with the cable provider TCI. The petitioned requested that AOL be granted access to TCI's high-speed data division, @Home.

Kennard declined the petition, saying that cable did not dominate the access market sufficiently to justify such a request. However, it didn't stop there: The battle ascended to the federal courts and later forced the FCC to issue rules designed to keep cable modem service classified as an information service rather than a telecom service, thus avoiding the onerous regulation that is a condition of telephone service delivery.

The second action that took place at that time was the FCC's decision to exempt DSL from line-sharing requirements, thus putting cable modem service (which commands the bulk of the U.S. residential broadband market) and DSL on an equal regulatory footing.

Clearly, regulatory agencies are trying to balance the need for a regulated telecommunications marketplace with the need for an unfettered development environment that can innovate technologically without fear of excessive fees and taxes. Michael Powell, who left his post in

2005 as the chairman of the FCC, clearly had a plan in mind when he chose to allow the line-sharing rules to lapse. It is now clear that his intent—and therefore the intent of the FCC—was to engender a spirit of facilities-based competition rather than rely on the unbundled network element (UNE)-based environment, which simply has not worked as well as was hoped.

Another development in this area of local loop competition has been the recent arrival of WiMAX and other broadband wireless access technologies. WiMAX offers 100 Mbps over a service radius of several miles. Because it is based on an OFDM transmission scheme, it does not require line of sight for connectivity. The technology is targeted at the "first mile" challenge for metropolitan area networks. It operates between 10 and 66 GHz and between 2 and 11 GHz (point-to-multipoint and optional mesh topologies) and supports multiple physical layer specifications for each frequency band. The 10- to 66-GHz standard supports two-way transmission options at a variety of frequencies, including 10.5 GHz, 25 GHz, 26 GHz, 31 GHz, 38 GHz, and 39 GHz. It also supports device interoperability so that carriers can use multiple vendors' products. The standard for the 2-GHz to 11-GHz spectrum supports both unlicensed and licensed bands; this is a real boon for the entrepreneurial innovators that push the limits of any new technology.

WiMAX allows Wireless Internet Service Providers (WISPs) to enter the market with a minimal investment in infrastructure and then offer a complete package of services to subscribers. When widely deployed, it will compete favorably with cable modem and DSL (in fact, some analysts refer to WiMAX as wireless DSL).

Several companies have been leading the WiMAX charge. The most prominent is Intel, which is making heavy investments in WiMAX as part of a strategy to take the lead in WiMAX the same way it did in WiFi with Centrino. Its research shows that many people use their PDAs, broadband-equipped mobile phones, and laptops to access data networks while mobile, a phenomenon that is causing many communities to build metro-based broadband access areas to serve their residents.

As a founding member of the WiMAX Forum, Intel promotes compatibility and interoperability among certified broadband wireless products. The forum's member companies support the industrywide acceptance of the 802.16 WiMAX standard as well as the European Telecom Standards Institute (ETSI) HiperMAN wireless local area network (LAN) standards.

One reason WiMAX represents such a powerful competitive technology is the interest shown in it by alternative providers, most specifically power companies. As was mentioned earlier in this chapter, the power cable that runs in great festooned loops across the countryside from pylon to pylon is made of aluminum but is still extraordinarily heavy. As a result, it is manufactured with a hollow core to reduce its span weight. Long ago, manufacturers observed that a bundle of optical fiber inside the hollow core did not add appreciably to the weight of the cable but added *significantly* to its strategic value. Power companies suddenly had an in-house transport network over which they could transport their own data for telemetry and load-sharing purposes. What they did *not* have, of course, was a local loop—until the arrival of WiMAX. By installing a WiMAX base station adjacent to a power substation, a power company can enter the broadband access game with a minimal investment in plant and equipment. Equally intriguing is the recent technological leap that allows power companies to "carve out" a high-frequency channel over the power infrastructure in much the same way DSL transports a high-bandwidth channel above the voice band over the twisted-pair local loop. Interest in this option is high: Google recently purchased Current, a software company that specializes in the middleware required to manage broadband delivery over power infrastructures.

This area of the industry is in a state of unbridled ferment at the moment, and regulators are struggling to keep up with the changes as much as the service providers and manufacturers are. The unbridled growth in VoIP has caused a sea change in the way the market views telephony and related services, leading regulators to respond in a variety of ways, one of them being the "special treatment" of VoIP as if it were a separate service.

On the one hand, this is not a bad thing because the Internet is something of an innovation engine and regulators are loath to disrupt or hobble its contributions to the innovative, evolving information economy. On the other hand, regulating VoIP as a service that is distinct from PSTN-based voice is wrong. The service is not VoIP; it's voice. VoIP is a technology option, not a service. Regulators should not be in the business of regulating technology per se but instead should be concerned with the application of technologies in accordance with the mandates discussed earlier. What comes out of the phone is still the same voice that has always come out of the phone. Although VoIP today enjoys a certain amount of immunity from regulatory scrutiny, that is a temporary situation: The time will come, and not all that long from now, when VoIP providers will reach "critical mass" and find themselves under the same degree of regulatory scrutiny as are more traditional providers. This is a great example of the old adage "Be careful what you wish for; you might get it." Cable companies and VoIP providers, beware. Today you may be classified as information service providers, but the day will come in the not too distant future when your services will be deemed to be on a par with traditional service, and regulatory parity will arrive.

4: Beware the Berserkers

In the role-play game Dungeons and Dragons, one character who appears randomly on the scene is a Berserker. A Berserker has no function other than to inject chaos into the game: sometimes good, sometimes bad, but *always* unpredictable. This telecom/IT industry is beset by an army of Berserkers that are in the process of redefining the roles of networks, computers, and the applications that reside in them. They also are changing the relationship between enterprise and end-user customers, service providers, and manufacturers irreversibly. Examples of Berserkers include Microsoft, IBM, Cisco, eBay/Skype, Vonage, Virgin, and Google. Let's look at each of them briefly (we'll discuss some of them in greater detail later in this chapter because of their emerging roles in the IMS development effort).

Microsoft is a Berserker purely because of its influence and vision. As I often tell people, "You don't have to *like* Microsoft, but you *do* have to *admire* it. And don't you *dare* take your eyes off it." Microsoft rapidly is becoming one of the most powerful and disruptive forces in the industry today. They clearly have their eye on network services, as evidenced by recent acquisition activity that put them squarely in the network management and operations support systems (OSS) space, strategic alliances with companies such as Skype, and the inclusion of an expanded voice client in their soon to be released Vista operating system, the replacement for XP. The client includes a softphone that will appear on the desktop: click and dial. Given the scope of Microsoft's influence and the sheer volume of machines running the Windows operating system, this minor inclusion poses a clear and present threat to service providers around the world. With almost $40 billion in cash at its disposal, Microsoft's ability to make decisions rapidly is accelerated significantly. More on Microsoft appears later in this chapter.

IBM is a Berserker because of its brilliant implementation of the adage "The quickest way to become a leader is to find a parade and stand in front of it." When the emergence of the services market was perceived to be imminent, IBM acquired a services company (PWC) and entered the fray with an established, well-respected organization. Today most people have forgotten that IBM is a manufacturer of hardware and software, and that's just the way IBM liked it. The $9 billion IBM has at its disposal gives it a large degree of institutional freedom. There is more on IBM later in the book.

Cisco is a berserking force because it has managed to create the perception that fully 100% of the Internet is built on Cisco gear. This is clearly a gross exaggeration, but perception is reality. Also, the eBay-Skype combination, with its nonlinear approach to its own role, is powerful for all the reasons discussed earlier. Similarly, Vonage, an Internet telephony company, poses a threat to traditional service providers because it offers low-cost global telephony with all the enhanced services available from a traditional telephone company.

Virgin presents a threat from another perspective. More than anything else, Richard Branson's company is a powerful brand management firm. As a virtual MVNO, the company has demonstrated consistently that ownership of the network is far less important than strategic brand management. Furthermore, its presence as an MVNO has given rise to other companies like it and a new family of companies known as Mobile Virtual Network Enablers (MVNEs).

The MVNE is an intermediary entity that positions itself between the MVNO and the hosting service provider (Figure 1-12), the company from which the MVNO buys its minutes and network access. Services offered by the MVNE include telecom management [VoIP, prepaid, roaming, interconnect management, SMS, Advanced Intelligent Network (AIN)], business support systems (BSS), and operations support systems (OSS: provisioning, usage settlement, revenue assurance, fraud management, service mediation), customer interface and care [device management, interactive voice response (IVR) management, call center management, revenue-sharing strategies], marketing (product development, promo-

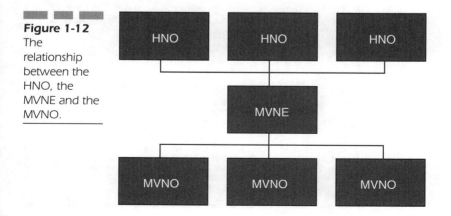

Figure 1-12
The relationship between the HNO, the MVNE and the MVNO.

tions, advertising, packaging, procurement, distribution), mobile data provisioning (platform management, content management, content aggregation, application management), training, sales, integration, and customer relationship management analysis. At the time of this writing there are about 40 MVNEs in operation, most of them having evolved from companies offering related services such as application service providers (ASPs), billing companies, IT companies, content providers, content aggregators, Internet service providers (ISPs), and hardware manufacturers.

The advertisement shown in Figure 1-13 of a Tandy (Radio Shack) desktop computer in 1989 represents the pinnacle of computing capability at that time. The machine ran at 20 MHz and had 2 MB of random-access memory (RAM) included (expandable to 16 MB), all for $8500, a price that did not include the monitor or the mouse or, apparently, a hard drive. Yet this was *the* business machine at that time.

Figure 1-13
Print ad for a computer, 1989. Note the price tag.

Tandy 5000 MC Professional System

NEW FOR 89 **8499⁰⁰**

Monitor and mouse not included

■ 20 MHz Intel® 80386™ Microprocessor ■ VGA Graphics
■ 2 MB RAM (16 MB Capacity) ■ Cache Memory

Our most powerful computer ever! The Tandy 5000 MC Micro Computer is strictly business, from the look of its 256,000-color VGA graphics to the tactile feel of its newly-designed keyboard. Its Intel 80386 processor operates at a lightning-fast 20 MHz, and a memory cache controller provides RAM-fast access to your data. IBM® Micro Channel™ compatible architecture provides a 32-bit wide data path for virtually simultaneous data transfer between peripherals. Will operate MS-DOS® 3.3, MS® OS/2, SCO® XENIX® 386 and network operating software. The 5000 MC's technology, performance and price all add up to an incredible value. VGA graphics, serial and parallel ports and mouse support included.
25-6000 . . . . 8499.00

The Greatest Berserker of Them All

One of the most powerful forces shaping the technology industry today is the emerging generation known as *the Millennials*. Although readers may scratch their heads and wonder why there is a sociological discussion in a book about advanced communications technologies, rest assured that there is perhaps no topic more important today. Millennials, typically characterized as children born between 1982 and 2004, are interesting for one seminal reason: The oldest of them entered the workplace in 2004; the youngest were *born* in 2004. Their generation is complete. However, their influence is being felt only now. Today they are entry-level supervisors in corporations; within five years they will have begun moving into positions of influence and decision making. These kids are your new employees, your new customers, but far more important—and relevant—*they are your new competitors*. Understand what they represent and the impact they will have in the workplace and market or you will suffer the consequences.

Sociologists have studied the generational cycles that characterize human social behavior patterns for years. In the United States and other Western nations, the identified patterns are somewhat unique because the United States and a few other nations tend to view the concept of the passage of time as a linear progression, whereas older, longer-established societies view time as a cyclical continuum. In the Mayan *Pictun*

(8000 years), the Hebrew *Yom* (1000 years), the lunar ecliptically aligned Babylonian Yuga (12,000 years), and the Buddhist *Kalpa* (4,320,000,000 years; how the Buddhists know that their Kalpa repeats its 4-billion-year cycle is beyond me), it is a repeating cycle that requires time to be Control-Alt-Deleted periodically to clear out the universe's head and get things back on track again. Furthermore, most societies view this temporal cycle as occurring in a repeating pattern of four identifiable quadrants with unique yet highly related characteristics.

The Generational Link

Behavioral sociologists study this phenomenon of repetition and relate it to human generations. Generations are defined as groups of people who are born during an identified period and who have a common set of experiences and therefore develop something of a collective generational personality. Each generation lasts about two decades, after which it fades into the background as the next generation comes into its own. This is a good thing: After all, how much more of the Baby Boomer generation can the world take? (Before you start firing off e-mails, I'm a Baby Boomer.) See Figure 1-14 for the life periods that define a generation.

There has been a great deal of discussion about whether generations of people guide societal direction or whether society guides the development of generations. In fact, most sociologists who study the relationship observe that the two are inextricably related, that they influence each other. In fact, societies as a general rule pass through four behavioral phases. Those phases are driven by powerful change agents that include the evolution of social values, shifts in political power, balances in demographics and social makeup, and economic upturns and downturns. Those phases, which are shown in Figure 1-15, blend one into the next like the seasons of life, with each season lasting about 20 years.

The first phase, by convention, is social strength, a time of growth and optimism during which business institutions grow stronger and the individual grows weaker as individuals place more trust in banks, health care

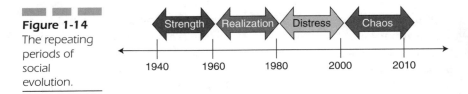

Figure 1-14
The repeating periods of social evolution.

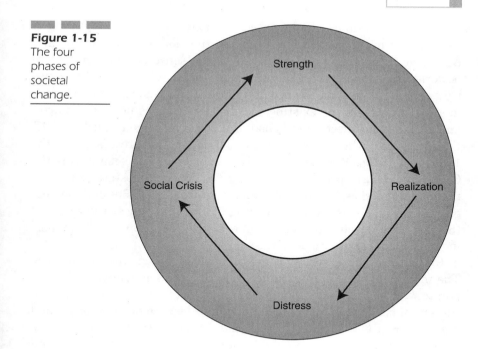

Figure 1-15
The four phases of societal change.

institutions, and large corporations. During this period the individual becomes relatively anonymous and places his or her trust in the institution to guide society. Think back to the 1950s and 1960s, when seemingly everybody worked for a large oil company, a bank, IBM, or AT&T (remember that there was a time when AT&T had a staggering 1 million employees). This is the period when the comedian Bob Newhart released his *Organization Man* album, which made light of corporate America. During this period a social norm emerges and flourishes as the strength of the previous norm declines. The most recent occurrence of this evolutionary phase was during the Truman, Eisenhower, and Kennedy presidencies in the United States During that time the United States became powerful and confident but also became highly conformist. A societal "Borg" formed as everyone danced to the tune of the large corporation. This was the "Leave It To Beaver" era when the corporate uniform was the white button-down shirt, dark blue suit, red tie, briefcase, and hat. At the same time, however, a feeling of spiritual emptiness gripped the country that prompted follow-on generations such as the Millennials to seek greater meaning in their lives. More about that later.

The second phase in this inexorable process is a period of realization that bubbles just below the surface for quite some time. During this period the individual, who has become anonymous with the vesting of social power in the institutions, begins to question "the meaning of life." As people increasingly are disturbed by the sense of being ever more powerless, a strong probing of social mores ensues. This period becomes loud and passionate, and as people's sense of spiritual emptiness begins to grow, attacks on the existing social order occur as new values arise and start to take effect. Think about the rise of movements such as EST, Lifespring, and others targeted at the self-affirmation process during the 1960s and 1970s. Most recently this phenomenon was seen during the Carter and Reagan presidencies, a time that saw manifestations such as the sometimes violent unrest that continued from the 1960s and the Reagan tax revolt. A certain "moral courage" came into play as the values of the past were rejected and a sense of personal liberation and a glimmering of individual power emerged.

In the third phase, society is in wholesale revolt against institutions. The individual rises in importance, rejecting the anonymity of the corporate workplace. A search for greater meaning in life begins as institutions weaken. During this period individuals become much stronger and more influential elements of the social fabric, institutions weaken as they decline in regard to public trust, and the values of the inbound "regime" take root and push out the remaining incumbent values. As the quest for meaning peaks during this phase, a sense of moral restlessness grips the country. The controversial presidencies of the first George Bush, Bill Clinton, and the younger Bush fall into this category.

The fourth phase arrives amid a strong sense of change. This is a period of secular crisis in society, a time when individuals search for relevance in their lives. This final phase is a period of crisis and social emergency, a time of strong social upheaval that continues as the new social infrastructure takes effect. The second term of George W. Bush's presidency is in the middle of this phase at the time of this writing as the country picks up the pieces from the devastation of 9/11 and the ensuing war in Iraq.

These four evolutionary periods have been cycling for as long as historians have been studying cultural change and, as might be expected, sociologists give each generation a name. In recent times the four archetypal generations, in the same order as the four phases described above, are the Hero Generation (born 1901 to 1924), the Silent Generation (born 1925 to 1942), the Baby Boomers (born 1943 to 1960), and Generation X (born 1961 to 1981). The most recent arrival, the Millennials, were born between 1982 and 2004. This is critical because the oldest of them have just entered the workplace; the youngest have just been born.

Note that we have named five generations, yet in the last few paragraphs we described four archetypes. In fact, the Millennials are the beginning of the next cycle and are identical in every way to the Hero Generation, the generation that rebuilt after World War II, the generation that Tom Brokaw called "the Greatest Generation" in his book of that name. This is a generation of fixers, a generation determined to right the wrongs left behind by the last two generations; at least that's how they see their role, and they are extraordinarily good at it.

It should be noted that these generational phases are not only a U.S. phenomenon: They occur throughout the world, within all social strata, and although they vary somewhat from region to region, the basic characteristics are identical. In fact, my research has turned up remarkable parallels among societal groups in diverse markets such as Singapore, South Africa, Romania, and Kansas.

And Today?

Today we find ourselves at the end of an inner-driven, introspective Baby Boomer–centric era. The narcissistic Baby Boomers, with their emphasis on accountability, wealth accumulation, and community values, left their mark on succeeding generations. Following the Boomers were the Gen-Xers, an alienated group of kids who felt abandoned by their dual-income parents. Behind them arrived the Millennials, sometimes erroneously called the Gen-Yers (wrong because "Y" implies that they are an extension of the Gen-Xers, and they decidedly are *not*).

So What?

What does this have to do with the technology industry in general and IMS specifically? In fact, a lot, and it behooves corporate leaders to pay very close attention.

A Tale of Three Generations

Each of these most recent generational groupings has definable characteristics that follow its members throughout their lives. The Baby Boomers are ideological to a fault, highly judgmental, focused unwaveringly on values, and inordinately narcissistic. They are the most egocentric generation to come along in a very long time (enough about you, what about me?), a characteristic that shows up often in the workplace. Baby Boomers feel a very strong need to be right and often argue their point of view unceasingly in meetings to ensure that they are heard. When it comes to work, they are driven: Remember that these are the children of the people who grew up during the Great Depression, people who saw their accumulated wealth disappear on a single fateful day. As a result, they inculcated in their children (the Baby Boomers) the belief that wealth is fleeting and therefore should be amassed and diversified.

Baby Boomers are the dual-income generation, a generation for whom work is life and the line between the two is increasingly ephemeral. They have a love-hate relationship with authority of all kinds (think 1960s, Berkeley, Kent State, the Blue Meanies of Chicago). These are the people who smoked so much dope in the 1960s that they don't even *remember* the 1960s, yet if they catch their own children smoking it, they ground them for the rest of their lives.[3] Baby Boomers are perfectionists by nature, somewhat spiritual, and quite community-oriented. They are also fairly optimistic and involved in life, concerning themselves with youth (their own as much as that of their children), health, and wellness. They are also somewhat schizophrenic when it comes to relationships: They have the highest divorce rate in history, often because work comes above all else. The all-important work–life balance often is lacking in their lives.

Finally, Baby Boomers are highly team-oriented, but with a bit of a twist: "It's all right for the team to win as long as I get the credit" is a thought process characteristic of them. The need to win, to be credited, is strong in this group.

The Generation-Xers are strikingly different from their Baby Boomer predecessors. They are skeptical and somewhat cynical about life, as one would expect. These are the children of the Baby Boomers, after all. Because both of their parents worked, their perception is that they grew up in the modern-day equivalent of a Charles Dickens novel, raising themselves and living on their own. As one Gen-Xer said to me in jest, "I lived on the street and had to kill small animals to eat." These are the latchkey kids who came home from school to an empty house and had to fend for themselves.

---

[3] There's wonderful saying about this generation: "If you remember the 1960s, you clearly weren't there."

As one would imagine, they are remarkably self-reliant, action-oriented, and self-accountable. They are also far more balanced in terms of the division of time between their work lives and personal lives. A typical interaction at work between a Baby Boomer and a Gen-Xer might go something like this: "Look, boss, I understand that to get paid, I have to work hard for you—*for eight hours*. After that, I go home. And as for this misplaced pathological idea you have that I'm going to carry a pager and a work cell phone so that you can call me after hours? That's just not going to happen." Imagine what happens when a driven Baby Boomer manages a group of Gen-Xers.

Similarly, they are unimpressed with authority, which is a puzzlement to law enforcement officers. In fact the most common verbal response to exercised authority from a Gen-Xer is—preceded by an exaggerated sigh and a rolling of the eyes—"Whatever...."

Gen-Xers have difficulty making long-term commitments, yet paradoxically they are family-oriented, diversity-aware, risk-friendly, and focused on achieving results. They are balanced in terms of managing their work lives and personal lives and extremely technically adept. Because they grew up to be self-reliant, they don't work well in teams. Put them in a room and ask them to come to a consensus and there will be blood on the walls before they reach a satisfactory conclusion. However, they do work well as individuals and are very good at troubleshooting, technical support, and other "stand-alone" jobs.

Now we turn our attention to the Millennials. The Millennials are as different from the Gen-Xers as the Gen-Xers are from the Boomers. Millennials tend to be confident, team-oriented, and refreshingly conventional. Unlike the Gen-Xers, who eschewed everything that would identify them with their parents, it's okay for Millennials to be smart. Also unlike the Gen-Xers, the Millennials actually *like* their parents.

Perhaps the most important thing to know about them is that they are on a quest for meaning. Millennials are looking for relevance, for a way to make a difference. They are not looking for a career; they are looking for a job. If the job gives them a sense of relevance, they will stay in it for a very long time and make it look like a career. However, place them in a position that has them doing the same meaningless task repeatedly with no sense of social value and they will leave without warning.

I recently had an opportunity to see this phenomenon firsthand in India. A large corporation that operates call centers in Bangalore asked me to spend some time with its management team to help them resolve a problem they faced with entry-level employees. They had a practice of hiring college graduates and placing them in call centers as operators, a position that for years had worked well as an entry point to the corporation and from which employees could move on to greater responsibility within the firm. New hires were given 10 days of training before being placed on the phones. The problem that this company was facing was that the average new hire was staying on the job for an average of *four days after the completion of training*. It didn't take long to realize that the vast majority of the new employees were Millennials and, after four days of answering phones day in and day out, they saw no relevance in the daily grind they were subjecting themselves to; therefore, they left in large numbers.

We conducted telephone interviews with both current and former employees and discovered that our conclusions were correct: They were leaving because of the lack of a sense of being valued by management or providing value to something greater than themselves. After asking them a few other questions that consisted of nothing more than a generic skills inventory, we returned to management and submitted our findings. "These kids," we told them, "come into your business with diverse skill sets that are important to them. Are you aware, for example, that that fellow over there [pointing out the supervisor's window to a young man in a cubicle] speaks 11 languages and that those languages are important to him? And did you know that that young lady in the far corner has very strong sales skills, yet you have her answering technical support questions?"

They weren't aware because, as far as they were concerned, the new employees were coming in as tabula rasa and had nothing substantive to add other than their energy and whatever they had learned in training. We suggested a few changes to the way the call centers were being run, the most substantive of which was that the Millennial new hires be given the freedom to use their skills in a way that would make them more valuable as employees. The control-oriented Baby Boomer managers reluctantly agreed and, within weeks, the retention rate rose to over seven months.

As a rule, Millennials tend to be strong achievers if they are properly motivated, optimistic about things, sociable, street-smart, and highly moral. In fact, this generation is one of the most moral, rule-abiding generations to come along in a very long time.[4] They play by the rules. For example, when the older end of this generation goes out to party on weekends, they appoint a designated driver *who does not*

---

[4] My wife and I have two Millennials on a long-term lease. As a result, I have a little Millennial laboratory that I can consult any time I like by simply observing our kids and their friends.

drink—period. When I was a kid, being the designated driver meant that you'd drink only beer. These kids take social responsibility seriously. In fact, for the first time in decades the number of people attending church, a number that had been in steady decline for nearly 40 years, is on the rise as Millennials seek a greater sense of meaning in their lives. Peace Corps sign-ups are climbing, and the numbers of college students involved in community projects is higher than it has been in a long time.

Another interesting thing about this generation is that they are *absolutely oblivious* to authority: not love-hate, not unimpressed, but oblivious. They are so morals-driven, so self-policing, that they don't understand the need for outside authority in their lives. This too is a puzzlement to law enforcement personnel, as much because of their obligation to enforce laws that the Millennials don't understand the need for as because of their need to understand the behavior and drivers of Millennial employees coming into law enforcement.

Another characteristic of Millennials is their commitment to long-term relationships with each other. As early as high school Millennials enter into serious relationships that last a very long time. This flows over into the way they make decisions. Millennials are the antithesis of the Baby Boomers, who wanted all the credit. Whereas the Baby Boomers are wont to say, "It's all right for the team to win as long as I get the credit," Millennials are more likely to say, "It's all right if I get a little credit as long as the team wins." Here's why.

What We Know about Millennials: The Important Stuff

Here's what we know about Millennials that is worth remembering. Keep in mind that this demographic and sociological data is important because these kids, who are your new employees, soon will move up into higher management levels and take on decision-making responsibilities. Not only will they be your employees, they will be your customers and competitors. Time taken today to understand what drives and motivates them is time well spent.

It should come as no surprise that Millennials are heavily influenced by and dependent on technology, particularly communications technologies. This is the first generation in history to grow up in a world that always had the Internet, always had the World Wide Web, always had mobile telephony, *and has no allegiance whatsoever to twisted-pair*.

A wired telephone to this generation is an anachronism, and its members are disconnecting them in growing numbers, relying instead on mobile devices. More and more of them, for example, are choosing to use their mobile phones as their primary mode of communication, eschewing the perceived safe harbor of 911 service and "carrier-class" voice quality in favor of freedom of mobility and on-demand connectivity.

Needless to say, this poses a substantial challenge for incumbent telephone companies that have invested billions of dollars in their in-place wireline networks and now watch as their costs remain the same while their revenues decline. Predictably, a Millennial's preferred communications modality is SMS or IM first, e-mail second and, if they absolutely have to, they'll talk on a phone, but it better not have a wire attached to it. They carry more gadgets on their hips and in their purses and backpacks than Batman and spend an amazing $109 *per week* on technology-oriented products and services. Never mind that the vast majority of that money comes out of their parents' pockets. What matters is that the Millennials direct the spending of it. Furthermore, they influence 70% to 80% of the spending in the home.

Millennials enjoy group activities and in fact work best in cooperative teams. As individuals they do not test well in problem-solving situations, yet they test *off the charts* in groups. Even in social situations they prefer larger groups. If you ever have the opportunity to attend a Millennial high school dance, do so just for the experience. They don't dance in couples; they dance in *clusters*. They don't date in pairs either; they date in large groups, enjoying the camaraderie of their peers.

In the center of Tokyo there is a large intersection (Figure 1-16) where five major roads come together. Traffic lights are timed to go red at the same time so that pedestrians can cross in any direction they like, similar to the "chicken walk" in downtown San Francisco (luckily, the lights at Shibuya Crossing do not all go *green* at the same time). Every time the lights go red, 3000 people cross the street; it's quite impressive. If you stand at the sidelines and look closely, you will see hundreds of Millennial kids at the periphery of the crowd, some walking through the crowd with an eerie sort of radar working for them and all banging away on the thumb pads of their SMS devices. The first time I saw this phenomenon, I asked quite a few of them what they were doing. Without exception the answer was "Setting up get-togethers with my friends." The SMS device serves as a location beacon and is used to "triangulate" the location of friends so that they can meet in a mutually convenient location.[5]

---

[5] Shibuya Crossing is also where I saw cantaloupes for sale for approximately $100 each. See Figure 1-17.

Figure 1-16
Shibuya
Crossing,
downtown
Tokyo.

Millennials also gave the world the concept of *flash mobs*: the practice of spontaneously gathering large numbers of people at a common public place, typically for no particular reason, although these groups have been used to great effect for political protest and to bring about social change. Flash mobs are characterized as the technique of rapidly assembling a large group of people from multiple directions in a single location for the purpose of attaining a particular goal. The goal may be

Figure 1-17
Cantaloupes in
a Tokyo fruit
market. Note
the price for
the "boxed
set."

social, political, or military; in the case of the Millennials, it is (for now) purely a social phenomenon. Typically, there are four phases in a successful swarm: identify the venue, gather, act, and disperse. For these four phases to work in a coordinated fashion, they must be synchronized among large numbers of people. What better way to perform this massing phenomenon than through the capabilities of the distributed mobile telephony network?

This grouping phenomenon has considerable implications in the workplace. Millennials are remarkable problem solvers when allowed to work in groups. They often subconsciously use a mobbing theme to resolve conflicts and problems that to biologists is reminiscent of the technique used by honeybees to make collective decisions about nest locations, flower availability, predator avoidance, and the like. When confronted with a problem, Millennials collectively analyze the problem, individually analyze the data, and then gather to make the requested decision collectively. All ideas "go into the discussion pot," and the discussion ensues. If an idea is deemed invalid, irrelevant, or simply wrong, it is discarded instantly and emotionlessly. It can come back into the discussion later if need be. As a result, the "fact tree" is pruned rapidly and a decision is reached rapidly.

I have watched this process in action on numerous occasions, and it's a remarkable thing. Individuals may peel off at a moment's notice to call or SMS a friend or colleague to ask a question, extending the knowledge web that produces the most accurate possible answer. This behavior is a living example of Metcalfe's law, which, as we discussed earlier in this chapter, states that the value of a connected network increases exponentially as a function of the number of nodes in that network. If the network is a Millennial decision-making process, it is easy to see why this technique is so astonishingly functional. It is also easy to see why a Baby Boomer or Generation-X manager watching this process might wonder what in the world is going on, because to the unschooled eye it looks an exercise in unbridled chaos.

Baby Boomers and Gen-Xers were taught to respect the laws of linear thinking, whereas Millennials are nonlinear problem solvers. Managers beware: Just because they don't approach a problem the way you would, that doesn't mean they're wrong. It does mean that their behavior as customers and competitors will be substantially different from the norm to which we have become accustomed. They will use every means at their disposal, most of them electronic and immediate, to employ their knowledge web to gather intelligence about a product or service. You must be prepared for this. Recognize also that this behavior of using the web of connectivity that is an inextricable component of their lives feeds directly into the IMS concept: anywhere, anytime access to content and computing, with services delivered to any device recognizable by the network.

It also is interesting to note that the Millennials are members of the first generation in the 54-year history of television that is watching *substantially* less of it, choosing to get their entertainment content elsewhere. As you might imagine, this is a serious, vexing concern for television advertisers, forcing them to place ads in venues such as video games.

One final observation about this generation: Because of immigration and emigration, globalization, and the growing number of multinational corporations that move employees freely and routinely around the globe, Millennials are more ethnically and racially diverse than any previous generation. But far more important, they are ethnically and racially *oblivious*: They don't see it. There may be hope for the world yet.

I saw a firsthand example of this several years ago when my daughter made friends with Angela (a pseudonym), another girl in her high school. Because of my ridiculous travel schedule, I didn't meet Angela for over two years. Whenever she was at the house I was on a trip, and whenever I was home she wasn't around. However, because she was part of my daughter's group of friends, I soon knew as much about Angela as I would have if I actually had met her. I knew where she lived, where she was from, who she was dating, and what her teenage problems were. When I finally met her, I did a double take because Angela is African-American. I wasn't shocked because she is African-American; I was shocked because *it never occurred to my daughter or to any of her friends to use skin color as a way to describe their friend.* Never once, in two years of hearing about their lives and activities, did that come up.

▮▮▮ Millennials in the Workplace

What do you need to know about Millennials to take advantage of their remarkable capabilities on the job? First, recognize that employees fall into four tiered roles, as shown in Table 1-1. In each tier employees interact with the values that will guide them throughout their careers and lives. The lowest tier is the entry-level position in which employees *learn*

Table 1-1 The relationship between generations, responsibilities, and values.

Role	Values	Today	20 Years Out
Corporate Leadership	Establishing Values	Baby Boomers	Generation-X
Corporate Energy	Applying Values	Generation-X	Millennials
Corporate Enthusiasm	Testing Values	Millennials	Millennials
Entry-Level	Learning Values	Millennials	???

the values that will establish professional behavior patterns throughout their careers. Most people have seen the Dell commercials that use the "interns theme" to demonstrate the company's capabilities. Those interns are Millennial employees. In most corporations today this role is held by the older Millennials who are just graduating from college and entering the workforce.

At the second tier we find the stratum of employees who generate corporate enthusiasm and exude limitless supplies of energy. These are the employees who often are found working at trade shows and marketing events, working 27 hours a day and loving every minute of it, displaying their tireless enthusiasm as they *test* the values they learned early in their entry-level training. Today they too are typically Millennials.

At the third tier we find the slightly older Generation X employees who are now in middle management and are *applying* the corporate values that have shaped them in their careers and personal lives. They are professional role models for the up-and-coming younger employees and are often supervisors. They are tirelessly energetic, often working at all hours in data centers, manufacturing plants, and call centers.

Finally, at the fourth, uppermost tier, we find the corporate leaders. With their professional longevity they are charged with creating the values that guide the corporation. Today they are for the most part Baby Boomers. The last shadows of the Silent Generation have retired, and the Gen-Xers for the most part have not yet penetrated this tier.

Now shift gears and look how the profile changes over 20 years, one generation beyond where we are today. The Baby Boomers have retired, and Gen-Xers have moved into the upper tier of the corporation. The Millennials are now in the middle and lower tiers of the management ranks, and that means they are hiring and firing employees, making purchase decisions, establishing sales and marketing strategies, and preparing to run their companies. This is why it is important to develop a strategy today to deal with Millennials in the marketplace tomorrow.

▆▆▆ Understanding the Millennials

To interact with or manage Millennials effectively, it is critical to understand what drives them and what shapes the values of their generation. There are also a number of perceptions employers must be aware of when working with Millennials. The first is the perception that there is "no such thing as reality." This is the Internet generation, after all, and if nothing else, the Internet has proved to this generation that it takes no effort to attach Pamela Anderson's head to Sylvester Stallone's body seamlessly or to create a gaming experience that seems quite real but clearly isn't. Yes, they know the difference between killing people in a video game and then taking a break and going out to do it in the real world. Remember, this group is morals-driven.

It is also important to know that Millennials are primarily experiential learners. They learn by doing, and learn quickly and accurately when allowed to interact with whatever they are attempting to learn. When you got that new mobile phone, who did you ask to program it? More than likely it was a Millennial. Note also that instruction guides are wasted on them. They'd rather just use something that's unfamiliar to them until they have learned what they need to know.

Another interesting thing about this generation is that the Internet is perceived to be far more fulfilling than television is. As we noted earlier, Millennials are watching less television than any generation before them. The result of this has been a shift in advertising revenues and a renewed interest in presence technology as a way to learn more about the demographic behaviors that are so important to sales and marketing efforts.

A great deal of material has been published on the subject of Millennials and attention deficit disorder (ADD) and whether this generation is more prone to it than were other generations (whatever *it* is). Articles have begun appearing in serious medical and psychological journals about this subject, but with a bit of a twist. Some health care professionals and behaviorists are beginning to ask whether ADD may simply be a neurological response to the Millennials' need to multitask as the number of simultaneous sensory inputs they are bombarded by grows. Whatever the case, Millennials multitask exceptionally well. If you don't believe that, stand behind one of them who is sitting at the computer engaged in seven IM sessions, talking on the cell phone propped between the head and a raised shoulder, ripping a CD, answering e-mail, listening to music, and doing homework—*all well*. I don't claim to be a psychologist, medical professional, or behavior theorist, but I read enormous volumes of information about the subject of evolving Millennial behavior and find that the accelerating level of interest in this subject is appealing.

One other observation while we are on the subject of computers: To a Millennial, they are *not* "technology" any more than the telephone and television were technologies to earlier generations. Also, they are not an option; they are a necessary part of everyday life, and their availability is not open for debate. Similarly, connectivity—and it better be broadband—is not optional.

Colleges and universities are finding this to be the case in a somewhat painful way. It used to be the case that a major profit center at institutions for higher learning was the campus telephone network. Dormitories were wired for voice service, and students paid a monthly fee to the university for the privilege of having a telephone in their dorm rooms. Today, students arrive on campus fully wired with mobile phones, wireless PDAs, Blackberries, WiFi-equipped laptops, and a solid understanding of the concept of free voice. Their message to the college? "Oh, thanks anyway, but I don't need your phone. I have a phone. What I need is broadband wireless, and it better be campuswide or I'll go somewhere else." And they do: Ubiquitous broadband wireless connectivity is becoming a criterion for school selection in colleges and universities. More than one school has gone through the onerous task of selling its campus switch because maintenance has become a major drain on resources, particularly given the fact that campus voice revenues largely have disappeared.

One last fact before we leave behind the subject of Millennials and technology: For those of you who bought a nice pen and pencil set as a graduation gift, *take it back*. Millennials compose well and collect and share ideas well, but they do it on computers and SMS devices. They don't write. A nice matched wireless keyboard and mouse, perhaps.

■ Other Millennial Tidbits

The list of Millennial characteristics continues to grow and becomes more fascinating the more we learn about them. Whenever I lecture on this subject, a handful of people always come up to me laughing, telling me that I just described their kids. It's true: The law of large numbers says that as long as the statistical sample is sufficiently large, it is valid to make general assumptions about the behavior of social groups. Here are some additional facts. Because Millennials play by the rules, they naturally expect others to do so as well. Baby Boomers, take note: *If you make a commitment to a Millennial and fail to meet that commitment, you will hear about it for the rest of your life.*

One seemingly unavoidable aspect of Millennial life is video games. In conversations with them I have learned that video games to them are "windows on the world," a technique for performing a subliminal form of scenario planning and what-if analysis. In fact, video game companies have picked up on this and are beginning to manufacture games for the major platforms that are actually very powerful business tools. For the right amount of money, video game companies will build "Sim-IBM" (assuming you work for IBM), complete with customers, competitors, products and services, employees, financial data, and competitive intelligence. Strategists can play the game, changing the variables to engage with different outcome scenarios to see how the company would fare in different market conditions. Gamers who have used these products rave about them because they tend to provide an accelerated view of how the company would behave in different sets of competitive conditions.

A recent example of this what-if scenario process occurred in 2004, when a half million players engaged in an Internet-based "scavenger hunt" for four months, often divided into teams and occasionally required to get together to solve complex problems. The game required players to gather in both the real world and online to solve their given tasks collectively by using information gotten from Web sources and then physically deliver information to locations in the real world. One piece of the exercise, for example, required participants to find and decipher Global Positioning System (GPS) location data, send players to phone booths scattered all over the United States and, upon calling a specific number, respond within a few seconds to unexpected questions from a live actor on the other end of the phone. To deliver the proper answer, each participant had to trust a group of people he or she had never met to provide instantly the information he or she needed to respond correctly.

The game was called ilovebees, and it centered on the website of a fictitious honey company that served as the starting point for the game. Interestingly, the real purpose of the game was to serve as a viral marketing tool for the Microsoft Xbox game Halo 2.

This kind of immersive gaming experience often is referred to as an *alternative reality game* (ARG). Although ARGs work well as marketing tools, they are actually instructive, teaching participants how to navigate through massive volumes of data and information and collectively swarm a problem to resolve it quickly and accurately.

According to the primary community coordinator of ilovebees, Jane McGonigal, these types of games create players "who feel more capable, more confident, more expressive, more engaged and more connected in their everyday lives."[6]

These immersive experiential environments evolve and change as the participants make their way through them, causing participants to change their responses to unexpected outcomes that occur within the game. One of the things that make these experiential environments so effective as learning and problem-solving tools is that there is a tacit agreement among the participants that they will suspend belief while playing and accept the fact that while they are immersed in the game, this *is* the "real world." As a result, the ARG experience becomes that much more effective.

One final observation about the Millennial Generation: They believe that content found on the Internet should be free to everyone—sorry, Metallica. They casually burn CDs of ripped music and routinely share the files with each other. Although this technically constitutes theft of intellectual property, here's the interesting thing: After they rip the music, they buy the CD. In fact, when the government shut down the file-sharing sites Napster and KaZaA a few years ago in response to pressure from the music industry, CD sales took a savage dip, as shown in Figure 1-18.

All these characteristics should lead the reader to understand that this is a distinctly different group of people from those found in the typical corporation today. They are a rich source of corporate capability and energy and, as long as they are motivated properly, they will prove to be a formidable component of the workforce. The question, of course, is how to do that.

Motivating the Millennials

What is the best way to motivate Millennials in the workplace? First, pay attention to the characteristics listed earlier and, to the degree possible, structure the workplace around them. Recognize Millennials' high level of required social interaction. Use experiential learning and team assignments wherever and whenever possible. Give them freedom with

---

[6] Harry Jenkins, "Chasing Bees, without the Hive Mind," *MIT Technology Review* (online edition), December 3, 2004.

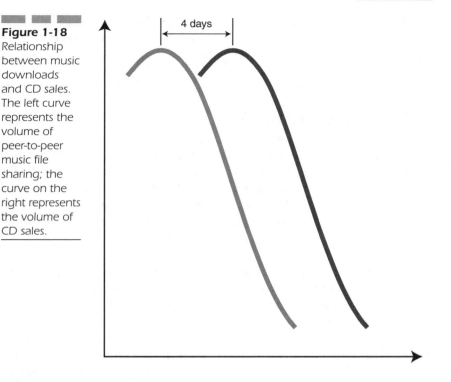

Figure 1-18
Relationship between music downloads and CD sales. The left curve represents the volume of peer-to-peer music file sharing; the curve on the right represents the volume of CD sales.

4 days

regard to where, when, and how they do their jobs. Put work in a nice place, such as their homes, and encourage telecommuting. As morally driven as this generation is, an employer will not be disappointed with the results. Note that the self-policing Millennials do not tolerate delays in themselves and others—they often are seen as being unrealistically impatient—and therefore will deliver on time. They also will not tolerate "being managed." The fact that they don't do the work the way you would do it is not a reason to assume that the work will be done poorly.

Next, make the work they are assigned meaningful. Nothing will turn off a Millennial faster than work that has no perceived value. Remember, they are looking for meaning, so give it to them. At the same time, they like variety, so give Millennials a chance to learn continuously and reward their learning with diverse, ever-changing jobs.

Remember, Millennials look at work differently than did the generations that came before them. They're not necessarily looking for a *career*; they're looking for *meaningful work*. If the work is meaningful and challenging, they may become long-term employees.

Finally, give them plenty of continuous feedback. When assigning work, state the desired outcome as clearly as possible and then step out of the way and let them run with it. It *will* get done and most likely will exceed expectations provided that the work is meaningful and challenging. This cannot be stated strongly enough.

Conclusion

Because the Millennials are a functional repeat of the famously capable Hero Generation, they are ideally suited to inherit the chaos of the early years of the twenty-first century. They will rebuild and strengthen the institutions that keep the country stable, create a longed-for sense of community and belonging, and restore order and purpose, leading the country out of the secular crisis that plagues it today. Fear not: We're in good hands.

Let me reiterate this for readers who are scratching their heads and wondering why a treatise on sociological norms is included in this book about IMS. Networks are only as valuable as the people using them, and their value is directly proportional to the degree to which they bring value to those users. Millennials are a very different group of people for whom technology is a lifestyle choice, not a visible set of tools they occasionally use. They expect to be fully connected all the time and want to have seamless access to content from a broad variety of devices, both mobile and fixed, without hassle. The network to them is immaterial because in the minds of Millennial customers *access* means *access to my stuff*. The network must adapt to ensure that it delivers the right content, to the right device, in the hands of the right person, in the right form, with the right features, at the right time, for the right price. End of discussion. In other words, the network must learn to adapt to the requirements of the user instead of the user having to modify her or his behavior because of the physical limitations of the network.

As we'll see later in the book, this is what IMS is all about: building a user-aware network infrastructure that has the ability to do what we've just described. Because Millennials soon will be not only employees but also highly influential customers and competitors, it is critical to start thinking now about how the network must evolve to accommodate their needs.

In Chapter 2 we look at the IMS marketplace scenario and the current state of technology before diving into the inner workings of IMS.

CHAPTER **2**

Beginnings

■■■ ■■ ■■
Figure 2-1
A business
computer, circa
1989, cheap at
$9,000. Note:
Mouse and
monitor **not**
included!

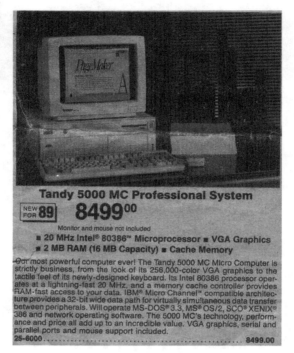

Tandy 5000 MC Professional System

NEW FOR 89 **8499**⁰⁰

Monitor and mouse not included
- **20 MHz Intel® 80386™ Microprocessor** ■ **VGA Graphics**
- **2 MB RAM (16 MB Capacity)** ■ **Cache Memory**

Our most powerful computer ever! The Tandy 5000 MC Micro Computer is
strictly business, from the look of its 256,000-color VGA graphics to the
tactile feel of its newly-designed keyboard. Its Intel 80386 processor operates at a lightning-fast 20 MHz, and a memory cache controller provides
RAM-fast access to your data. IBM® Micro Channel™ compatible architecture provides a 32-bit wide data path for virtually simultaneous data transfer
between peripherals. Will operate MS-DOS® 3.3, MS® OS/2, SCO® XENIX®
386 and network operating software. The 5000 MC's technology, performance and price all add up to an incredible value. VGA graphics, serial and
parallel ports and mouse support included.
25-6000 . . . . 8499.00

We laugh at the woefully inadequate capabilities of the machine shown
in Figure 2-1. It hit the market 17 years ago, in 1989. Yet it is immensely
more powerful than Ed Roberts's Altair, which became available to the
public 14 years before the Tandy machine. I ask you this: In 2011, a mere
five years from now, what will cause us to look back on 2006 and laugh
at the silly technology we are so proud of today?

The future that is fast approaching is a tantalizing one and will be
here before we realize it. Let's take a look at what it portends by describing the typical home and work environment of my good friend Dennis
McCooey as he prepares for his week several years in the future. I ask
you to suspend skepticism as you read the next section because it will
help you understand (1) what is coming and (2) which companies are
going to deliver on the promise of the future described here.

■■■■ In the Not Too Distant Future

Dennis woke slowly to the incessant chime of his PDA at 6:15. There
were times, like this one, when he hated the thing. Smart enough to note

the 8 A.M. meeting in its database, the PDA automatically set an alarm to wake him on time.

Sitting up, Dennis removed the device from its cradle and checked the other entries on his schedule. Other than the flight to Madrid that afternoon, it was a fairly light day. Before placing the PDA back in its cradle, he used the stylus to bring up the device's applications list. Selecting an icon that looked like a coffee cup, he scrolled down and selected "brew" from the list of options. As he walked into the shower, the PDA broadcast a signal to the coffeepot in the kitchen, which blinked on and began to fill the house with the smell of freshly brewed Costa Rican La Minita coffee.

Turning on the shower, Dennis brushed his teeth while waiting for it to warm up. A minute later he climbed into the stall, turned to the back wall, and said, "NPR." Instantly the voice of Bob Edwards filled the shower. He listened for about 10 minutes while bathing, then, as he shaved, said, "Voice mail." After a brief delay a disembodied voice responded, "Office, nine messages; mobile, two messages; home, zero messages. Say 'yes' to list the originators." Reaching for a bottle of after-shave lotion, Dennis declined, saying instead, "Mobile." Within seconds the messages collected for his mobile device began to play over the speakers in the bathroom. He responded to the first message, with his voice picked up and transferred by the microphones in the room, but the second was a long rambling message from a coworker that contained detailed information he needed for the meeting in Madrid the next day. "Stop," he commanded, then, "Save. Text. PDA." The disembodied voice replied, "Message saved to PDA. File size, 4K. You have 3.2 MB of storage remaining on your PDA." Dressed, he wandered into the kitchen.

At the kitchen table Dennis read the paper while drinking his coffee. Reaching across to the counter, he powered up the Macintosh and watched as the photograph of Madrid's Plaza Mayor that he used as his wallpaper faded up from black and listened as HAL's voice from *2001: A Space Odyssey* said, "I'm completely operational, and all my circuits are functioning perfectly." He downloaded 58 e-mail messages, scanned them quickly while sipping the coffee, and decided they could wait until he reached the office. Shutting down the desktop machine, he returned to the newspaper.

When the time came to leave for the office, he turned off the coffeepot, grabbed his mobile phone from the charger near the door, picked up his briefcase, and headed outside. Before leaving, he wrote a note to his wife, who was in California visiting family but would return in a few days. He set his briefcase on the porch and then went back inside for his suitcase, which he had packed the night before for the trip to Madrid that afternoon.

As he walked to the car, his phone gave off a gentle beep. Looking at the screen, he watched as the display changed from "LEAVING HOME BASE STATION" to "CONNECTED TO VERIZON WIRELESS," followed by "CALL-FORWARDING HOME NUMBER TO MOBILE." The system knew to do this because of his prerecorded preferences stored somewhere deep in the network.

As he drove down the main street of town, listening to NPR on the radio, lost in thought, Dennis had his reverie interrupted by the sudden ringing of his mobile phone. "Answer phone," he instructed the device, and after a brief hesitation the speaker activated and said, "Good morning, Mr. McCooey. Today, whole-bean Costa Rican La Minita is on sale at Speeder and Earl's for 30% off the normal price in quantities of a pound or more. To take advantage of this great value, please turn right at the next corner and immediately turn right into our parking lot. If you'd like, press pound now, and we'll have your usual two pounds ready to go with a free cup of black coffee." Pressing the pound key, he followed the message's instructions, picked up the coffee, paying for it with his phone, and continued to the office, where he parked in the lot, grabbed his briefcase, and headed inside.

As Dennis approached the door of the building, his phone again gave a gentle beep, and he knew that it was connecting itself logically to the corporate PBX while automatically forwarding calls from his home and mobile numbers. As he greeted the security guard and approached the gate, the indicator light on the portal turned from red to green, and the door opened. He passed through and headed to his office.

At his desk Dennis booted his PC, watching as Windows came to life and eventually gave way as the Plaza Mayor again faded up from black. Booting Eudora, he scanned the 58 messages he had reviewed quickly earlier on the Mac at home and began to respond to them. Some he answered, and some he discarded; most he left for later because they were not urgent or required more thought than he had time for at the moment. When he finished, he headed off to a series of boring meetings that started at 8:00, during which he answered a few of the remaining e-mail messages with his PDA. He also brought up the text-based voice mail message that he had saved that morning, read it over carefully, and responded. The meetings weren't a complete waste, he decided.

In the last one, however, he was asked to generate a report showing the results of a variety of business scenarios that could occur in certain circumstances. Using the need to get started as an excuse to leave the meeting, he beat a hasty retreat to his desk, where he set up the DecisionPoint software, plugged in the necessary parameters, and set the system to its task. He smiled as he thought about what it used to take in the way of machine resources to run this kind of application; they used to have to run them at night, and then only with permission because they were such resource hogs. Even on night shift, when system utilization was at the lowest level, those jobs often took hours to complete. As he pondered this, the PC beeped softly, indicating that the number crunching was complete. Printing the report, he wandered off to the cafeteria to have one more cup of coffee and look it over before turning the report over to those who had requested it.

Shortly after lunch Dennis shut down his PC, said good-bye to a few people, and drove to the airport. He was on his way to Madrid for a meeting with several clients who had semiconductor manufacturing operations on the south side of that city. Their businesses were going well, but they were concerned that the overgrowth of manufacturing capacity in Asia might result in a downturn in the domestic manufacturing sector and wanted to discuss planning for the future to ensure their longevity. He would be in Madrid for the week, long enough to take care of business and enjoy his favorite city again. Thoughts of *cochinillo asado, paella a la Valenciana*, and *arroz con leche* made his mouth water.

On the plane he managed to get work done, responding to the remaining e-mail and voice mail messages that had accumulated since his departure from the office. He watched a movie, read most of the latest John Grisham novel that he had on his PDA, took a nap, and ate the pseudomeal that they served. Animal, vegetable, or mineral? he wondered as he picked listlessly at the unrecognizable food on the tray. Thoughts of the culinary marvels he would enjoy in the days ahead bolstered his spirits, and he threw his napkin over the tray and went back to reading.

On arrival at Barajas International Airport, he passed through passport control and customs without incident, hailed a cab, and headed downtown to the Meliá on Princesa. Recognizing him as a frequent visitor (hearing fluent Castilian Spanish coming from the mouth of an obvious non-Spaniard always helped), the desk clerk checked him into an upgraded business suite and promised to have his bags sent up immediately. Dennis thanked him, picked up his briefcase, and headed for the elevator.

The room was nicely appointed, airy, and spacious, with a view toward the Moncloa arch and a modern PC on the desk. When the bags arrived, he tipped the boy who brought them up, unpacked, hung up his clothes, and jumped into a hot shower. It was early in the morning in Madrid and he was exhausted, and so he hung the do-not-disturb sign on the door and jumped into bed for a quick nap. He knew that this would be a late night and that he'd never make it without some sleep.

In what seemed like only a few minutes, his cell phone jarred him awake. Groggily he looked at the clock and saw that he had been asleep for nearly five hours. Answering the phone, he heard the telltale voice of his old friend Manuel: "So, are you here yet? Let's go; time's wasting. I have reservations for dinner this evening downtown, after which we're going to a flamenco show some friends are putting on. Did you sleep?" Dennis smiled at his old friend's exuberance. An artist who always claimed to be starving but probably made more money than Dennis, Manuel was tied into the art scene in Madrid like no one else and always could be counted on to put together entertainment for any evening Dennis had available. They agreed to meet at 9 P.M. in a restaurant Dennis had never heard of. "I just transmitted the GPS coordinates to you, so no excuses this time about getting lost," chided Manuel.

After a long walk up Avenida Princesa to Plaza España, Dennis returned to his room and took another shower before getting ready for dinner. After shaving and getting dressed, he turned to the PC on his desk. He entered his log-in ID and password in the appropriate fields and pressed his thumb against the biometric pad adjacent to the keyboard. After a few seconds the familiar photo of the Plaza Mayor appeared on the screen along with all his files and applications. HAL's voice informed him that this machine was as alive and well as the Mac in the kitchen at home, and so he booted Outlook Express and checked messages. Luckily, there weren't many; the few that had come in could wait until the next day.

Satisfied, he grabbed a light jacket, left the hotel, and hailed a taxi. Instructing the driver to take him to the Puerta del Sol, the plaza that is the emotional center of Madrid, he watched as the city passed by his window. He instructed the driver to drop him on the southwest corner of the plaza; stepping out, he inhaled deeply the smells of the old city as he walked west toward the Plaza Mayor and his nearby meeting place with Manuel. Turning south, he walked down a short, narrow street that smelled of chorizo and fish and diesel. Passing under an archway that looked as if it had been there since before there was dirt, he walked into the square and once again was overcome by the beauty of the place. In the center of the plaza was a bronze statue of Phillip III on horseback, and it was under the rear end of that horse that he and Manuel traditionally had met as teenagers. Passing the statue, he continued down the far staircase into the windy streets of the oldest section of the city, the voice of the PDA talking softly through the Bluetooth headset, giving him walking directions.

Turning the corner, he spotted the place. Sure enough, there was Manuel, oblivious to the world, watching the people go by without really seeing them. Dennis was less than 10 feet away when Manuel finally recognized him. Embracing, they greeted each other warmly before heading down the stairs into the older part of the city to eat in a restaurant that was unknown to the myriad tourists who visited Madrid.

They sat in the restaurant for three hours, and at midnight the flamenco show started. This was not the flashy, colorful flamenco that visitors to Spain see; it was the dark, gritty flamenco that rises from the depths of the Gypsy soul and hangs in the air like torn black cloth, bouncing erratically off the sharp staccato notes of the guitar. Over strong red wine, fiery brandy, and dark Spanish coffee they listened until the singers could sing no more. At 3 A.M. the restaurant ushered everyone out into the night, the cool crisp air feeling good after the smoke-filled evening in the restaurant. Good thing his meetings didn't start until noon the next day, Dennis thought. What a civilized country. Before leaving *TablaoFlamenco*, he pulled his PDA from his pocket, searched Amazon for one particular performer, and ordered two CDs of the man's work.

His PDA woke him at 10:30 in the morning. Slightly fuzzy-headed, Dennis stumbled into the bathroom to get ready for the day ahead. The hot water revived him; half an hour later he was ready to go. Plucking his PDA and cell phone from their charging cradles, he headed off to the first meeting. He knew he had to begin this one with a PowerPoint presentation about the current state of the industry because the attendees were all over the map with regard to their collective opinions about the company's position in the game. This shouldn't be too difficult, he thought. They had good products and a strong management team but weren't dealing with the competition particularly well and weren't attuned enough to customer requirements to be effective. He walked out to the street and descended into the metro, taking the train to the other side of town, where the client's offices were.

When he arrived, he signed in at security and picked up the badge they had left for him. Taking the elevator to the twelfth floor, he quickly found the conference room where he knew the meeting would be held. He had been in that room before and knew where the ceiling-mounted projector controls were. He walked over to the PC at the front of the room, turned it on, and waited for it to complete the boot process. As soon as it was ready, he logged in as he had done in his hotel room, placing his thumb on the reader. Without incident his desktop appeared, and he brought up the PowerPoint presentation he needed for this meeting. By then people had begun to drift in, some of whom he knew. They introduced him to the new faces.

The meeting went very well, as did the others later in the day. He finished around 5 P.M. and took a taxi back to Sol, having decided to walk from there to his hotel. It was a nice day and still warm, and it would do him good to walk after sitting in meetings all day. He passed familiar-smelling shops filled with dried ham and sausages and fresh vegetables, enjoying the sights and sounds of the city.

His reverie was broken by a soft beep from his PDA. Opening it, he found a message on the screen: "SWORD FOR SAM, BASQUE PAPRIKA AND SAFFRON FOR HELEN. ALL AVAILABLE AT JOYAS SEVILLA, ONE BLOCK UP ON RIGHT. 15% DISCOUNT FOR AMERICAN EXPRESS PURCHASES." He had forgotten about the gifts he wanted to pick up. As he deleted the message, another popped up on the screen: "MESSAGE FROM DOWNLOAD SERVICE: 28 PAGES REMAIN UNREAD OF CURRENT E-BOOK. YOU HAVE ASKED TO BE NOTIFIED OF AVAILABILITY DATES OF NEW WORKS BY SELECTED AUTHORS. *SWORD OF TERROR* BY RICHARD PARLATO IS NOW AVAILABLE; DOWNLOAD?" Responding positively to the message, he put the PDA back in his pocket. Arriving at the store, he found the spices for his wife but decided to wait on the sword. Tonight he'd search online for the one he wanted for his son.

As he approached the hotel, Dennis realized that he wasn't ready to go inside yet, and so he paused at the Plaza España and sat on a stone bench in front of the statue of Don Quixote. His mind wandering aimlessly, he decided to check his e-mail. Pulling the PDA from his pocket, he quickly scanned through the messages, answering a few and discarding the rest. Clicking to another application, he caught the latest broadcast from CNN Headline News, followed by the latest from NPR and BBC. Satisfied and growing hungry, he rose and headed back to the hotel.

The Underlying Technologies

The scenario in the preceding section may seem whimsical but is in fact representative of the direction in which the technology sectors is going and the promise of IMS. Furthermore, a number of key players in those industry sectors are proving to be the force behind this evolution. We'll discuss them and their role in a moment; first, let's peek into the future at the underlying technology.

Consider all the routine activities that McCooey engaged in on the preceding pages.

- A converged-function PDA awakened him in the morning and then used a wireless link (probably Bluetooth) to start the coffeepot.

- Voice recognition allowed McCooey to turn on the radio and select a specific station and then allowed him to access and seamlessly (and effortlessly) operate three different voice mail systems.

- Network signaling allowed him to access the same e-mail content from multiple machines in multiple countries.

- A user-aware network gave him the opportunity to call-forward his home and mobile lines automatically to his office number. Note that it required no action on his part; the process occurred automatically as the result of a user-configurable database entry.

- Location-based services combined with mobile voice service directed him to his favorite coffee establishment and later helped him find gifts for his family in Madrid.

- The RFID (Radio Frequency Identification) tag built into his phone, the credit card in his wallet, or his PDA automatically opened the security gate at the office.

- Grid computing allowed him to create a virtual supercomputer that enabled him to perform the massive job requested at his morning meeting.

- An enhanced signaling network facilitated the follow-me capability that allowed McCooey's mobile phone to be reachable anywhere in the world. A similar enhancement allowed him to travel without a laptop since all his network resident files were accessible from the PC in his hotel room or visitor office.

- Prearranged services, billed on a transaction basis, allowed him to enjoy television and radio broadcasts with his PDA with no effort whatsoever: no network selection process, no payment options, just delivered service.

This may seem remarkable, but as it turns out, there is nothing among these technologies that is new. What's new is (1) the way the technologies are combined and used and (2) the way network service providers think about their relationship with the customer.

Nine emerging technology-related factors will redefine the way we live, work, play, and engage with each other. Although I characterize these as future characteristics, most of them are here now, and some have been around since the 1970s. I will describe each in turn.

The Changing Technology Services Model

The story of "a week in the future life of Dennis McCooey may seem slightly whimsical, and today perhaps it is. In a few years, however—a *very* few years—the capabilities made possible by evolving technologies and by the companies developing them will exceed those described in the story. Let's assume, then, that the capabilities described here will come to pass and examine the technological underpinnings that will be required to make them real.

Those underpinnings fall into five categories: (1) computing, which defines the processing power that serves as the source and sink of data, (2) content, which is the reason for having computing and network capability in the first place and is fast becoming a financial sector to be reckoned with, (3) capability, which is a function of the software that acts on transported data and makes it useful, (4) carriage, which is another term for access and transport, and (5) communications, which represents the signaling capability required for service delivery. These are the Five Cs. We'll look at each of them in the sections that follow (Figure 2-2).

Putting the Five Cs to Work

Today business travelers carry laptops with them not because it's empowering to have that shoulder bag up there destroying their rotator cuffs but because the machine has their *stuff* on it. They are obligated to carry the computer because they must have access to what is on that machine to do their jobs. Furthermore, the applications required to manipulate *the stuff* also reside on the laptop, and that is another reason for carrying it. But what if this were not necessary? What if a business traveler such as Mr. McCooey could access his personal files from any computer anywhere in the world and bring up any application on

Figure 2-2
The five Cs.

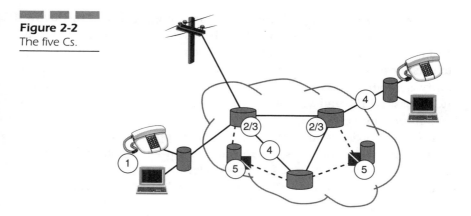

demand on any of those computers? That means *any computer*, whether the machine is a desktop, laptop, tablet, or PDA. It also means that the operating system—Windows, Mac OS, LINUX—is equally immaterial. Furthermore, an enterprise user could have access to as many computing resources as necessary to do its job, similar to the model relied on for the delivery of water, power, and natural gas. Is there any reason computing resources could not become the next deliverable utility?

For this remarkable capability to become available, several key changes in the overall architecture of the network must take place. First and foremost, all the applications and (to the degree that customers will permit this to happen based on trust) some or all of the content must be moved into the network so that the user can access his or her data and boot all relevant applications in a machine- and location-independent manner. This disassociation of content and applications from the end-user device is fundamentally important. Furthermore, the data, which unquestionably will be delivered from disparate sources, must be encoded in a standardized way so that any application running on any machine (and, by extension, operating system) can access and read data encoded by a different machine. This capability most likely will be delivered through the widespread use of Extensible Markup Language (XML).

Second, there must be software in place that creates the "virtual computer" on the remote device. This ensures that when the user boots the remote application, it appears on his or her remote machine in a manner that is reminiscent of local execution.

Third, there must be adequate bandwidth between the user machine and the computer hosting the content and applications to ensure that application execution and remote file access occur with enough rapidity so that they appear to be executing locally.

Fourth, there must be a logical capability that facilitates the follow-me computing model. This will allow McCooey to roam the world freely and have his computer applications and content follow him seamlessly to each destination. This is really no different from the roaming capability available today in the mobile phone world via Home Location Registers (HLRs) and Visitor Location Registers (VLRs), although it is somewhat more complex.

Fifth, if the goal is to migrate content and applications from the end-user device to the network, there must be an execution environment there with massive adjacent storage capacity.

Sixth, voice recognition must become a flawless addition to the package, since it plays a fairly important role in the example we described above. Voice is an intuitive interface between a machine and a person; keyboards and styli are not. Today voice recognition is a best-effort function; it must become much better if it is to succeed.

Seventh, the network must become more user-aware. Consider one aspect of the Amazon business model: A customer visits his or her website and selects and purchases a book. Within minutes Amazon sends the user an e-mail receipt, followed by a thank you message. Embedded in that message is often a secondary message that points out to the customer that many other customers who bought the same book also bought "the following books." This is obviously an incentive to buy, but it is an intelligence-based incentive: It relies on data-mining efforts Amazon conducts that identify and analyze individual and group buying patterns and then point them out to both Amazon and the consumer. The result is a measurable upward impact on sales.

It often is said that the telephone network is the largest machine ever built. It is certainly the most extensive and pervasive. Imagine what a powerful marketing tool it could be if it had the ability to collect noninvasively and analyze customer buying patterns—not just of telecom services but of other products as well. If done properly, the network could become a powerful implement that serves the market management needs of the telecom service provider, its customers (both enterprise and end user), and companies that sell products electronically, similar to Amazon, Dell, and hundreds of other companies.

In our example McCooey is notified of a coffee sale around the corner because the network "knows" his preferences and matches them to his current behavior, which ties into our eighth component: location-based services. By adding GPS technology to a mobile device—a PDA or mobile phone—the network can combine historical customer buying patterns with location data, perform network-based analysis, and then notify the user about purchase options. When McCooey's phone notified him of the coffee sale and told him to turn at the next corner, or when his PDA told him that the gifts he wanted to buy for his family in Madrid could be had at the store just ahead on the right, this technology innovation was being invoked.

Carried to the enterprise level, the network could become the catalytic trigger that collects information about network utilization, for example, and leads to recommendations that are based on that behavior about different calling plans and network service packages that could be offered to the customer and better meet her or his specific needs. Or it could direct IT and telephony buyers to visit a particular site because of low-priced bandwidth, arbitraged to the lowest possible price because of market fluctuations and availability.

Ninth, all this global roaming and potentially wireless connectivity implies the need to deal with a host of security considerations. Various forms of data encryption will be required to protect transmitted data, and some form of extremely secure user identification will be required, most likely based on biometric identification technology (fingerprint scanner, retinal scanner, handprint reader, facial mapper, etc.). The perception of increased vulnerability undoubtedly will be one of the (temporary) unfortunate results of this technological evolution and the applications that ensue, but it is a well-known fact that perception tends to be perceived as reality; therefore, perception must be managed carefully. Security must be a leading included factor, not a reactive response.

Finally, a billing methodology that works across this massively complex environment must be put in place.

This billing system may be the single most complex component in the whole mess. Not only must data be collected about buying preferences and actual usage, actual billing preferences must be taken into account. For example, some customers may want to be billed a negotiated, recurring monthly charge for the services they use, whereas others (Millennials fall into this category) may want to be billed on a usage basis, paying by the kilopacket, download, or program. The challenge is this: Where will the usage data be collected? Because of the massively decentralized architecture of the modern network, data collection most likely will be performed at the point that is closest to the user, which probably means at the user's device. This means that some kind of usage client will have to be installed on every device so that the information can be collected, aggregated, analyzed, and billed.

So what are the Five Cs in this explanation? Computing is fairly obvious and refers to the creation of a centralized (or physically distributed but logically centralized) computing resource within the network that provides processing on demand and also hosts applications and content while at the same time providing the functional logical connectivity to the end-user device. Content is the data/information transported across the access and transport network and acted on by the hosted applications to create value for the user. There undoubtedly will be concerns about network-resident personal content; some users will prefer to carry a memory device (memory stick or microdrive) with them instead. It also includes the storage capacity required to house it. Capability refers to the applications that act on the transported data, converting it from data to information that then can be used to create knowledge.

Carriage refers to the broadband access and transport network that provides functional connectivity between the user of the network (enterprise or end user) and the network itself. Finally, communications refers to the overlay signaling environment that facilitates the "follow-me" capability, similar to what is done today in the mobile voice environment, and creates the logical relationship between content, applications, and the transport network. Today this is done largely by Signaling System Seven (SS7) in the legacy wireline network, but more and more the signaling function is being performed by NOPE: Session Initiation Protocol (SIP) in the IP domain. Both probably will coexist for some time; interfaces between the two will have to be written.

In the sections that follow we examine each of these in detail and the companies that may well deliver them.

Computing

Web services is one technological phenomenon that has emerged on the services scene and has been made possible to a large degree by the migration of computing resources into the network. These are application-based services that are accessible via the Web and are largely distance- and location-independent. For example, most e-mail systems now offer a Web version that allows subscribers to access their ISPs or corporate e-mail accounts online to avoid the cost of a long-distance phone call to their remote home servers. This is a simple and early example of the concept but a highly illustrative one.

The concept of network-centric computing is not new by any means. Oracle, Sun, and Microsoft have talked about it for years but, for the first time, the technology has reached a state where it is commercially feasible.

When Lou Gerstner left IBM and Samuel Palmisano took over the reins of that corporation, his first major announcement was that he intended to earmark $10 billion in research and development (R&D) money for the development of *utility* or *grid computing*. The concept is simple: In the same way that power, water, and gas are delivered from a central grid on demand to users, computing cycles [millions of instructions per second (MIPS)] can be delivered in precisely the same fashion. IBM is, after all, highly (although not entirely) dependent on hardware sales as a major contributor to its revenue stream. Forty percent of its revenues come from services; that amounted to $34 billion in 2001, with gross margins of roughly 28%.

Since services play such a major role in its business model, IBM's ability to extend that model to include a variety of services in addition to those it already offers makes sense. Consider IBM's grid computing model. A large percentage of the mainframes (it is interesting that IBM now calls them *enterprise servers*) in corporate data centers today are leased to those corporations by IBM; the hardware and operating system software remain IBM's property. As the grid model evolves, and as IBM takes greater advantage of high-bandwidth connectivity between these machines around the world, a new, expanded service provider model evolves. IBM evolves from being a hardware vendor to a full-blown services provider in every sense of the term, and the network cloud expands its reach. This drives a cooperative evolution between the telco service provider, which delivers connectivity and bandwidth, and IBM, which delivers computing power [central processing unit (CPU) cycles or MIPS] over that transport infrastructure.

IBM is also the number one supporter of Web-based services. These are applications that use the Internet as the basis for automatic communications between various applications as a way of sharing data, again supporting the concept of a network that is intelligent enough to adapt to network user behavior. In late April 2003, IBM announced a relationship with Akamai, a developer of network-based applications. The result of their collaboration is a new service called Akamai Edge Computing, which is used by IBM WebSphere customers. This is an example of the model we are describing.

Naturally, IBM with its "On-Demand Outsourcing" is not the only vendor rallying to the concept of utility computing. Hewlett-Packard (HP) and Sun also are investing heavily in the concept, and others will follow. HP's Adaptive Infrastructure Strategy and Utility Data Center products support the grid model and, like IBM, that firm offers a "salad bar" billing concept under which customers pay a monthly service fee that is based on what they consume rather than a fixed monthly fee. Sun's product line offers hardware, software, and services, but with a twist: HP and IBM are on track to become full-blown, vertically integrated computer utilities; Sun's intent is to offer resources that will facilitate the ability of a customer corporation to manage and operate its own utility functions. The company historically has targeted the telecom marketplace, but beginning with Solaris 9, and then with Solaris 10, it has placed an even greater focus on the industry.

Although telecom convergence translates into multiple opportunities to identify and benefit from new sources of revenue, convergence management, particularly between legacy and IP networks, creates a major challenge because of the many disparities between the two. The pressure to reduce the total cost of ownership (TCO) as IP-based services come into the picture is a high priority for most service providers.

The Solaris 10 operating system addresses this challenge, offering performance-related improvements in all areas of the system. The company has added innovative capabilities such as DTrace for real-time debugging, predictive self-healing, and IP QoS improve the performance, reliability, and availability of these emerging (and evolving) "hybrid" networks. Equally compelling is the company's focus on cost reduction. Solaris's "container" concept, which essentially allows for the creation of multiple "virtual processors" within the same machine, combined with Sun's ZFS self-healing file system concept, reduces the cost and time required to manage complex file systems, thus reducing overhead. Solaris 10 also supports next-generation network components, including SIP, Stream Control Transmission Protocol (SCTP), and Advanced Traffic Conditioning Agreement (TCA), all of which will find their way into the IMS domain in short order.

Finally, Microsoft is also in the game. Its Dynamic Systems Initiative supports a "lights-out" operating environment in corporate data centers.

What about the financial viability of this model? According to Forrester Research, corporations can save as much as $2 million over five years by engaging in dynamic server resource allocation and $3 million by offering virtual storage solutions.

The keys to this model, then, are the system manufacturers: IBM, Sun, HP, and Microsoft. Their focus on the utility model of computing and the products they offer to accelerate its implementation lie at the heart of the evolution. They are, however, only one part of the puzzle.

 # Content

The term *content* refers to the information for which networks are built in the first place: voice, video, images, data, audio, and multimedia combinations. One of the most talked about directions in which the industry is going today is *convergence*: the transport and delivery of multiple disparate content types across a single network infrastructure for the sake of reduced cost and complexity. One of the first examples of converged content was *unified messaging*. First introduced by Avaya, unified messaging allows a call agent in a call center to access multiple media types from a single device regardless of the media over which they arrive. When the call agent logs in to the system, his or her PC lists all the messages that have been received, allowing the agent to manage the information contained in those messages much more effectively. Today unified messaging systems also support remote workers. A traveling or remotely located employee can dial into a message gateway and download all messages—voice, fax, e-mail—from that single central location, simplifying the process of staying connected when one is away from the office.

One of the driving forces behind converged or unified messaging (i.e., content) is the ability to create bundled service packages. If a service provider can offer voice, distributed video, high-speed Internet access, and perhaps even wireless, it can create a strong barrier to exit for its customers. Cox Cable, for example, which offers bundled service packages to its customers, experiences a 53% lower churn rate among subscribers who buy packages compared with those who buy individual services. Furthermore, there is ample evidence that customers, particularly enterprise customers, find the idea of a single converged bill for all their telecom services attractive. Traditional telco service providers facing the prospect of a declining revenue stream as a result of substitution (wireless, cable, DSL cannibalization of second lines) and natural price erosion are intrigued by the potential ability to add entertainment content to their service offerings.

Evidence of this is provided by the increasing interest in the so-called triple play: the ability to deliver voice, video, and data over a single network interface, often to a single or small subset of devices. Most recently there has been talk about the quadruple play, through which companies also offer wireless as part of the bundle. Time-Warner, for example, resells Sprint wireless service as part of its quadruple-play package.

The players in the content sector are those you might expect and some you wouldn't. The obvious ones are Sony, Vivendi, AOL Time-Warner, and Microsoft, plus a host of smaller players in various niche market segments. The content these organizations host is quite varied. It ranges from AOL's "walled garden" model, which offers wholly owned unique content, to Microsoft's game-specific content via its Xbox Live service.

Microsoft has invested more than $2 billion in Xbox in the last five years, much of it directed toward the Xbox Live service. The service was launched in Japan in February 2003 and in five European countries in March 2003. The Xbox hardware has a built-in broadband adapter and a hard drive on which downloaded content can be stored. The pricing model is intriguing: The first year's service, which includes a headset for talking to other players over the broadband connection, sells in the United States for approximately $49, roughly the cost of a traditional game CD. It's a big market: The traditional gaming industry's revenues grow exponentially year after year, and mobile gaming, that is, games designed to be played on a mobile phone or PDA, will exceed $2 billion in 2006.

Closely associated with the network-based computing model is the role of the storage solution provider. If we accept the belief that a migration of system content (applications) and personal content is under way from the edge (server or end-user device) to the core (enterprise server or mainframe), that content must become resident on a massive and easily accessible storage array within the network. This implies two things: that the content providers themselves become key drivers behind this evolution and that storage solution providers offer a critical component of the overall architecture. A simple but highly visible example of this phenomenon is Google's GMail, a free e-mail service available to anyone "invited" by a colleague to join. Upon registration, the user is given 3 GB of online storage and encouraged never to delete anything; Google will allocate more storage when the user's allocated space nears exhaustion.

Remember Microsoft? It is in this game for obvious reasons: Its entire future vision relies on network-centric storage. Its .Net strategy, which will be discussed in detail shortly, is linked closely to a network-centric philosophy. Because of .Net's dependence on centralized storage as its applications and content migrate toward the network, Microsoft wants to play a major role in the storage market by making its operating system so compelling that storage companies such as Network Appliance, HP, and EMC2 will be challenged seriously.

Content, then, includes two main areas: the content itself, which traverses the network and lends capability to the user, and storage, which comes in many forms and is playing a greater role than ever in the evolutionary process of migration to a network-centric architecture.

Microsoft

It is worthwhile to spend a few minutes discussing Microsoft (the entire corporation as it was in 1978 is shown in Figure 2-3), certainly one of the most influential companies of all time. As a corporation that has revenues on the order of $30 billion a year, Microsoft has the kind of influence most companies dream about. It is also extremely visible because of its massive size and therefore is subject to substantial public scrutiny.

Over the years Microsoft has reinvented itself constantly. From 1977, when Bill Gates and Paul Allen wrote system software in Albuquerque, New Mexico, for Ed Roberts's Altair, to the present day, when the Microsoft Corporation is providing software to computing equipment all over the world and supporting the development efforts of more than 40,000 partner companies, the company has wheeled and danced with its market partners, shape-shifting to ensure its place in the industry and, to a large extent, history.

One thing Microsoft has ready access to is cash—today reportedly more than $38 billion of it. Over the years the company has made strategic investments. In recent years it invested $50 billion in AT&T and Comcast, strategically committing itself to the belief that cable would become a significant competitor for broadband data transport (it has). In the deal, Microsoft requested that Windows rather than Java be the preferred operating system in the set-top box, a move that opened a new market segment.

What business is Microsoft in? The answer is plural: Microsoft is in *many* businesses. It certainly is active in the home and enterprise sys-

Figure 2-3
The entire Microsoft Corporation Circa 1978. Bill Gates is at lower left, Paul Allen at lower right. (Photo courtesy Microsoft Corporation)

tem (Windows) and application (Office) software markets for desktop machines, laptops, palmtops, and enterprise servers, having the bulk of the market. Few competitors have been able to penetrate the Microsoft armor, although LINUX has had a substantial impact on the enterprise server space, by some estimates controlling as much as 40% of the market. Nevertheless, Microsoft dominates the sector and has announced its intention to consider entry into and support of the open-source movement.

The company also is courting the game sector. Over the years Microsoft has acquired several small video game developers, including 49% of Rare, the manufacturer of the popular video game *Donkey Kong Country*.

Other entertainment efforts have gotten Microsoft's attention as well. In January 2003, the company announced its intention to build a global FM radio network to support its Smart Personal Objects Technology (SPOT) efforts, a solution that will embed an FM receiver that works anywhere in the world.

SPOT is an addition to .NET that is designed to take the capabilities of .NET beyond the PC and laptop, focusing instead on everyday devices that could be enhanced by its availability. SPOT enhances the likelihood of product miniaturization, lower power requirements, and lower cost, allowing devices such as electronic watches to be enhanced.

At CES 2003, Microsoft announced that the Smart Watch would be the first commercial implementation of SPOT. At that time it announced that SPOT soon would find its way into home appliances and other devices that could benefit from the power of networking.

SPOT uses FM broadcasting to deliver Web-based data to smart objects. Smart Watches, for example, receive more than 200 channels of information that are broadcast to users on spectrum leased by Microsoft.

Microsoft created its DirectBand Network to transmit data to Smart Watches and other SPOT-enabled devices. DirectBand consists of a specially designed radio receiver chipset in the watch and a nationwide network based on FM-subcarrier technology. DirectBand transmits Web-based data over subcarrier frequencies, using protocols designed for Smart Watches.

The DirectBand broadcast range currently includes over 100 metropolitan areas in the United States and a handful of cities in Canada. To achieve this, Microsoft partnered with ClearChannel and Infinity Broadcasting, allowing Microsoft to broadcast data over an existing radio network rather than having to build its own.

To add DirectBand to an existing radio station, technicians install a broadcast generator that inserts data directly into the Smart Watch transmission. The encrypted data originates from the DirectBand Data Center in Tukwila, Washington, and is transmitted from the Microsoft Network (MSN) via a collection of facilities, including private frame relay networks, satellite hops, and IP networks.

This concept obviously opens an opportunity for content delivery and an alternative delivery mechanism. Microsoft also announced that it will license its Windows Media technology at significantly reduced prices to manufacturers of consumer electronics products such as camcorders, DVD players, and portable media players, a move that will have a dramatic effect on Microsoft's competitive position in the entertainment sector if it is taken up on its offer.

Microsoft also has entered the mobile segment with great vigor on several strategic fronts. Although the firm shut down its Teledesic project, an ambitious satellite-based service delivery network, other wireless projects are under way. In January 2003, Microsoft released a CDMA software bundle for its Pocket PC and Smartphone platforms: a module that provides the interface between the "physical layer" air interface and Microsoft's new Windows-based mobile operating systems. United Kingdom–based Orange has agreed to use Microsoft Windows–powered Smartphones, exposing Microsoft to another influential market segment. Other firms are expected to follow suit.

Of course, not everything has been completely rosy for Microsoft as it has penetrated the mobile marketplace. Although Microsoft was eager to license Windows to PC manufacturers and was quite successful at it, it has been less successful selling to the mobile market. Concerned about a repetition of the Microsoft monopoly in the PC world, mobile manufacturers pulled together and created Symbian, a software consortium charged with the goal of creating a Windows-like mobile phone software product that would not be dominated by Microsoft. Symbian supporters include Nokia, Motorola, Siemens, SONYEriccson, Panasonic, and Samsung. Its efforts have been successful, and today Symbian dominates the mobile OS world with about 80% of the market. That number may not hold, however. One factor working against Symbian is the fact that, in spite of the number of companies that have licensed it, for the most part it is deployed in Nokia handsets within GSM territories. Windows Mobile, in contrast, has the advantage of being largely enterprise-focused and able to synchronize with the Microsoft Exchange Server, a factor that can improve the very important enterprise customer's usage experience.

Also lingering in the wings is LINUX. Although its use as a mobile device operating system is intriguing and has gotten a great deal of attention and implementation in Asia, it remains somewhat in the shadows in North American and European mobile markets.

Some analysts believe that Symbian will lose significant market share over the next few years because of the growing influence of Microsoft and the appearance on the scene of contenders such as LINUX and Palm. PalmSource has announced its intention to convert the Palm operating system into a middleware bundle that will run atop LINUX, preserving the interface for users. Although some analysts continue to issue favorable reports on Symbian, disruptive forces are at work: Consider the impact of the Windows Mobile Treo Smartphone announced in September 2005 by Palm, Microsoft, and Verizon. The juggernaut may not be stoppable.

Changing the World: .Net Although Microsoft continues to expand into what are perceived as new markets, it also is undergoing a massive reinvention of its own philosophical direction. The new direction, called .Net ("Dot-Net"), represents a fundamental change not only for Microsoft but for the computing and content industries as well. .Net is as much a technical philosophy as it is a product direction and supports the concept of network-based computing.

.NET is Microsoft's Web services strategy, designed to interconnect users, information, systems, and devices through a common software platform. Designed to integrate across the entire Microsoft platform, .NET gives users the ability to build, deploy, and manage connected, secure network-based solutions that use Web services. .NET gives businesses the ability to integrate their systems rapidly and benefit from anytime, anywhere, any device information. Sound familiar? .Net includes Web hosting servers, development tools, applications, and more than 35,000 Microsoft Certified Partner organizations to provide support.

Microsoft's definition of Web-based services is straightforward: They are "an approach that helps the business connect with its customers, partners, and employees. They enable the business to extend existing services to new customers. They help the business work more efficiently with its partners and suppliers. They unlock information so it can flow to every employee who needs it. And they reduce development time and expense for new projects."[1]

Adding to the promise of .Net is the system's reliance on the widely accepted XML standard, the increasingly relevant de facto standard for Internet data exchange and Web services deployment. If a database structure is coded using XML, its contents can be read by any system

---

[1] From Microsoft's .Net home page, http://www.microsoft.com/net/Basics.mspx.

regardless of the programming language in which the application is written. Because Web services are delivered over the Internet by widely recognized standards such as Simple Object Access Protocol (SOAP), the Universal Description, Discovery, and Integration (UDDI) Protocol, and XML, their role as a universal data delivery technique is largely assured.

A collection of evolving components make up the new architecture. The first is Office 12, which incorporates the capabilities of the traditional Office suite. Next is Jupiter, a server concept that melds BizTalk, Content Management, and Commerce Server functionality so that business documents can be routed according to predetermined and optimally defined workflows. Microsoft calls this "connected business." Related to this is the .Net Speech Software Development Kit. The idea behind this product is to enhance demand for Smartphones, Windows-based PDAs, and speech recognition software. Speech recognition figures prominently in Microsoft's future model; in support of its role, the company recently acquired Vicinity Corporation for $96 million. Vicinity's product allows Microsoft to deliver maps and directions to mobile devices, yet another thrust into the content arena. The product is based on VoiceXML; call centers are another major target.

Another component is Xdocs. Xdocs allows XML-formatted documents to be shared across multiple applications. As described earlier, XML is "next-generation Hypertext Markup Language (HTML)" and is designed to address three things: functional workplace collaboration, business process management, and real-time data visibility.

All these components make up the overall evolutionary scheme called .Net, which has four basic components supported by the elements described above. They are described in detail below.

First, all functional software (and, to the degree possible, content) becomes network-resident. Instead of residing on each desktop machine, Office and other applications will reside on servers at the edge of the network and will be accessed by remote devices as required. Furthermore, each application will be divided into "applets," small functional applications that can be downloaded on demand as the user's activities require them.

Second, all software will be sold on a subscription basis rather than on a purchase model, guaranteeing that every user always will have the most up-to-date version of the software available. Payment will be based on a subscription model, with customers paying either on a monthly basis or according to usage.

Third, the software will be functionally device-independent. Windows machines obviously will be the preferred platform, but the software will execute on any operating system and any hardware platform, guaranteeing software portability and an ongoing and substantial revenue stream for Microsoft.

Fourth, XML will replace HTML as the content formatting language, a move that will enhance the ability to separate the content from the formatting mechanism and further the ability to provide device-to-device portability of content and application functionality.

In effect, this shift in Microsoft's product design allows the company to become in effect the universal provider of system and application software as well as wholly owned content. What it does *not* do is obligate Microsoft to take on any role in the network itself, although .Net is fundamentally dependent on the availability of broadband access for its success.

Microsoft keeps and protects its competitive position by effectively managing its own intellectual property (the other IP) and by being very good at spotting trends in the industries it serves. The company tracks developments across many industry segments by monitoring the types of software tools it receives requests for from 40,000 external development partners. By managing its content libraries effectively, Microsoft can innovate internally and help its 40,000 partners innovate externally. Furthermore, the company focuses its efforts on platform development instead of application development; that allows it to share "code blocks" among applications, resulting in both cheaper and faster development and cross-application commonality.

As I said in Chapter 1, "You don't have to *like* Microsoft, but you *do* have to *admire* them. And don't dare take your eyes off of them—they move far too quickly to be ignored." The company is a prime example of the observation made elsewhere in the book: "In this brave new world, you have two choices when it comes to business success. You can have *some* of the money or *none* of the money. Nobody will get it all." By sharing its success with a large population of partners, Microsoft wins, and the partners win as well. The company has a clear and compelling vision of the future of information technology that includes computers, networks, content, and storage and is positioning itself to play significant roles in all those areas. Watch this company closely.

Capability

Capability represents the applications that act on the content stored in network databases. These applications range from traditional office automation utilities such as Microsoft Office to sophisticated database management and analysis tools that perform data mining, knowledge management, enterprise relationship management, and customer relationship management routines such as those offered by Oracle and SAP. The latter applications have taken on greater importance in recent years because of the growing need of corporations to create stronger relationships with their customers. The best way to do this is to develop an understanding of the challenges the customers face, and the best way to do *that* is through analysis of their day-to-day behavior in the marketplace, facilitated by data-mining applications that run in the network and depend on a broad spectrum of data points as their information sources.

Along these lines, network management, sometimes called operations, administration, maintenance, and provisioning (OAM&P) or operations support systems (OSS), must take on an enhanced set of responsibilities. Most network management centers, like the one shown in Figure 2-4, are almost exclusively inward-looking, focusing their activities on the management of network elements that support service provisioning, accounting and billing, configuration, network security, fault identification, repair, and network performance. Under the new capability model, these systems also must focus on the users of the network: the enterprise and end-user customers that rely on network resources. By tracking their activities and creating databases that chart how customers use network resources, a service provider can develop enhanced strategies for improving the relationship it has with its customers, becoming a trusted adviser rather than simply a vendor. Along the same lines, the network could facilitate the ability to collect infor-

Figure 2-4
A modern network management control center. Photo courtesy AT&T.

mation about customers for the service providers' immediate customers. The most recent arrival in this area is the Next-Generation Operations Support System (NGOSS), which takes into account the requirements of emerging network architectures and applications such as IMS. We'll discuss NGOSS later in the book.

Carriage

Carriage, which includes both access and transport, is a necessary component of the future of networking and computing because broadband access is required for the success of the network-centric model. It's a showstopper; without it the concept fails because of the volume of traffic generated between the remote user and the network-centric application.

Of course, the technology implications are interesting. DSL is the best-known option for broadband access, yet its success to date in the United States has been tepid at best. Cable modems captured nearly 70% of the overall broadband access market because of regulatory decisions that drove incumbent telephone companies to stall on their own deployments. Although DSL is catching up, it still is fighting a daily battle against cable modem–based broadband, which continues to offer excellent service along with whatever its provider bundles it with.

Equally interesting is wireless. As companies such as Verizon move into wireless data with their data-only service and plan infrastructure that will allow them to move from EV-DO (Evolution—Data Only) to EV-DV (Evolution—Data&Video), wireless becomes a viable alternative to wired broadband infrastructure. Furthermore, 802.11 (WiFi), 802.16 (WiMAX), and 802.20 products are now on the market, including products that support voice over 802.11, such as Cisco's 7920 WiFi phone.

Transport (as opposed to access) is not dramatically different, with a few exceptions. T- and E-Carrier systems will continue to be important, as will Synchronous Optical Network (SONET) and Synchronous Digital Hierarchy (SDH) optical infrastructure. New to the party, however, is Ethernet, which has become a contender in gigabit form, as well as emerging standards such as Resilient Packet Ring (RPR), based on the IEEE 802.17 standard. In the metro arena gigabit Ethernet and 10-gigabit Ethernet have become de facto standards for service delivery because of Ethernet's ability to transport high-speed data with configurable QoS capability through the 802.1Q protocol.

▇▇▇ Communications

Today mobile telephone users can roam freely throughout their country of residence or even throughout a wider area, such as the entirety of Europe, and receive seamless service. This is the result of the interplay between the universal signaling network, SS7, and the global telephone network. SS7 is a dedicated packet-based data transport network that relies on distributed databases to deliver a wide variety of services to both fixed and mobile users and to manage roaming functions through databases known as Home and Visitor Location Registers, which facilitate the delivery of calls to users traveling outside their home operating areas.

The same signaling network can be extended in scope to provide similar roaming capabilities for enterprise users who wish to access network-based applications and content. If one assumes that the migration indeed occurs (and it undoubtedly will), the signaling network must be able to create a logical link between the traveling user and his or her database content and applications, as we saw when McCooey traveled in Madrid. SS7 is ideally suited for this function and undoubtedly will evolve accordingly.

As IP extends its reach into the telephony domain and convergence becomes an even stronger force, the communications function will have to evolve in lockstep. Although SS7 is a marvelously capable protocol for the PSTN, it is less suitable for IP networks. SIP was designed to serve as an alternative to its predecessor, H.323, and to provide the same capabilities for IP networks that SS7 provides for legacy circuit-switched environments. H.323 originally was rolled out to control the delivery of multimedia traffic on LANs; SIP, in contrast, was created specifically with converged VoIP applications in mind. It defines a set of standard "objects" and a messaging hierarchy for communicating among the various elements of a typical VoIP network.

SIP is a collection of modules that provide signaling functions across the IP network. These modules, which are shown in Figure 2-5, include user agent clients; a location server, which relates a client device to a specific IP address; proxy servers, which are responsible for forwarding call requests from one server to another on behalf of SIP clients (hence the name *proxy*); and redirect servers, which transmit the called party's address back to the calling party so that the connection can be made.

SIP messages perform basic signaling responsibilities: session establishment, session maintenance, and session teardown. These messages include *Invite*, which is used to establish or join a call session; *ACK*, which is used to acknowledge an invitation; *register*, which is used to reg-

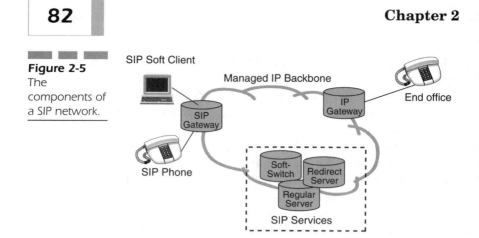

Figure 2-5
The components of a SIP network.

ister a user with a server; *Options*, which are used to petition for data about the capabilities of the server; *Cancel*, which cancels a previous request; and *Bye*, which ends a session.

SIP was created by the Internet Engineering Task Force (IETF), an organization responsible for many Internet-oriented standards. Its responsibility lies with session creation and destruction; the actual in-progress session and connection details are left up to the communicating endpoint devices. This is a departure from traditional SS7-controlled sessions.

The protocol relies on a text-based command structure that uses the now universal Hypertext Transfer Protocol (HTTP) syntax and Uniform Resource Locator (URL) addressing, both of which are ideal for delivering telephony over an IP network, where the convergence of voice, video, messaging, conferencing, and Web access can create an enhanced customer experience. Designed with the assumption that end-user devices are intelligent (and therefore do not require a great deal of intelligence in the core), SIP is designed to facilitate connectivity among a group of proxy and location servers. As a result, it is immensely scalable, one of the key concerns among enterprise IT personnel who see growing user populations and unbounded demand as a major challenge to their ability to satisfy QoS demands.

The Trusted Third Party: A New Player

A function we have not yet discussed is the content manager. If content and applications become network-based and become the driving force behind enhanced revenue, they must be managed.[2] To a large degree, the applications will be managed by the company that creates and sells them—Microsoft, for example, with its Office suite—or hosted applications such as security and VoIP. The content, however, is a different story. Microsoft has no interest in managing third-party content, and the traditional telecom service provider is not suited to the task. This has nothing to do with capability; it is simply not, nor has it ever been, those providers' functional domain. A third alternative will emerge in the form of the trusted third party, a company with experience managing, optimizing, and distributing database content. This company also must be experienced with safeguarding the security of the data entrusted to it. One company that falls into this role is Verisign, a firm with significant experience in database management.

In the wireless world the emergence of the MVNO has given rise to the MVNE. The MVNO proves that network ownership is not a requirement for profitable telephony service provisioning. The MVNE, in contrast, offers infrastructure services to the MVNO, including network element provisioning and OAM&P and OSS/BSS support. In some cases the MVNE administers HLRs, Short Message Service Centers (SMSCs), Multimedia Service Centers (MMSCs), and other support entities.

The primary advantage the MVNE brings to the MVNO is financial: It facilitates the deferral of MVNO CAPEX and operating expense (OPEX), allowing the MVNO to focus instead on customer relationships and market build-out. Furthermore, the MVNE makes it easier for the MVNO to customize service offerings and enter new markets since the lag time typically associated with network build-out is alleviated. Some MVNEs also provide wireless data services, including Generalized Packet Radio System (GPRS), Enhanced Data for Global Evolution (EDGE), hosted applications, content, and e-commerce.

■ Putting the Five Cs Together

Computing, content, capability, carriage, and communications: the Five Cs. To them we probably should add two more: *consumer* and *customer*. After all, they are the reason for the existence of the other five and the source of the revenue that the Five Cs are in a position to generate. How do these pieces work together? If we assemble the five capability compo-

---

[2] A famous adage states, "That which gets measured gets managed."

nents, we find an intriguing model of the future that establishes a framework for rapid and accurate delivery of services to the enterprise customer and the end user, on *their terms*, that offers a great deal of flexibility to companies that are wheeling and dodging in response to changing demands from customers.

The model is an elegant one. Microsoft, Sun, Oracle, and other application-oriented companies, through .NET, N1, and other models, support a world in which application software no longer is owned by the user but instead will be leased or billed according to usage. Software will be modularized, and users will encounter only the functional modules they need and be billed only for those they actually use. The consequence is that users always will have access to the most current version of the software they need and will be shielded from the complexity of the application.

Similarly, content may migrate from the end-user device into the network, assuming that levels of trust are in place that allow customers to be comfortable with the idea of storing their wholly owned content on a central hosting facility administered by a trusted third-party firm that guarantees security, privacy, and confidentiality. Even if corporate database content does not migrate into the network's edge—it could stay on the user's machine, a portable large-capacity hard drive, or even a small server—there still will be a fundamental architectural change beyond the edge. For example, users of network-based applications who formerly archived their database content on hard drives in desktops or laptops more commonly will store those files on high-capacity, nonvolatile memory cards simply because they can. RAM-based storage requires far less power than does a motor-driven hard drive, and this has positive implications for battery life.

Another implication is access. If customers are to access remotely based content and applications, they will do so only if the access bandwidth is sufficient to make the experience acceptable. Broadband access, therefore, whether DSL, cable, or some form of wireless, is a crucial component that one hopes will become more available as regulatory decisions and changes in technology, economics, and availability sort themselves out. Broadband transport has been a widespread reality for decades; broadband access, in contrast, is a relatively new phenomenon.

Similarly, storage solution providers will play pivotal roles inasmuch as their products serve as the destination for the network-bound applications and content as Web services become a reality and demand for ad hoc access to applications grows.

Finally, it would appear that computing as a "sellable resource" is moving inexorably toward commodity status and being reinvented as the ultimate utility in the same way that water, gas, and electricity are sold today as utilities. As we discussed earlier, IBM, HP, and Sun are reassessing their product lines to support this evolution. What an interesting shift in priorities: Hardware companies are reinventing themselves as services firms, access and transport companies are becoming (or attempting to become) content providers, and all sectors are forming strategic alliances with each other as a way to anticipate and respond to customer service requests.

The implications of this evolution are intriguing. If the hardware manufacturer becomes a vendor of processing capacity and works closely with the access and transport provider to ensure uninterruptible network connectivity between the user (enterprise or residence) and the processor/storage providers, and the content and storage providers play an enhanced role in this future network architecture, what other significant shifts might occur? One is a potentially new role for the network equipment manufacturer.

■■■ The Network Equipment Manufacturer

Today the large manufacturers of network hardware—Lucent, Cisco, Nortel, Alcatel, and so on—play a somewhat limited role because of the legacy role they historically have played as vendors of hardware and some software. These companies, however, have access to an incalculably valuable resource in the form of their R&D departments. Consider the contributions, for example, of Bell Laboratories, some of which are shown in the sidebar. Until relatively recently these organizations were treated largely as stand-alone research organizations that made great contributions to the public good but had minimal involvement in the day-to-day sales activities of the parent company. That has changed. These organizations have become or are becoming central contributors to the sales process, offering potent, targeted expertise to the customer-facing sales team. In a situation such as the scenario at the beginning of this chapter, there is ample evidence to suggest that a network hardware manufacturer could take on the responsibility of the management and operation of its clients' networks, optimize them to reduce CAPEX and

The Innovations of Bell Labs

The laser	Touch-tone
Information theory	High-fidelity audio
The transistor	The fax machine
The UNIX operating system	Synchronized sound movies
Optical fiber transmission	Electronic speech synthesis
Satellites	The solar cell
Cellular telephony	The first transatlantic cable
Electronic switching	The pager
The digital signal processor (DSP)	Light-emitting diodes (LEDs)

OPEX spending, and then either continue to operate the networks as a contract outsourcing agent or hand the optimized network back to the client—all for an appropriate fee.

Equally important is the expanding role of the strategic alliance between firms that, on the surface, are clearly competitors. Alliances already have been formed among many of them.

There also may be a revision in the role of the traditional access and transport service provider. Today the service provider is often the "center of the deal universe" because its physical facilities actually touch the customer. In the evolving service-dominated telecom sector, however, that could change because of the strong logical relationships that exist between network-based applications providers and the users of those applications, corporate or otherwise. For example, a professional services firm could become the "general contractor" for a network sale, serving as the "prime" contact between the customer and the various service components—infrastructure, computing, software, storage, and so on—that together represent the ultimate solution to the customer's business challenge. In fact, this is perhaps the most likely model of interaction between the technology industry and the enterprise customer. The professional services firm operates as the principal contact with the customer and aggregates capability as required from access and transport providers (wireless, wireline, cable, etc.), hardware system manufacturers, software providers, storage providers, computing utility companies, ASPs, and so on. In effect, it becomes the center point around which a virtual corporation emerges. This virtual corporation becomes the true *service* provider, delivering a converged collection of services, platform components, and capabilities that together address specific customer needs.

All this, of course, hinges on the belief that bandwidth, CPU cycles, and gigabytes of storage are marching arm in arm inexorably down Commodity Lane. It also is based on the belief that the upper reaches of the technology food chain represent the end state because, according to the physics of value, money rises to the surface.

Climbing the Value Chain

Let's examine the value chain shown in Figure 2-6. The highest layer in the chain is the value layer, and value is the ultimate deliverable. However, value is the one item among the seven layers that is defined by the customer, not by the deliverer of the service. At a high level, however, delivered value falls into four categories in which service providers must focus their efforts. These categories transcend industry segments and thus are applicable in all industries. A provider of service must do one or more of the following things to be successful and effective in the eyes of its customers: reduce the customer's operating costs, increase the cus-

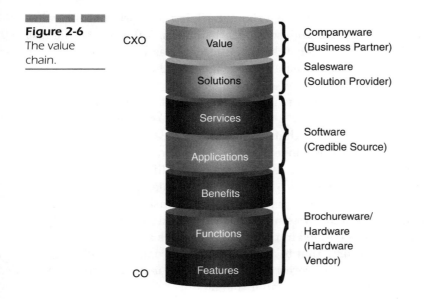

Figure 2-6
The value chain.

CXO

Value — Companyware (Business Partner)

Solutions — Salesware (Solution Provider)

Services

Applications — Software (Credible Source)

Benefits

Functions — Brochureware/ Hardware (Hardware Vendor)

CO — Features

tomer's revenues, improve the customer's competitive position, help lower marketplace risk, or some combination of the four.

How companies do this is almost immaterial in the grand scheme of things. What matters is the outcome, and that is defined by six characteristics that detail the relationship between the customer and the deliverer of service: trust between the partners, integrity, clearly defined complementary strengths, willingness to engage in an enduring relationship, a commitment on both sides to the relationship, and openness between the two parties. The "touch point" between the customer and the deliverer of service is usually a technology solution. However, if the service provider delivers the characteristics listed above and, if the nature of the relationship is defined by these characteristics, technology as an obstacle is taken off the table.

Consider the nature of the seven layers of the chain. The bottom three layers—*features*, *functions*, and *benefits*—typically define the characteristics of the underlying technology in terms that are important to those who have to plan, design, install, maintain, and repair the hardware, which most likely is resident in the central office (CO). These are also the words that most typically appear in product literature.

Applications and *services*, which are slightly higher in the value chain, represent the first appearance of software and its influence on the hardware. This is where services first begin to appear as a differentiable additive element in the overall hierarchy.

Solutions, the sixth layer in the value chain, represent the functional transition point between the underlying network and the value it brings to enterprise and end-user customers. Value is the highest layer in the chain; it can take on different meanings provided that each unique meaning satisfies one or more of the key characteristics described earlier.

The seven layers are further clustered into the four subcategories shown at right in Figure 2-6. The bottom three layers qualify as "brochureware," meaning that they tend to appear on sales literature. Nothing in those words conveys any information about the functional characteristics of the device. As a result, it is difficult to formulate a value opinion about the device being described unless, of course, the person formulating the opinion is an engineer responsible for the operation and maintenance of the system. A salesperson who focuses exclusively on the characteristics defined in these three layers is a classic vendor, selling hardware features that to a large extent are common to all competitors at that level. If this were a poker game, these features would qualify as the stakes required for a seat at the table.

As we observed earlier, applications and services represent the arrival of software and therefore flexible, adaptable functionality that enhances the value of the underlying network hardware. Sales organizations that focus their efforts here in addition to the lower three layers typically are classified as credible sources of information because they display the ability to deliver not only a solid hardware solution but also the software that addresses specific challenges faced by the customer.

The solutions layer is important because it adds further qualifications to the sales effort on behalf of the customer. This is a touchy area, however, because every vendor on the planet has added "solutions" to its general vocabulary and the term is close to losing its inherent meaning through overuse. The solutions layer is salesware, a necessary component that adds a focus on resolution to enterprise challenges and issues.

The value layer at the top of the food chain is different from the other six for a number of reasons. First, as we noted earlier, it is defined by the customer, not by the vendor. Second, there is no temporal component associated with it. In other words, the applications that are important today will change over time, and the features and benefits found at the hardware layer will evolve. The value a well-designed solution brings to the customer, however, remains the same because it offers the three eternally necessary components: increased revenues, reduced costs, and an improved competitive position.

Adding Value to the Value Chain

As the corporate value chain shown in Figure 2-7 illustrates, a series of tightly interdependent functions leads to the relationship between the customer and the vendor. R&D efforts yield marketable concepts on which manufacturing can base product development and around which operations can develop business plans. The marketing organization serves two bosses: the internal customer with whom it must work to

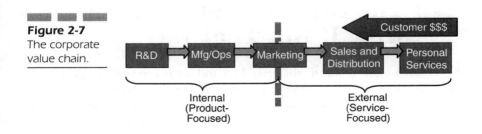

Figure 2-7
The corporate value chain.

develop the message about products that will be delivered to the market and the external customer who will receive the message.

When the product is developed and ready to be sold, the sales and distribution organization steps in and develops the strategy required to move the product into the marketplace effectively. Once it is placed there, interaction with the customer will ensure the sale through highly personal, targeted relationships.

Customer revenue, of course, flows upstream, and its magnitude is directly attributable to the degree of personal service the customer experiences during the interaction that leads to the sale. All the functions listed as internal—R&D, manufacturing, operations, and a piece of marketing—are important to the overall process but are (and should be) largely invisible to the customer. In fact, many corporations are engaging in a radical thought process that leads to the inevitable conclusion that most of those functions can be outsourced. Most strategically focused leaders are shifting their attention from the internal functions with which they are most comfortable to the external functions (external product marketing, sales, product distribution, customer service) that have the greatest impact and bring the greatest perceived value to the customer. This does not *in any way* imply that the internal functions are less important; it does imply, however, that strategic value lies on the right end of the continuum and operational and tactical value lies to the left. The message, of course, is that the checkbook typically lies at the strategic end of the chain.

As the seven-layer model illustrates, the players in the technology game must expand their perspective to ensure that they focus not only on the care and feeding of the CO and what goes on there but also on the CxO and what is important to them. Then and only then will they evolve from being service providers to being a *service provider*, where service is defined by the customer, not by the company that provides it.

The Current Network and How It Got That Way

Now that we understand what could be and what the contributing components are, let's take a moment to examine the developmental impact points in today's network. We are at a point of transition between the legacy PSTN and the emerging VoIP network. Tantalizing possibilities such as IMS and IP television and Internet telephony are just over the horizon. We can see the glow; we're just not sure yet what's causing it. What we *do* know is that the glow is approaching, and fast.

Shaping Today's Telecom Industry

It begins with a single dot of paint on a blank canvas and then another and another. Weeks later a masterpiece emerges from the profusion of paint dots. The artistic school is Pointillism; it was perfected by Georges Seurat, and it yielded such masterpieces as his *Sunday on the Island of La Grand Jatte* (Figure 2-8).

Our industry is Pointillism at its best. So many disparate vectors guide the industry that it is often difficult to step back and see the masterpiece as opposed to a collection of unrelated dots of technological paint. As you read the following vignettes, think of them as inconsequential pieces of fabric in a quilt or spots of paint on a canvas whose combination yields something complex and dazzling. Think also about the five forces we discussed in the last section and how they are related to the material that follows. Most important, think about the concept of IMS: a network environment that adapts to user requests for service.

Many factors have combined to create the telecom industry as we know it today. One of the earliest was the arrival of widespread mobile telephony and the "training" of the marketplace to accept lower-quality service in exchange for freedom of mobility. This is an important construct primarily because it trained the market to accept lower-quality

Figure 2-8
Georges Seurat's Sunday on the Island of La Grand Jatte, an example of Pointillist art.

service and therefore paved the way for the arrival of VoIP. By the time it became prevalent, cellular voice had been around for a couple of decades, and the marketplace was somewhat inured to the idea of service that was of lower quality than carrier-grade.

Equally critical was the growth in broadband access availability and the widespread use of and reliance on the Internet and the World Wide Web. As more and more users took advantage of the capabilities of broadband, demands for improved QoS caused technologists to focus on the forces responsible for less than desirable service: jitter, latency, and packet loss. Soon networks and users benefited from higher bandwidth; improved routing, switching, and algorithms; and more expansive buffers.

As convergence progressed, applications emerged. Avaya, Lucent's former customer premises equipment (CPE) division, announced a product that allowed a user to sit at his or her PC *and listen to his or her voice mail messages.* Today we laugh at the idea, but in those days it was remarkable and was one of the first real implementations of functional convergence. The promise of application integration, bundling, and unified messaging in turn led to experimentation with packet voice and ultimately to the introduction of VoIP.

As application capabilities emerged, demand for end-to-end broadband throughput grew to unprecedented levels. Broadband access, high-speed routing at the edge of the network, Multiprotocol Label Switching (MPLS), and growing support by carrier-grade routers from the likes of Cisco and Juniper moved the perceived bottleneck out of the network core and into the application running on the end user's device.

In 2001 the telecom bubble, which had been growing to untenable heights, collapsed under its own weight, taking the telecom, telephony, and IT markets with it as $7 trillion in market value evaporated. The market, which was accustomed to the frenzy of capability that was so important a part of the bubble, developed intense heartburn over the collapse. Customers' love affair with technology came to an abrupt end, and a budding romance with services and business enhancement began. Customer intimacy, solution selling, customer relationship management (CRM), enterprise resource planning (ERP), data mining, and knowledge management became the most common phrases in the business lexicon.

Technologists jump out of the driver's seat (or, more likely, are pushed); the customer jumps in with four simple questions. You burned me once, they say; you won't do it again. If I buy from you, if I invest in this new technology you are offering, will it raise my revenues? Will it reduce my costs? Will it enhance or at least stabilize my competitive position? Will it mitigate the downside risk I face operating in an increasingly and aggressively competitive market? Scratching their Information Superhighway road rash, service providers and manufacturers are looking to reinvent themselves. Along the way, they are learning a new word: *solutions*. Too bad nobody seems to know what the problem is.

In response, customer service demands reach an all-time high. Call centers and contact centers grow like crabgrass. Outsourcing and off-shoring become the watchwords of the day, and corporations race to move operations to India, the Philippines, and Eastern Europe. Enterprise speed and agility, particularly as they relate to customer service, become prime differentiators. The ability to maintain customer contact and continuity is viewed as a critical contributor to customer satisfaction—and revenue assurance.

The customers continue their push. Recovery from the burst bubble leads to industry consolidation, buy-down, and intensifying competition. SBC acquires AT&T, proving that the child is father to the man. Qwest pits itself in a futile, all-out acquisition battle with Verizon, but in the end Verizon walks away with MCI. Sprint and Nextel agree to merge.

Customers, seeing fewer players on the field, react predictably, pitting one vendor against another in a pricing and service delivery frenzy.

Watching the industry die the death of a thousand cuts, regulators wait quietly and pensively in the wings. The Telecommunications Act of 1996 was by many accounts a failure; they are loath to repeat the bloodletting. Regulatory reform favors the incumbent and facilities-based competition, leading to an upsurge in cable, wireless, and power companies offering voice over their newly deployed IP infrastructures. They do it because they can and because voice was, is, and always will be the killer application. Suddenly IP represents the fundamental underpinning of the "triple play" (voice, video, and data) and the growing realization that the ILEC is no longer the only game in town for carrier-grade service.

The incumbents, however, are not content to lie there while their market is picked off by a pack of fast-moving would-be competitors. VoIP and related technologies continue to evolve and improve as networks become broader, faster, and more capable. In response to the broadside attack on their market, the telcos counter, announcing service packages that include entertainment and broadcast content delivered over DSL, in effect, their own triple (and in some cases quadruple) play. SaskTel offers a full complement of cable content over its DSL network in Saskatoon and Regina. Telus announces TelusTV. Qwest, Bellsouth, Verizon, and SBC all announce broadband access build-outs and deeper fiber penetration, all intent on capturing a place in the lucrative content game.

Where has this taken the industry? One predictable side effect is that the game has become one of offering boutique services in a commodity market. Basic technology indeed has become a commodity, as have Internet access, storage, wireline voice, long distance, content of many types, switching, routing, and wireless. As if commoditization were not enough, the industry reels from attacks by the modern equivalent of Visigoths and Vandals riding down from the north to wreak havoc on the electronic villages. Blows against the beleaguered empire come from Skype and Vonage, Yahoo! and Google, Virgin Wireless, Microsoft, and an increasingly demanding and technologically adept customer base. Skype and Vonage successfully undermine the ILECs' position of circuit-switched power, demonstrating just how good—*and free*—VoIP (over Internet) can be. Although the ILECs lose access lines at the frightening rate of 10,000 per day, Skype *adds* 150,000 every day. Yahoo! and Google make IP-based mail, chat, and storage applications available to the masses at no charge. Google's GMail offers 3 gigabytes of storage to every user, telling users not to delete files: Google will add storage on demand. Virgin Wireless proves (1) the power of brand and (2) the increasing irrelevance of owning the network—and the power inherent in owning the customer and working the brand loyalty game.

Microsoft codifies everything, extending its desktop- and set-top-hungry tentacles into every possible customer touch point: desktop, set-top, palm-top, mobile, gaming, content, application, operating system, and central office. They don't want the infrastructure; they just want the customer. Thus, they revamp Windows XP, call it Longhorn, change its name to Vista, and upgrade their embedded Istanbul-code-named Messenger service to include a carrier-grade VoIP client. When the PC boots and the desktop populates, a softphone will appear in the corner. Click and dial.

And the customers? They just want more.

These forces—Skype and Vonage, Yahoo! and Google, Virgin Wireless, Microsoft, and the customers—behave like biological viruses. They infect and multiply, and the world around them changes as a result. In concert, devices converge, get smaller, become more capable. Desktop phones integrate IP-based Web browsers. Mobile devices combine full-function PDAs and phones and connect to the network at high speed. Vendors roll out WiFi telephones, further facilitating convergence over the enterprise network and offering untold bypass opportunities.

This is a time of blurring lines. The consumer and enterprise markets bump and rub against each other as corporations send waves of employees home to work, erasing the line between enterprise and consumer. These SOHO workers, together with the burgeoning small-to-medium business (SMB) market, create demand for centralized service quality delivered over a fully distributed network to increasingly remote workers. Follow-me and find-me services, sometimes called "presence applications," become highly desirable as mechanisms for logical convergence.

At roughly the same time, the convergence of IT and telecom nears completion. In the enterprise, where VoIP has been deployed widely, voice has morphed into "just another data application." It is, after all, nothing more than a sporadic contribution of packets to the overall network data stream and, with the broad deployment of edge bandwidth and digital compression, an increasingly small percentage of that data is devoted to voice. As this realization dawns, chief technology officers (CTOs) throughout the enterprise domain make a bold move: They issue mandates that cause their IT organizations to absorb the functions and responsibilities of their historically dedicated voice service organizations. This move does two things: It formalizes enterprise recognition that VoIP is *clearly* an enterprise application and further recognizes that *voice* is *not*. Consider this: The packets emerging from a traditional data application such as e-mail are remarkably forgiving of delay and jitter because the asynchronous application that creates and consumes them is equally forgiving. If the message is delayed in its arrival by an additional 10 minutes, for the most part no one cares. In contrast, e-mail is extraordinarily intolerant when it comes to packet loss. The loss of a single packet can result in catastrophic data corruption.

Voice has precisely the opposite behavior. The human ear is such a poorly engineered listening device that 40% packet loss often goes undetected. But introduce 30 milliseconds of delay into the packet stream and customers become surly.

Equally problematic is the fact that we now have a group managing voice *that knows nothing about voice*. We all have seen this broadcast message appear on our desktop or laptop PCs:

E-MAIL SERVER C030TY7 WILL BE BROUGHT DOWN IN FIVE MINUTES FOR EMERGENCY MAINTENANCE. PLEASE SAVE YOUR WORK AND LOG OFF. ESTIMATED TIME OF RESTORAL: ONE HOUR.

We shrug our shoulders, grumble a bit, and amble down to the cafeteria for coffee. But imagine what happens when this message appears instead:

THE VOICE SYSTEM WILL BE BROUGHT DOWN IN FIVE MINUTES FOR EMERGENCY MAINTENANCE DUE TO A WORM THAT HAS

PASSED THE FIREWALL. PLEASE HANG UP. ESTIMATED TIME OF RESTORAL: ONE HOUR.

I suspect that this message will engender a very different response. It's one thing to be without e-mail for an hour; it's another thing to be entirely without voice. The availability of never-failing carrier-grade voice is a deeply inbred expectation; once it becomes "just another IT application," a different picture will have to be painted.

The coming together of voice and data is a powerful and compelling thing as far as the customer is concerned. For the service provider, however, the result is a complex architectural and logistic problem whose management is not optional. Many companies have jumped on the VoIP bandwagon, but not always for the right reasons. The rationale ranges from "gotta go VoIP because it's cool" to "huge reduction in expense" to "unified messaging." Implementers, however, must never forget one thing: *Voice is the application. VoIP is a technology option.* The sounds that emanate from a standard telephone and the sounds that emanate from an IP-based device are identical. Customers don't convert to VoIP because of that cool stream of packets emanating from the handset. The decision to go with a VoIP solution therefore must be based on a clear and emotionless understanding of the inner workings of a typical telephone network, how it differs from a VoIP network, and the pros and cons of each one.

The power that comes from a wisely thought out telecom strategy is all about knowledge: *knowing* why you are choosing to evolve; *knowing* what to expect; *knowing* when to make the change; *knowing* how it will all happen; knowing where the technology, service, application, human resources, and management changes will take place; and *knowing* how

to respond to them all. There's a wonderful line, reputedly from *Alice in Wonderland*: "If you don't know where you're going, any road will take you there." Of course the only way to know where you're going is to know where you've been. In response to that, an old quote from Texas cattle drives seems appropriate: "When you're driving a herd to market, take a look back now and again to make sure they're still there."

Next in line is the inevitable growing interest in open-source software. The industry goes public—and free. LINUX takes the operating system world by storm and does damage to Microsoft's firm grasp on the enterprise server world. XML becomes the de facto standard for data representation in the IP world and soon spreads beyond it. In October 2004, in New Delhi, at a meeting of semiconductor manufacturers, STMicroelectronics stunned delegates by announcing that the firm would make public 1 million lines of code to the industry at large, the first step toward a single standard for chip design that has come to be known as Generalized Open Source Programmable Logic (GOSPL). It is valued at $150 million, and 77% of the attendees agreed to use the standard.

Next comes a tectonic industry shift as computers come of age and with them the gaming industry. The year 2010 appears to be magical because, in that year, around the world, 450 million homes will have broadband and there will be 1 billion VoIP connections. Processor speeds will increase eightfold from where they are today and, because storage grows 12 times faster than processor speeds, the average PC will have a terabyte of onboard storage in 2010. *That is four years away.*

The battlefield, long waged in the access domain, moves to the living room as IPTV takes root and players jockey along the ramparts. Microsoft and Alcatel form a strategic alliance to create the first commercial IPTV platform. With this movement of the battlefield comes a new army: The Millennials arrive, and with them a redefined industry.

Here we are. The industry has been taken apart, examined, revamped, and put back together. Instructions from the market are clear: Out with the old and in with the new, but down with the price and up with the services. I'll buy, but on my terms.

▬ The Next Steps

What does this portend for the industry at large? One thing is clear: The old measures of success no longer apply. Consider the following list.

From Circuit Switching to Circuit Routing

A frequently heard phrase in telecom is "we're going from circuit to packet." This is certainly true to a point, but the statement leaves a major question unanswered. As the network evolves to an IP construct, we do not abandon circuits along the way because circuits are fundamentally important to the delivery of quality-based service. What *is* happening is a move from *physical circuits* to *virtual circuits*. We still ensure a logical end-to-end flow; we just do it in a different fashion.

From Traffic That Responds to the Network to a Network That Responds to the Traffic

In line with the prior comment, the move from circuit to packet brings about a major relationship change between the network and the traffic it transports. In circuit switching, a physical path is established on an end-to-end basis over which all traffic must pass; in effect, the traffic must respond to the network. In packet environments, however, the opposite is true: As packets arrive at nodes within the network, the network reads the destination of each packet by using a variety of techniques and *adapts to the requirements of the traffic.*

From "Wireless and Wireline" to "Access"

As the Millennials become more influential, and the market at large becomes more aware of the enhanced capabilities of the network, the line between wireline and wireless will disappear slowly as customers demand simply *access.* If the network has the ability to adapt to *me* instead of the other way around, it shouldn't matter what access modality I have. In theory the network should be able to find me, interrogate whatever device I'm using, and download the appropriate material in the right format.

From MVNO to MVNE

As Virgin, ESPN, Disney, 7-Eleven, and other MVNOs succeed with their new models of network-free service delivery, a new focus emerges, this time on the back-room systems that enable high-quality service delivery to the customer.

From Mobility to Ubiquity

Both mobility and ubiquity are important constructs in the emerging model of network utilization, but they are not the same. Mobility implies the ability to connect to the network via a wireless local loop, whether EV-DO via CDMA, EDGE via GSM, or pure IP via WiFi or WiMAX. Ideally, it offers predictable high bandwidth, dependable connections, and secure transmission. Ubiquity, in contrast, implies the ability to connect to the network anywhere and at any time regardless of the characteristics of the loop. Ubiquitous access may include wireless as an option but also includes wired solutions such as Ethernet, T-1, and DSL.

As I observed earlier, customers are not looking for the next great killer application but rather for a killer way to access the applications they already have, because those applications offer solutions to most of the challenges they encounter. Consider, for example, typical business users. As long as they are in their home office environment, wired connectivity is perfectly acceptable for both voice and data. When they leave the office and get in the car, *mobile telephony* becomes important. Mobile data has no application (thankfully!) in the car other than the applications optimized for that environment—OnStar service, for example, or GPS-based guidance systems, or specific applications related to public safety. If, however, the user stops for coffee before going home and decides to check her or his e-mail one last time, *ubiquitous* connectivity, whether wired or wireless, provides value to the user from a data perspective while *mobile* telephony remains valuable for voice. An RJ-45 connection on the tabletop is just as serviceable as a WiFi connection, not to mention far more secure and predictable.

Ultimately, *mobility* defines the characteristics of a *lifestyle choice* that involves networking, whether personal or work-related. Ubiquity defines the *characteristics of the technology infrastructure* required to support that mobile lifestyle. "Anywhere, anytime connectivity" has become the mantra of the mobile user and, although WiFi is the most loudly proclaimed option, it is *not* the only option. This, I believe, is part of the reason that revenues associated with WiFi remain elusive. It is sexy, cool, and functional. However, among those three characteristics the only one that has revenue potentially associated with it is *functional*, and there are too many alternatives to wireless that offer lower cost, greater security, and more predictable connections. Until a service provider comes up with a compelling argument for WiFi's performance superiority, the only companies that will make money on it will be those that build wireless access points and routers.

From QoS to QoE

Service providers are driven by the quality of service they deliver. The measures are well known: five nines of reliability (99.999%), carrier-grade, toll-quality, mean time to repair, mean time between failures, and so on. Note, however, that *none* of these measures are meaningful to the customer because they are all network-focused. The *result* of these measures should have a bearing on the customer and therefore should drive a very different measure of service quality delivery: quality of experience. Quality of experience is an outward-looking measure and should include measures of the degree of positive change in the user's interaction with the network and the service provider behind it. A network that is available 99.999% of the time has no value to the users if the databases they wish to access are not available.

From a Network-Aware User to a User-Aware Network

This lies at the heart of IMS. Today the customer must be constantly aware of the eccentricities and limitations of the network and adapt his or her behavior accordingly; hence, there are separate phones and numbers at home, at the fax machine, at the office, on the mobile, and on the second line. With IMS comes a new model in which the *network* adapts to the *user*. A single number works for all devices, and the network "senses" the user's current situation and modifies its service delivery approach accordingly. What a concept!

From Broadcast Content to Unicast Content

As companies, services, and devices converge, demand for varied content delivered to a broad array of devices grows accordingly. Customers want to receive *their* content on *their* device regardless of location, network bandwidth permitting, of course. Furthermore, they want to have the option of downloading only the content for which they are motivated to pay. In the new world of networking, the network will host a database of preferences and will download only the programs the user wants to see, with the profile easily modifiable by the user.

From Access to the Network to Access to My Stuff

Along the same lines, there is a growing recognition on the part of the customers that they don't view the networks the same way the network service provider does. To the service provider, access means "access to the network." To the customer it means "access to my stuff."

From Data-Centric User to User-Centric Data

As sophisticated (and largely automated) CRM capabilities creep into the network, a shift in the role of data occurs. Users are data-centric because their interactions with the network require them to be. For example, I carry my laptop not because it makes me look impressive but because it has all my data on it and I need access to those files. Once the level of sophistication of the network climbs to the point where it becomes user-aware, as described earlier, a shift to *user-centric data* occurs. At this point databases are mined, analyzed, and acted on, creating knowledge the service provider can use to increase sales and maximize the stickiness of the customer.

From Recurring-Charge Billing to Transaction-Based Billing

Perhaps the single greatest untapped opportunity within the telecom/IT space is the need to rewrite billing and operations support systems. Today most service provider OAM&P systems are based on a recurring-charge model and the assumption that most customers care little for call detail records. This assumption is flawed, however, particularly among enterprise customers and the emerging Millennial market sector. A strong interest in transaction-based billing has emerged, and service providers will be forced to adapt their systems to it. For example, many subscribers want to be billed for connect time, number and size of downloads, and so on. Consider the immense success of iTunes and services like it. This is a *massive* opportunity: The first company to demonstrate its ability to "granularize" its billing model will win long-term customer loyalty.

From Regulating Technology to Regulating the Experience

Regulators have "revamped" their approach to their responsibilities, thinking as much about the ultimate customer experience as about the details of the regulated components. One change element is an increased focus on the *result* of the delivered service. This results in both an internal and an external view of the regulated environment.

■■■■ Recipes for Success in the IMS World

What comes out of all this discussion? As we enter the world of an IMS-dominated network environment, all players, most notably the manufacturers and service providers, must take certain key steps to drive a different relationship between themselves, their served markets, their regulators, and the technologies they develop and deploy.

The Service Providers

We begin with service providers. These companies must:

- *NOT consider the roll-out of a new product or servic*e before they answer four critical questions:
  - Will it raise the customer's revenues?
  - Will it reduce the customer's OPEX and CAPEX costs?
  - Will it stabilize or enhance the customer's competitive position?
  - Will it mitigate the downside risk a customer faces as he or she operates in an increasingly competitive marketplace?
- *Develop a culture of regulatory compliance* if they are to survive.
- *STOP focusing on preservation of access lines and minutes of use and START* focusing on preservation of customers.
- *Let go of technology as a differentiator.*
- *Accept the fact that* in the new technology business model they can have some of the money or none of the money. To that end they must

learn to enter into alliances and partnerships that don't involve hegemony.

- *Pay a great deal of attention to the Millennials.* They will soon be the most important and influential employees, customers, and competitors these companies have.
- *Chart a path toward becoming a content provider* and recognize that they already are. Voice is the single most important content component.
- *Stop trumpeting the value of their solutions.* Instead, they should strive to make the market understand that they know what the problems are.
- *Develop a comprehensive telecom / IT attack strategy,* given that telecom is being subsumed by IT in the enterprise space.
- *Challenge the existing paradigms:* local loop, application demand, mobile requirements, and customer demand.
- *Challenge everything by asking at every turn these three questions:* "What's it for?" "Why are doing this?" and "Are you sure?" Then and only then can service providers be sure they are ready to proceed to the next step.
- *Consider the nature of the ideal access appliance* or appliances.

The Manufacturers

Meanwhile, the manufacturers must:

- *Take the lead* by reorienting compensation plans so that rewards are based on customer satisfaction and solution effectiveness rather than on sales levels of the "product du jour."
- *Create a chief integration officer* whose organization is tasked with the functional elimination of product line silos (Figure 2-9).
- Become a contractor or architect. Their product is business problem resolution; the tool is the combined efforts they and their business partners offer.
- *Recognize that wireline and wireless are not distinct product lines.* They're access, no more and no less. If you disagree, ask a Millennial.

Figure 2-9
The role of the
Chief
Integration
Officer

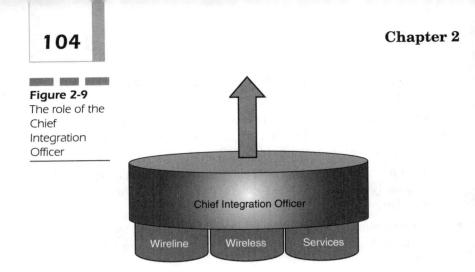

In Summary

We've spent quite a bit of time addressing the past, present, and future behavior of the market. It should be obvious that this is a whole new industry with a whole new set of drivers, customers, technologies, and demands. As the network becomes more user-aware, the applications shift and open new opportunities for the players in the game. We now turn our attention to IMS, the innovation that lies at the heart of this evolution. In Chapter 3 we begin with a brief overview of the PSTN and the Internet. After all, they represent major organs within IMS's anatomy; it behooves us to spend some time analyzing their physiology.

Network
Basics

We begin this chapter with an overview of the telephone network, followed by an overview of the public switched telephone network and the Internet. Readers familiar with these architectures can flip ahead to the beginning of the story of IMS; those less familiar with the inner workings of networks, read on.

Figure 3-1 shows a typical telephony network layout. A customer's telephone is connected to the service provider's network by a *local loop* connection (so-called twisted-pair wire). The local loop in turn connects to the local switch in the central office. This switch is the point at which customers first touch the telephone network, and it is responsible for performing the initial call setup, maintaining the call while it is in progress, and tearing it down when the call is complete. This switch is called a *local switch* because its primary responsibility is to set up local calls that originate and terminate within the same switch. It has one other responsibility, though: to provide the necessary interface between the local switch and the long-distance switch so that calls between adjacent local switches (or between far-flung local switches) can be established.

The process, then, goes something like this: When a customer lifts the handset and goes off-hook, a switch in the telephone closes, completing a circuit that allows current flow that in turn brings a dial tone to the customer's ear. Upon hearing the dial tone, the customer enters the destination address of the call (otherwise known as a telephone number). The switch receives the telephone number and analyzes it, determining from the area code and prefix whether the call can be completed within

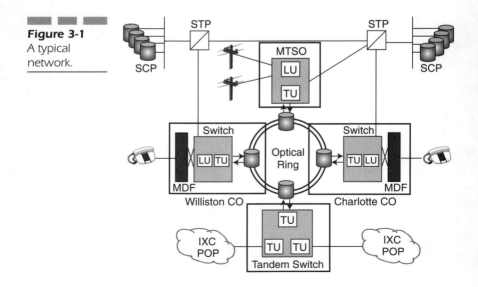

Figure 3-1
A typical network.

the local switch or must leave the local switch for another one. If the call is local, it merely burrows through the crust of the switch and then reemerges at the receiving local loop. If it is a toll or long-distance call, it must burrow through the hard crunchy coating of the switch, pass through the soft chewy center, and emerge on the other crunchy side on its way to a long-distance switch. Keep in mind that the local switch has no awareness of the existence of customers or telephony capability beyond its own cabinets. Thus, when it receives a telephone number it is incapable of processing, it hands it off to a higher-order switch with the implied message "Here: I have no idea what to do with this, but I assume that you do."

The long-distance switch receives the number from the local switch, processes the call, establishes the necessary connection, and passes the call on to the remote long-distance switch over a long-distance circuit. The remote long-distance switch passes the call to the remote local switch, which rings the destination telephone and, ultimately, the call is established.

Network Overview

When a customer places a call, a complex process begins that ultimately establishes a temporary end-to-end communications path between the caller and the person being called. When the caller picks up the telephone, the act of lifting the handset (going off-hook, which sometimes is done by pushing a button on a cordless handset) closes a circuit, allowing current to flow from the switch in the local central office to the phone. Using various methods, the switch delivers a dial tone to the caller's ear. The dial tone notifies the calling party that the switch is ready to receive the dialed number.

The customer now dials the telephone number by pressing the appropriate buttons on the phone. The switch then performs a rudimentary analysis of the number to determine whether it is served out of the same switch. In North America a telephone number has three pieces: a three-digit Numbering Plan Area (NPA, often called the area code), a three-digit prefix that identifies the switch that hosts the called number, and the four digits that uniquely identify the called party. Each network number exchange (NXX) can serve 10,000 numbers, and a modern central office switch typically can handle as many as 15 to 20 exchanges of 10,000 lines each.

In this example we assume that the called party and the calling party do not reside in the same switch. Consequently, the call must be routed to a different central office. Before that can take place, however, the calling party's local switch routes a query to the signaling network, which is known as Signaling System Seven (SS7). The signaling network is a separate stand-alone network buried deep within the telephone network that is responsible for establishing, maintaining, and tearing down calls and, at the same time, providing access to enhanced services such as Custom Local Area Signaling Services (CLASS), 800 Number Portability, Local Number Portability (LNP), Line Information Database (LIDB) lookups for credit card verification, interconnect services between wireline and wireless networks, and other enhanced features. In a sense it makes the local switch's job easier by centralizing many of the functions that formerly had to be performed locally. Today's signaling network is called SS7, and it represents one of the first successful "hybridizations" between telecom and IT.

The original concept behind SS7 was to separate the actual calls on the public telephone network from the process of setting up and tearing down those calls as a way to make the network more efficient. Consider the impact of Mother's Day in the United States. Mother's Day is the busiest calling day of the year by a significant margin. During the busiest calling time of that day, it is common to pick up the handset and, after dialing one's mother's number, be given a "fast busy." The network is not designed to handle the massive influx of calls that typically besiege it on that day. As a result, there are not enough network resources to handle the volume, and some people have to wait. This is done intentionally by the telephone company, and for good reason.

First of all, it doesn't make sense to engineer the network to handle the call volume of Mother's Day, which occurs only once a year; that would be an irresponsible waste of money. Furthermore, there are certain services that the telephone company must preserve, such as 911 and other emergency services, even during the Mother's Day onslaught. To do this the company uses the intelligence of SS7 to "meter" the inbound calls and ensure that emergency calls are given top priority. One way the network does this is by taking advantage of the size of the country and its four time zones. When it's 8:00 A.M. on the East Coast, for example, it's 5:00 A.M. in California, which means that people there haven't even *thought* about their first low-fat low-foam decaf double cappuccino yet. Consequently, network resources on the West Coast are highly underutilized and for the most part lying dormant.

SS7 takes advantage of this in an interesting way: It isn't unusual for a call from Florida to Manhattan, for example, to be routed through California's network infrastructure as a way to alleviate the congestion in the East Coast's telephone network.

When the decision to isolate the call setup and management process from the call itself was made, it had the effect of moving the call management intelligence out of the PSTN and into a separate network where it could be centralized somewhat and therefore made available to a much larger population. It also made the process infinitely more efficient. In the original design of the network, the call setup information traveled across the same path as the call itself. If I called my friend Dennis in California from my office in Vermont and he was on the phone, an indication that his line was unavailable would be returned to the originating switch in Vermont, which in turn would put a busy tone in my ear. The consequence of this was that I tied up network resources between Vermont and California only to hear a busy signal, and the telephone company made no money in the process. When the call setup path is separated from the actual call path, no billable network resources are engaged until it is conclusively known that the call can be established successfully. In fact, once it is known that Dennis's line is available, the network resources over which the conversation will travel are reserved only while the network waits for someone to answer the phone. Once Dennis answers, then and only then is the call connected.

The SS7 network, which is shown in Figure 3-2, is made up of very large packet switches known as Signal Transfer Points (STPs) and intelligent database engines known as Service Control Points (SCPs). The SCPs are basically mainframe computers with massive associated databases. The STPs and SCPs are interconnected to each other and to the telephone network via software modules resident in the local switches that are known as Service Switching Points (SSPs). Physical interconnection occurs via digital links that typically operate at 56 to 64 Kbps.

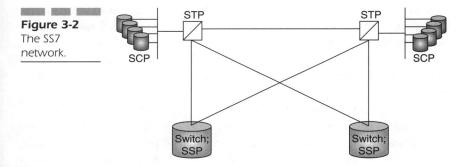

Figure 3-2
The SS7
network.

The collocation of STPs and SCPs represents another example of the "coming together" of telecom and IT.

Historically, the central office is a rather dark and altogether unelegant environment. SCPs, because they are mainframe computers, require a data center–like environment. Consequently, the face of the central office has changed dramatically over the years and now has "regions" that look far more like a data center than like a traditional central office.

When a customer in an SS7 environment places a call, the local switching infrastructure issues a software interrupt via the SSP so that the called party and calling party information can be handed off to the STP in the SS7 network. The STP routes the information to an associated SCP, which performs a database lookup to determine whether any special call-handling instructions apply. For example, if the calling party has chosen to block the delivery of caller ID information, the SCP query will return that information. If the called party has set up a relationship with the caller such that their calls are associated with a distinctive ring, SS7 takes care of that as well.

Once the SCP has performed its task, the call information is returned to the STP, which consults routing tables and then selects a path for the call. Upon receipt of the call, the destination switch will cooperate with SS7 to determine whether the called party's phone is available; if it is, it rings the phone. If the customer's number is not available due to a busy condition or another event, a packet will be returned to the source indicating that fact, and SS7 will instruct the originating SSP to put a busy tone or fast busy in the caller's ear.

At this point the calling party has several options, one of which is to invoke one of many custom calling services, such as *Automatic Ringback*. With Automatic Ringback, the network will monitor the called number for a period of time, waiting for the line to become available. As soon as it is, the call will be put through, and the calling party will be notified of the incoming call via some kind of distinctive ringing.

Thus, when a call is placed to a distant switch, the calling information is passed to SS7, which uses the caller's number, the called number, and SCP database information to choose a route for the call. It then determines whether there are any special call-handling requirements to be invoked and instructs the switches along the way to process the call as required.

These features constitute a set of services known as the *Advanced Intelligent Network* (AIN), a term coined by Telcordia (formerly Bellcore; sold to Science Applications International Corporation, and recently sold again to Providence Equity and Warburg Pincus). The SSPs (local switches) are responsible for basic calling, and the SCPs manage the enhanced services that ride atop the calls. The SS7 network, then, is responsible for the signaling required to establish and tear down calls and invoke supplementary or enhanced services. This is critically important, even more so today as the network begins the complex process of migrating from a circuit-switched model to a VoIP packet-based model. Furthermore, as IMS becomes a reality and full-blown convergence takes root, the signaling network, in whatever form it ultimately takes, will become all the more critical.

Related to SS7 in today's network is the SIP. SIP was created to serve as an alternative to H.323. H.323 originally was rolled out as a "control protocol" to manage and oversee the delivery of multimedia traffic across LANs. SIP, in contrast, was created specifically for VoIP, which is considered one of the major evolutionary building blocks of IMS. SIP defines a set of standard "objects" and a message hierarchy for communicating among the various components of the typical VoIP network.

Like SS7, SIP is a collection of modules that work together to provide signaling capability across the network. These modules (see Figure 3-3) include *user agent clients*; a *location server*, which relates a client device to a specific IP address; *proxy servers*, which are responsible for forwarding call requests from one server to another on behalf of SIP clients (hence the name *proxy*); and *redirect servers*, which transmit the called party's address back to the calling party so that the connection can be made.

These devices rely on a set of SIP messages that perform basic signaling tasks—establishment, maintenance, and teardown—just as SS7 does. The messages include *Invite*, which is used to establish or join a call session; *ACK*, which is used to acknowledge an invitation; *Register*, which is used to register a user with a server; *Options*, which are used to petition for data about the capabilities of the server; *Cancel*, which can-

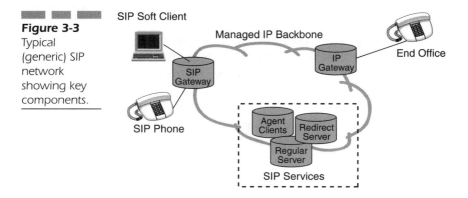

Figure 3-3
Typical
(generic) SIP
network
showing key
components.

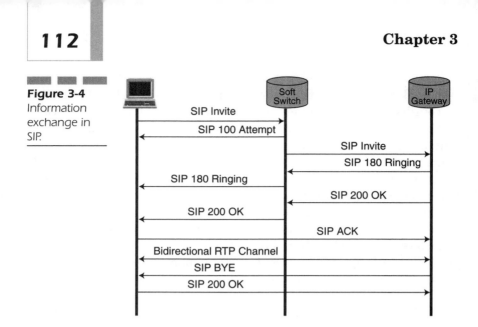

Figure 3-4
Information exchange in SIP.

cels a previous request; and *Bye*, which ends a session. Figure 3-4 shows a typical exchange of information using SIP.

SIP was created by the Internet Engineering Task Force (IETF), the organization responsible for most Internet standards. Its responsibility is session creation and destruction; the actual in-progress session and connection details are up to the communicating endpoint devices. Again, the assumption is that the devices communicating in an IMS domain are relatively intelligent.

As we discussed in Chapter 2, SIP uses HTTP syntax and URL addressing. It was designed to establish communications among a large group of servers and, as a result, it is immensely scalable. One of the major concerns among enterprise IT personnel is the growth of user populations and the apparently unbounded demand for services. SIP's scalability and ease of deployment therefore are highly desirable.

SIP was designed to establish peer-to-peer sessions between Internet routers. The protocol defines a variety of server types, including *feature servers, registration servers*, and *redirect servers*. SIP supports fully distributed services that reside in the actual user devices and, because it is based on existing IETF protocols, it provides a seamless integration path for voice-data integration. Not surprisingly, SIP has been accepted by most major telecom equipment vendors, including Lucent, Nortel, Cisco, Ericsson, Siemens, and Alcatel. Also, because it is designed for use in large carrier networks with the potential for millions of managed ports, its success is reasonably assured.

Originally, H.323 was to be the protocol of choice to make this possible. Although H.323 is clearly a capable suite of protocols and is indeed quite good for VoIP services that derive from ISDN implementations, it remains quite complex. As a result, it has been relegated for use as a video control protocol and for some gatekeeper-to-gatekeeper communications functions. Although H.323 continues to have its share of supporters, it slowly is being edged out of the limelight. SIP supporters claim that H.323 is far too complex and rigid to serve as a standard for basic telephony setup requirements, arguing that SIP, which is architecturally simpler and imminently extensible, is a better choice.

The intense interest in moving voice to IP is driven by simple and understandable factors: cost of service and enhanced flexibility. However, it is critical to understand the differences between simple voice and full-blown telephony with its many enhanced features. It is the feature set that gives voice its range of capability. A typical local switch such as Lucent Technologies' 5ESS offers more than 3000 features, whereas IP devices offer far less. Naturally, this will change as demand grows and, to that end, it is critical to understand how SIP works in modern networks.

SIP Functionality

SIP, which is documented in RFC 2543, is part of the IETF's standards collection for managing the transmission and control of multimedia data. It is built on a client-server model and is used almost exclusively in IP telephony networks.

SIP sets up and tears down multimedia sessions between communicating endpoints. These multimedia sessions may include multiparty conferences, telephone calls, and the distribution of multimedia content.

SIP is a lightweight, text-based protocol that is transported via TCP or User Datagram Protocol (UDP) and is designed to operate in accordance with the rules established for all Internet protocols. It is easy to implement, simple to operate, efficient, and scalable.

How SIP Works

SIP exchanges capabilities between communicating devices by using "invitations" as a means to create *Session Description Protocol* (SDP) messages. The role of those messages is to set up call-control channels and ensure that call participants can negotiate the network requirements for their calls.

Equally important is SIP's support of user portability. In an environment where users move around (and in the IMS world, we already have seen that this is the hallmark of the environment), it is crucial that network administrators have the ability to reconfigure the network as people move, without incurring inordinately high move, add, and change (MAC) costs. SIP is a major part of the answer to this challenge. The protocol uses proxy and redirect services to match an incoming call to a user's *logical* location, and the logical location then is tied to a physical port. A user (in this case an IP telephone as opposed to a human being), for example, can inform the SIP server of its current physical location by transmitting a "registration message" to a software "registrar." Thus, a human user can move from one location to another, take his or her IP phone along, plug it in, and immediately be recognized and connected, with appropriate access and security delivered on a user-by-user basis. *The network adapts to the user instead of the other way around.* Once again, this is a hallmark of IMS.

In proxy mode (Figure 3-5), SIP clients (end-user devices) transmit server requests to the proxy server, and the proxy server either handles

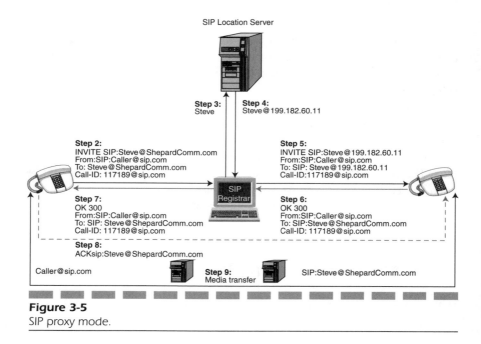

Figure 3-5
SIP proxy mode.

the service request directly or forwards it to another SIP server. One advantage of proxy operation is that the proxy server can disguise users by transmitting a "proxy" rather than the original user-generated signaling message. As a result, other users cannot "see" the original message. Instead, they see a message from the proxy server.

In redirect mode (Figure 3-6), the call setup request is transmitted to a SIP server. The server performs a lookup on the destination address, which it then returns to the originator of the call. The originator in turn signals the SIP client.

Other than the fact that SIP uses a different network architecture and relies on a different set of control protocols, it should be obvious that the basic *functions* performed by SIP are identical in purpose to those performed by SS7 in the traditional telephone network. The establishment of a call, the invocation of a set of supplementary IT-based services that generate additional revenue, and the eventual disconnection of the call are the basic responsibilities of both environments. In fact, as SS7- and SIP-based networks have come to coexist and reside alongside one another, interface protocols such as Nortel's IPS7 have been written to bridge the gap between them and ensure that signaling information can be shared as required. Again, because IMS assumes that the network infrastructure is subordinate to delivered services, it makes sense that this capability would be a basic requirement for the ongoing evolution of the so-called next-generation network.

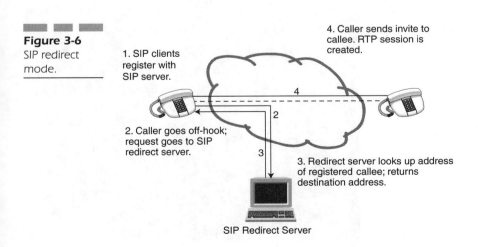

Figure 3-6
SIP redirect mode.

1. SIP clients register with SIP server.

4. Caller sends invite to callee. RTP session is created.

2. Caller goes off-hook; request goes to SIP redirect server.

3. Redirect server looks up address of registered callee; returns destination address.

SIP Redirect Server

■ Network Topology

Let's return to our discussion of network topology and explain how the elements of the traditional network work together. This will help us later as we "build" the IMS environment, because it is important to preserve the revenue-generating functions of the network as we proceed. Refer back to Figure 3-6.

In a traditional environment the customer's telephone is connected to a device on the outside of the house or office building called a *protector block* (Figure 3-7). This is a high-voltage protection device that protects both the subscriber and the switching equipment from lightning strikes.

The protector connects to the network via a twisted-pair local loop that arrives on what is known as the *drop wire*. It is either aerial, as shown in Figure 3-8, or is buried underground. In the traditional outside plant environment there may be multiple pairs in each drop wire because today the average household typically orders a second line for a home office, computer, fax machine, or teenager. This practice is declining, however, much to the chagrin of the telephone company; because DSL obviates the need for a second line (both voice and data service are multiplexed across the same pair), customers are not ordering the second line. Because the Millennials don't see the relevance of wireline telephones (they *live* on their mobile devices), they aren't ordering them.

Figure 3-7
Protector block, shown at left.

Figure 3-8
Aerial drop
wire.

Once the drop wire reaches the edge of the subscriber's property, it typically terminates on some kind of a terminal box, such as the one shown in Figure 3-9. There, all the pairs from the neighborhood or office complex are connected to the main cable that runs up the center of the street.

When outside plant engineers started designing networks, each customer was given a cable pair from her or his house to the central office; that was an expensive design because of the thousands of miles of copper

Figure 3-9
Terminal box,
sometimes
known as a
"B-Box."

that had to be put into the ground. With the arrival of time division multiplexing, however, engineers were able to design a system over which customers could share access to the network, as shown in Figure 3-10. This technique is known as a *Subscriber Loop Carrier*, and it uses a collection of shared facilities to combine the traffic from a group of subscribers in a shared facility, reducing the amount of wire required to connect them to the central office.

The only problem with this design is that customers are restricted to the 64 Kbps of bandwidth that carrier systems assign to each subscriber. As a result, subscribers who want to buy *more* than 64 Kbps, such as those who want DSL, are out of luck. New versions of loop carrier standards and technologies such as GR-303 and the deployment of optical remotes that use fiber instead of copper for the trunk line between the remote terminal and the central office terminal help solve the problem by making bandwidth allocation far more flexible. SBC, Verizon, and Bellsouth are all engaged in optical architecture rollouts that they claim will eliminate the problem in the next few years by giving every customer access to an optical local loop—or at least access to a node in his or her neighborhood that is connected to an optical facility and is thus capable of delivering massive bandwidth to the subscriber that is in keeping with the growing requirements of multimedia applications.

Either way, the customer's local loop makes its way over the physical infrastructure on its way to the core of the network that begins in the local central office. It may be aerial (Figure 3-11) or underground (Figure 3-12). The wire pairs that make up local loops are aggregated into cables, which in turn are combined to form larger cables, as shown schematically in Figure 3-13. As the cable gets closer to the central office, it gets larger; for example, four 250-pair cables may be combined to create a

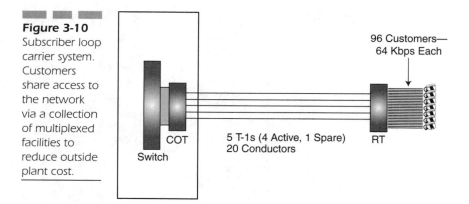

Figure 3-10
Subscriber loop carrier system. Customers share access to the network via a collection of multiplexed facilities to reduce outside plant cost.

96 Customers—
64 Kbps Each

COT

Switch

5 T-1s (4 Active, 1 Spare)
20 Conductors

RT

Figure 3-11
Aerial plant.
Telephony is
the lowest set
of facilities on
the pole.

1000-pair cable, which may be combined with others to create a 5000-pair cable that enters the central office. Once inside the office, the cables are broken out again for distribution of the cable pairs. This is done in the cable vault; an example is shown in Figure 3-14. The large cable on the left side of the splice case represents the cable pairs from the smaller cables on the right.

The Central Office

The cable enters the central office via buried conduit that feeds into the *cable vault*, the lowest subbasement in the office. Because the cable vault

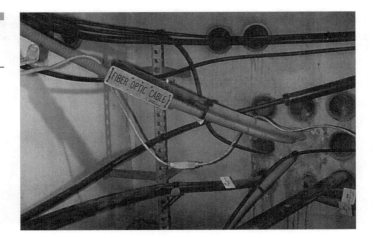

Figure 3-12
Underground
plant.

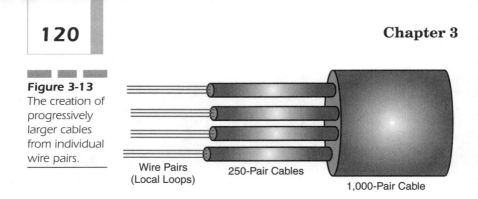

Figure 3-13
The creation of progressively larger cables from individual wire pairs.

Wire Pairs
(Local Loops)
250-Pair Cables
1,000-Pair Cable

is connected to the underground conduit system, which shares space with natural gas lines, sewer pipes, and other facilities that transport noxious and potentially explosive gases that could flow inadvertently into the cable vault and be set afire by a piece of sparking electrical equipment, these rooms are monitored by gas detectors that sound an alarm if gas is detected. A cable vault is shown in Figure 3-15.

The cables that enter the vault are quite large, but once they arrive at the central office, they must be broken down again into their constituent parts and eventually into individual cable pairs. Once this has been done, they leave the cable vault via fireproof foam-insulated ducts and travel upstairs to the *Main Distribution Frame* (MDF). The MDF (Figure 3-16) is a large iron frame that provides physical support and technician access for the thousands of pairs of wire that interconnect customers' telephones to the switch. The cables from the cable vault ascend and are hardwired to the *vertical side* of the MDF, as shown in Figure 3-17.

The vertical side of the MDF is wired to the *horizontal side*. The horizontal side (Figure 3-18) is connected to the central office local switch.

Figure 3-14
In the cable vault, the large cables shown on the left are broken down into the smaller cables on the right for distribution throughout the office.

Figure 3-15
Another view
of the cable
vault.

Note the wire lying on each shelf of the frame: These are the cable pairs that belong to the customers who are served by the office.

Remember that the job of the local switch is to establish temporary connections between customers or between computers that wish to communicate. *Line units* (LUs) in the switch provide a connection point for every cable pair served by the switch. In practice, then, the switch connects with ease one subscriber in the switch to another subscriber in the same switch. After all, the switch maintains directory tables—a database, of course—and so it knows the subscribers it hosts.

Connecting subscribers served by different switches is somewhat more complex. When the switch receives the dialed digits, it analyzes them to determine whether the called party is locally hosted. If the

Figure 3-16
Main
distribution
frame, or MDF.

Figure 3-17
Vertical side of
MDF, showing
protectors.

number is in the same switch, the call is established independently by
the switch; no complex signaling activity is required. If the number
resides in a different switch, the local switch must pass the call on to a
local tandem switch, which provides access to the *points of presence*
(POPs) of the various long-distance carriers that serve the area. The

Figure 3-18
Horizontal side
of MDF.

tandem switch typically does not connect directly to subscribers; it connects only to other switches. It also performs a database query through SS7 to determine who the subscriber's long-distance carrier of choice is so that it can route the call to the appropriate carrier. The tandem switch then passes the call to the long-distance carrier, which transports it over the long-distance network to the carrier's switch in the remote (receiving) office. The remote long-distance switch then passes the call to a remote tandem switch, which hands it to the remote local switch that serves the called party.

Interoffice Trunking

As Figure 3-19 illustrates, an optical fiber ring with add-drop multiplexers often interconnects central offices so that interoffice traffic can be transported efficiently. The switches have *trunk units* (TUs) that connect the back side, called the trunk side, of the switch to the wide area network, in this case the optical ring.

Let's return to the call example with which we started this section. The caller dials the requested number. The call travels over the local loop, goes across aerial and/or underground facilities, and enters the central office through the cable vault. From the cable vault the call travels up to the main distribution frame, which passes it to the local switch. The called number is received by the local switch, which invokes an SS7

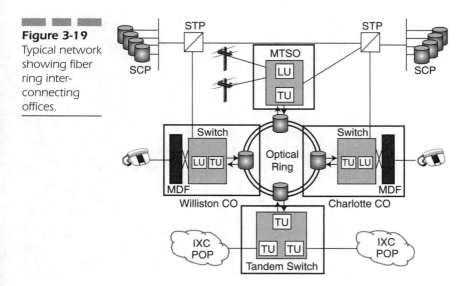

Figure 3-19
Typical network showing fiber ring interconnecting offices.

database lookup to determine the proper disposition of the call and any special service information about the caller's service. The local switch routes the call over intraoffice facilities to a tandem switch, which connects the call to the POP of the appropriate long-distance carrier. The long-distance carrier invokes the capabilities of SS7 to determine whether the called line is available. If that line is available, it passes the call to the remote local service provider. When the called party answers, the call is put through and progresses normally.

If the local loop had been wireless, the call from the cell phone would have been received by a cell tower (Figure 3-20) and transported to a dedicated cellular switch called a *Mobile Telephone Switching Office* (MTSO). The MTSO would process the call and hand it to the wireline network via interoffice facilities. From that point on, the call would be handled like any other. It either would terminate on the local switch or pass to a tandem switch for long-distance processing. The fact of the matter is that the only part of a cellular network that is truly wireless is the local loop; everything else is wired.

Figure 3-20
A cell tower,
disguised as a
palm tree.

This is an important point as we consider the impact IMS will have on future network architectures. I often ask audiences, "What percentage of cellular calls go through the wireline network?" Or I may ask, "What percentage of Internet traffic passes through the telephone network?" The answer to both questions is 100%. The only part of the cellular network that is wireless is the local loop: the connection between the mobile phone and the tower to which it connects. Although the second one is a bit of a trick question, the answer is still 100%. Although Internet IP traffic may not flow across the public switched telephone network, it does flow across facilities owned by the telephone company and leased as private line circuits to whatever entity owns that piece of the network.

The reason I mention this fact is that those who are planning celebration parties for the imminent demise of the legacy telephone network might want to hold off for a while. The telephone network does precisely what it was designed to do: carry traffic very well around the globe in a seemingly effortless fashion and in a remarkably efficient way. IMS, which erases the lines between infrastructures, will still be reliant on the core of the network for some time to come, particularly the transport pieces. It's very easy to say that IP "will replace the telephone network," but it's just not true. A very large part of the existing infrastructure will continue to play a major role in the evolving network. Although the architecture may look different, utilize a different set of protocols, and behave in an entirely different fashion, much of the physical infrastructure will continue to be relevant, as we'll see later in the book.

Now that we have our arms around the PSTN, let's turn our attention to the Internet and the services it makes possible.

Origins of the Internet

The Internet as we know it today began as a U.S. Department of Defense (DoD) project designed to interconnect a small collection of DoD research facilities. In 1968, the government research agency known as the Advanced Research Projects Agency (ARPA) awarded a contract to design and build the packet network that ultimately would become the Internet.[1] It had a proposed transmission speed of 50 Kbps and, in 1969,

---

[1] ARPA's interests have evolved since then. In 2003 it issued a call for papers from any researchers who had demonstrated practical implementations of time travel. See http://www.darpa.mil/baa/baa03-02mod3.htm.

the first node was installed at UCLA. Others were installed on roughly a monthly basis at Stanford Research Institute (SRI), the University of California at Santa Barbara (UCSB), and the University of Utah. ARPANET spanned the continental United States by 1971, and had connections to research facilities in Europe by 1973.

The original protocol selected for the ARPANET was called the Network Control Protocol (NCP). It was designed to handle the minimal requirements of the ARPANET network. As usage climbed, however, the protocol proved to be inadequate and, in 1974, the Transmission Control Protocol (TCP) was implemented, designed for end-to-end network communications control. In 1978, a new design split the responsibilities for end-to-end versus node-to-node transmission between TCP and a new addition, the Internet Protocol. Since TCP and IP originally were envisioned as a single protocol, they are known as the *TCP/IP protocol suite*, a collection that also includes protocols and applications that handle routing, QoS, and error control.

In 1983, the ARPANET was split into two networks. One part, still called ARPANET, continued to be used to interconnect research and academic sites; the other, called MILNET, carried military traffic and ultimately became part of the Defense Data Network.

The network that ultimately would become today's Internet continued to grow and evolve. In 1986, the National Science Foundation (NSF) built a backbone to interconnect four supercomputing centers to the National Center for Atmospheric Research. That network, known as NSFNET, continued to expand and eventually became what is now the Internet. Although the original NSFNET applications were multiprotocol implementations, TCP/IP was used for overall interconnectivity.

In 1994, a structure was put in place to reduce the NSF's responsibility in the Internet. The new structure, which still is in use, consists of three principal components. The first was a small number of *network access points* (NAPs) where ISPs would interconnect to the Internet backbone. The NSF originally funded four NAPs in Chicago (operated by Ameritech, now part of SBC), New York (really Pensauken, NJ, operated by Sprint), San Francisco (operated by Pacific Bell, now part of SBC), and Washington, DC (MAE-East, operated by MFS, now a division of MCI). Yes, those in the know *do* refer to the San Francisco facility as MAR West.

The second component put into place was the *Very High Speed Backbone Network Service*, a facility that interconnected the NAPs, which were operated at that time by MCI. It was installed in 1995, and originally operated at OC-3 (155.52 Mbps) but was upgraded to OC-12 (622.08 Mbps) in 1997.

The third component was the *Routing Arbiter*, which was designed to ensure that appropriate routing protocols for the Internet were available and properly deployed.

While all this was going on, Internet service providers were sprouting like mushrooms after a rain. Many of them received government funding to help establish the breadth and richness of the Internet, but after a period of time that ended. Ultimately, ISPs were given five years of diminishing funding to become commercially self-sustaining. The funding ended in 1998, and at approximately the same time, a number of additional NAPs were launched.

As a matter of segmentation, control, and management, three levels of ISP have been identified. *Tier 1* refers to ISPs that have a national presence and connect to at least three of the original four NAPs. National ISPs include AT&T, Cable & Wireless, MCI, and Sprint. *Tier 2* refers to ISPs that primarily have a regional presence and connect to fewer than three of the original four NAPs. Regional ISPs include Adelphia, Verizon.net, and BellSouth.net. Finally, *Tier 3* refers to local ISPs, those which do not connect to a NAP but offer services via the connections of another ISP.

Managing the Internet

It's a wonder the Internet is manageable at all. Like the telephone network, the Internet is really a network of networks, interconnected by high-speed facilities that for the most part are leased from telephone companies. It is incorrect to think of the Internet as a stand-alone network; it is a collection of leased lines that interconnect the devices that provide the sophisticated routing functions that make the Internet so powerful. As such, it is owned by no one and owned by everyone, but more important, it is *managed* by no one and *managed* by everyone. There is no single authority that governs the Internet because the Internet is not a single monolithic entity but rather a collection of entities. Yet it runs well, perhaps better than more centrally managed services.

That being said, there are certainly organizations that provide oversight and management for the Internet, as shown in Figure 3-21. These organizations, which are described below, guide the development of the network.

One of the longest-standing among those organizations is the *Internet Activities Board* (IAB), which is responsible for administrative and technical activities for the Internet as a whole. It works closely with the

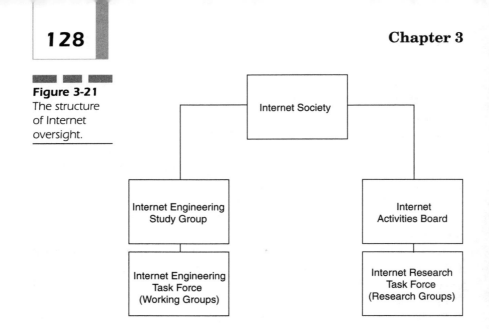

Figure 3-21
The structure
of Internet
oversight.

Internet Society (ISOC), a nongovernmental organization, established in 1992, which coordinates Internet internetworking and applications development. ISOC also provides communications for the IAB.

The *Internet Engineering Task Force* is one of the best-known Internet organizations and is part of the IAB. Mentioned earlier, the IETF creates working groups responsible for the production of technical specifications and protocol development. Because of the IETF's long-standing commitment to the Internet's success, the International Organization for Standardization (ISO) accredited it as an official international standards body at the end of 1994.

Similarly, the *World Wide Web Consortium* (W3C) has no official role but is the primary developer of protocols for the World Wide Web that promote its evolution and ensure its interoperability. This organization has more than 400 member companies.

Smaller organizations play important roles as well. The *Internet Engineering Steering Group* (IESG) provides direction to the IETF and is in fact a subgroup of the IAB. The *Internet Research Task Force* (IRTF) performs research on the future Internet. The *Internet Engineering Planning Group* (IEPG) coordinates worldwide Internet operations and helps ISPs achieve interoperability. Finally, the *Forum of Incident Response and Security Teams* coordinates *computer emergency response teams* (CERTs) globally.

Naming Conventions in the Internet

The Internet is based on a system of *domains* that identify its operating geography. For example, alcatel.com is a domain, as are sbc.net, cia.gov, and ShepardComm.com. The domains help guide traffic from one user to another by following a hierarchical addressing scheme that includes a top-level domain, one or more subdomains, and a host name. The postal service relies on a hierarchical addressing scheme, and it serves as a good analogy to the way Internet addressing works. Consider the following address:

William P. Gates III
Really Rich Guy Estates
1 Money Tree Court
Redmond, Washington 98134 USA

In reality the address is upside down because a package addressed to William must be read from the bottom up to be delivered properly.

The assignment of Internet IP addresses historically was handled by the *Internet Assigned Numbers Authority* (IANA), whereas domain names were assigned by the *Internet Network Information Center* (Inter-NIC), which had overall responsibility for name dissemination; "regional NICs" handled non-U.S. domains. The InterNIC also was responsible for the management of the *Domain Name System* (DNS), the massive distributed database that reconciles host names and IP addresses throughout the Internet.

The InterNIC and its overall role have gone through a series of significant changes in the last decade. In 1993, *Network Solutions, Inc.* (NSI), was given responsibility for operating the InterNIC registry by the NSF and had exclusive authority for the assignment of domains such as .com, .org, .net, and .edu. In October 1998, NSI became the sole administrator for those domains, but a plan was created to allow users to register names with other companies. At the same time responsibility for IP address assignments was migrated to a newly created organization called the *American Registry for Internet Numbers* (ARIN). Shortly thereafter, in March 2000, NSI was acquired by VeriSign.

The most recent addition to the domain management process is the *Internet Corporation for Assigned Names and Numbers* (ICANN). Established in late 1998, ICANN was appointed by the *U.S. National Telecommunications and Information Administration* (NTIA) to manage the DNS.

Of course, it makes sense that sooner or later the most common top-level domains, which include well-known suffixes such as .com, .gov, .net, .org, and .net, would be deemed inadequate. In November 2000, the first new top-level domains, seven in all, were approved by ICANN. They are .aero for the aviation industry, .biz for businesses, .coop for business cooperatives, .info for general use, .museum for museums, .name for individuals, and .pro for professionals.

Let's now examine the protocol that makes the Internet work so well.

TCP/IP

TCP/IP has been around for years. Although we often think of it as a single protocol that governs the Internet, it is actually a collection of protocols that provide the functions of the various layers of the protocol. We will explore each layer in the sections that follow.

The Network Interface Layer

Based on what they had seen during the Internet's raucous development, TCP/IP was created by its designers with the understanding that it would not be particularly well behaved. They assumed that the Internet would become a network awash in numerous unrelated and often conflicting protocols, transporting traffic with widely varying QoS requirements. The fundamental component of the protocol, the IP packet, is designed to deal with all these variables, and TCP manages QoS.

Network Interface Protocols

Two network interface protocols are particularly important to TCP/IP. The *Serial Line Internet Protocol* (SLIP) and the *Point-to-Point Protocol* (PPP) provide data link layer services in situations in which no other data link protocol is present, such as leased-line environments. Most TCP/IP software packages for desktop applications include these two protocols even though dial-up is fading rapidly in the presence of growing levels of broadband. With SLIP or PPP, a remote computer can attach directly to a host and connect to the Internet by using IP rather than being limited to an asynchronous connection.

The Point-to-Point Protocol

The PPP was created for point-to-point links. It has the ability to manage a variety of functions at the moment of connection, including password verification, IP address resolution, compression (where required), and encryption for privacy or security. It also supports multiple protocols over a single connection, an important capability for dial-up users that rely on IP or some other network layer protocol for routing and congestion control. It also supports inverse multiplexing and dynamic bandwidth allocation via the *Multilink-PPP Protocol* (ML-PPP), which is used commonly in ISDN environments where bandwidth supersets are required over the connection.

The PPP frame (Figure 3-22) is similar to a typical *High-Level Data Link Control* (HDLC) frame, with delimiting flags, an address field, a protocol identification field, information and pad fields, and a frame check sequence for error control.

The Internet Layer

The Internet Protocol is the heart of the TCP/IP protocol suite and the Internet itself. IP offers a connectionless service across the network that sometimes is referred to as *unreliable* because the network does not guarantee packet delivery or packet sequence. IP packets typically contain an entire message or a fragment of a message that can be as large as 65,535 bytes in length. The protocol does *not* provide flow control.

IP packets, like all packets, have a header that contains routing and content information (Figure 3-23). The bits in the packet are numbered from left to right starting at 0, and each row represents a single 32-bit word. An IP header must contain a *minimum* of five words.

IP Header Fields

The IP header contains approximately 15 unique fields. The *Version Field* identifies the version of IP that is being used to encode the packet

Figure 3-22
PPP frame
format.

Flag | Address | Control | Protocol | Data | CRC | Flag

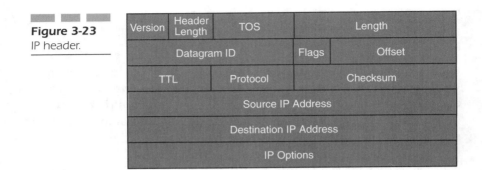

(IPv4 versus IP v6, for example). The *Internet Header Length* (IHL) *Field* identifies the length of the header in 32-bit words. The maximum value of this field is 15; this means the IP header has a maximum length of 60 octets.

The *Type of Service* (TOS) *Field* gives the transmitting system the ability to request different classes of service for the packets it transmits into the network. The TOS Field typically is not supported in IPv4 but can be used to specify a service priority (0 to 7) or route optimization.

The *Total Length Field* indicates the length (in octets) of the entire packet, including both the header and the data within the packet. The maximum size of an IP packet is 64 KB (okay, 65,535 bytes).

When a packet is broken into smaller "chunks" (a process called *fragmentation*) during transmission, the *Identification Field* is used by the transmitting host to ensure that all the fragments from a single message can be reassociated at the receiving end to ensure message reassembly.

The *flags* also play a role in fragmentation and reassembly. The first bit is referred to as the *More Fragments* (MF) bit and is used to indicate to the receiving host that the last fragment of a packet has been received so that the receiver can reassemble the packet. The second bit is the *Don't Fragment* (DF) bit, which prevents packet fragmentation (for delay-sensitive applications, for example). The third bit is unused and always is set to 0.

The *Fragment Offset Field* indicates the relative position of this particular fragment in the original packet that was broken up for transmission. The first packet of a fragmented message will carry an offset value of 0, and subsequent fragments will indicate the offset in multiples of 8 bytes.

This field represents some serious forward thinking on the part of the designers of the protocol. Consider this: A message is fragmented into a stream of packets at its origin point, and the packets are sent on their way to the destination address. Somewhere along the way packet number 7 takes a detour and ends up in a routing loop on the far side of the world, trying in vain to reach its destination. If we left it alone, it would continue to live forever, being passed back and forth between routers like the guy trapped on the mass transit train who can't get out at his station. To prevent this packet from living forever on the Internet, IP includes a *Time-to-Live* (TTL) *Field*. This configurable field has a value between 0 and 255 and indicates the maximum number of hops this packet is allowed to make before it is discarded by the network. Every time the packet enters a router, the router decrements the TTL value by one; when it reaches zero, the packet is discarded and the receiving device ultimately invokes error control to ask for a resend of the discarded packet.

The *Protocol Field* indicates the nature of the higher-layer protocol that is carried within the packet. Encoded options include values for Internet Control Message Protocol (ICMP) (1), TCP (6), UDP (17), and Open Shortest Message First (OSPF) (89).

The *Header Checksum Field* is similar to a Frame Check Sequence in HDLC and is used to ensure that the received IP header is free of errors. Keep in mind that IP is a connectionless protocol. This error check does not check the packet; it only checks the header.

In transmitting packets it is always a good idea to have a *Source Address* and a *Destination Address*. You can figure out what they are for.

Understanding IP Addresses

As Figure 3-24 shows, IP addresses are 32 bits long. They typically are written as a sequence of four numbers that represent the decimal value of each of the address bytes. These numbers are separated by periods

▄▄▄ ▄▄ ▄▄

Figure 3-24
32-bit IP address. Each "segment" of the dotted decimal address (192, 168, 1, 1) comprises eight bits.

192.168.1.1

("dots" in telecom parlance), and the notation is referred to as *Dotted Decimal Notation*. A typical address might be 168.152.20.10. These numbers are hierarchical; the hierarchy is described below.

IP addresses are divided into two subfields. The *Network Identifier* (NET_ID) subfield identifies the subnetwork that is connected to the Internet. The NET_ID most commonly is used for routing traffic between networks. The *Host Identifier* (HOST_ID) subfield identifies the address of a system (host) within a subnetwork.

IP Address Classes

IP defines distinct *address classes* that are used to discriminate between different size networks. Classes A, B, and C are used for host addressing, with the only difference between them being the length of the NET_ID subfield. A Class A address, for example, has an 8-bit NET_ID field and a 24-bit HOST_ID field. They are used for the identification of very large networks and can identify as many as 16,777,214 hosts in each network. To date, only about 90 Class A addresses have been assigned.

Class B addresses have 16-bit NET_ID and 16-bit HOST_ID fields. They are used to address medium-size networks and can identify as many as 65,534 hosts within each network.

Class C addresses, which are far and away the most common, have a 24-bit NET_ID field and an 8-bit HOST_ID field. These addresses are used for smaller networks and can identify no more than 254 devices within any specific network. There are 2,097,152 possible Class C NET_IDs, which commonly are assigned to corporations that have fewer than 250 employees.

There are two additional address types. Class D addresses are used for IP multicasting, such as transmitting a television signal to multiple recipients, and Class E addresses are reserved for experimental use. Class D addresses may receive more attention as IPTV gains a foothold.

Some addresses are reserved for specific purposes. A HOST_ID of 0 is reserved to identify an entire subnetwork. For example, the address 168.152.20.0 refers to a Class C address with a NET_ID of 168.152.20. A HOST_ID that consists of all 1's (usually written "255" when referring to an all–1s byte but also denoted as "–1") is reserved as a broadcast address and used to transmit a message to all the hosts on a particular network.

Subnet Masking

One of the most valuable but least understood tools in IP management is called the *subnet mask*. Subnet masks are used to identify the portion of the address that specifies the network or the subnetwork for routing purposes. They also can be used to divide a large address into subnetworks or combine multiple smaller addresses to create a single large "domain." In the case of an organization subdividing its network, the address space is apportioned to identify multiple logical networks. This is accomplished by further dividing the HOST_ID subfield into a *Subnetwork Identifier* (SUBNET_ID) and a HOST_ID. We won't go into the details of how the process works because it's beyond the scope of this book, but there are ample resources online that explain the subnet masking process in great detail.

Adding to the Alphabet Soup:
CIDR, DHCP, and Others

When the Internet became globally popular in the early 1990s, concerns began to arise about the eventual exhaustion of available IP addresses. For example, consider what happens when a small corporation with 11 employees purchases a Class C address. It now controls more than 250 addresses, of which it may be using only 25. Clearly, this is a waste of a scarce resource. Although the next generation of the IP is well on its way (IPv6), it isn't here yet and its implementation will be complex.

One technique that has been accepted for "address space conservation" is called *Classless Interdomain Routing* (CIDR). CIDR effectively limits the number of addresses assigned to an organization, making the process of address assignment far more granular and therefore efficient. Furthermore, CIDR has had a secondary yet equally important impact: It has reduced the size of the Internet routing tables dramatically because of the preallocation techniques used for address space management.

Other important protocols include Network Address Translation (NAT), which translates a private IP address that is being used to access the Web into a public IP address from an available pool of addresses, further conserving address space, and *Port Address Translation* (PAT) and *Network Address Port Translation* (NAPT), which allow multiple systems to share a single IP address by using different "port numbers." Port numbers are used by transport layer protocols to identify specific higher-layer applications.

Addressing in IP:
The Domain Name System

IP addresses are 32 bits long. Although they are not all that complicated, most Internet users don't bother to memorize the dotted decimal addresses of their systems. Instead, they use natural language host names. Most hosts, then, must maintain a comparative "table" of both numeric IP addresses and natural language names. From a host perspective, however, the names are worthless; the host must use the numeric identifiers for routing purposes.

Because the Internet continues to grow at a rapid clip, a system was needed to manage the growing list of new Internet domains. Consider this: In January 1995, there were 4,852,000 recognizable hosts on the Internet; in November 2005, roughly 10 years later, there were about 320,000,000! That naming system is called the *Domain Name System*. It is a distributed database that stores host names and IP address information for all the recognized domains found on the Internet. For every domain there is an *Authoritative Name Server* that contains all DNS-related information about that domain, and every domain has at least one secondary name server that also contains that information. A total of 13 *Root Servers* maintain a list of all the Authoritative Name Servers.

How does the DNS actually work? When a system needs another system's IP address based on its host name, the inquiring system issues a DNS request to a Local Name Server, as shown in Figure 3-25. Depending on the contents of its local database, the Local Name Server may be able to respond to the request. If it cannot, it forwards the request to a Root Server. The Root Server consults its own database and determines the most likely Name Server for the request and forwards it appropriately.

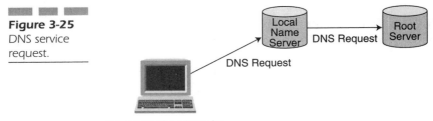

Figure 3-25
DNS service request.

DNS Request

"I need an IP address for hostname ShepardComm.com"

Early Address Resolution Schemes

When the Internet first came into the public psyche, most users ultimately were connected to the Internet via an Ethernet LAN. LANs use a local device address known as a *Medium Access Control* (MAC) address, which is 48 bits long and nonhierarchical, which means they cannot be used in IP networks for routing.

To get around this disparity and to create a technique for relating MAC addresses to IP addresses, the *Address Resolution Protocol* (ARP) was created. ARP allows a host to determine a receiver's MAC address when it knows only the device's IP address. The process is simple: The host transmits an *ARP request packet* that contains the MAC broadcast address. The ARP request advertises the destination IP address and asks for the associated MAC address. Since every station on the LAN hears the broadcast, the station that recognizes its own IP address responds with an ARP message that contains its MAC address.

As ARP became popular, other address management protocols came into play. *Reverse ARP* (RARP) gives a diskless workstation (a dumb terminal for all intents and purposes) the ability to determine its own IP address by knowing only its own MAC address. *Inverse ARP* (InARP) maps are used in frame relay installations to map IP addresses to frame relay virtual circuit identifiers. *ATMARP* and *ATMInARP* are used in Asynchronous Transfer Mode (ATM) networks to map IP addresses to ATM virtual path/channel identifiers. Finally, *LAN Emulation ARP* (LEARP) maps a recipient's ATM address to its LAN Emulation (LE) address, which is typically a MAC address.

Routing in IP Networks

Three routing protocols are used most commonly in IP networks: the *Routing Information Protocol* (RIP), the *Open Shortest Path First* (OSPF), and the *Border Gateway Protocol* (BGP).

OSPF and RIP are used primarily for intradomain routing, within a company's dedicated network, for example. They sometimes are referred to as *interior gateways protocols*. RIP uses hop count as the measure of a particular network path's cost; in RIP, it is limited to 16 hops.

When RIP broadcasts information to other routers about the current state of the network, it broadcasts its entire routing table, resulting in a flood of what may be unnecessary traffic. As the Internet has grown, RIP has become relatively inefficient because it does not scale as well as it should in a large network. As a consequence, OSPF was introduced. OSPF is known as a *link state protocol*. It converges (spreads important information across the network) faster than RIP does, requires less overall bandwidth, and scales well in larger networks. OSPF-based routers broadcast only changes in status rather than the entire routing table.

BGP is referred to as an *exterior gateway protocol* because it is used for routing traffic *between* Internet domains. Like RIP, BGP is a distance vector protocol, but unlike other distance vector protocols, BGP stores the actual route to the destination.

The Not So Distant Future: IP Version 6

Because of the largely unanticipated growth of the Internet since 1993 or so (when the general public became aware of its existence), it was concluded that IP version 4 was inadequate for the emerging and burgeoning needs of Internet applications. In 1995, IP version 6 (IPv6) was introduced to deal with the shortcomings of version 4. Changes included an increase in IP address space from 32 to 128 bits, improved support for differentiable QoS requirements, and improvements in security, confidentiality, and content integrity.

Header Format

IPv6 differs substantially from IPv4. Whereas IPv4, which has a variable-size header depending on the included options, the IPv6 header is fixed at 40 bytes. This provides a substantial advantage: A fixed-length header can be read into hardware and interpreted rapidly, speeding the processing of the header information. Options are dealt with through separate *extension headers*, which routers can ignore for the most part because they are designed to be processed by the end-user devices.

Most of the IPv4 header consists of address information. Thirty-two bytes each are needed for the source and destination IP addresses. In IPv6, there are no longer Header Length fields, Identification fields, Flags and Fragment Offset fields, or the Header Checksum field. Elimination of the Checksum field accelerates header processing, and since there is a checksum calculated at the transport layer, there is no need for another one at layer 3.

Fragmentation, long a function carried out by routers in the network, is no longer a major issue under IPv6. As a result, the other fields mentioned earlier disappear, further simplifying the process of packet analysis and treatment.

Among the remaining fields, TTL has evolved into a Hop Limit field, although the function remains precisely the same as in IPv4. The Protocol field now is called Next Header; it serves to indicate whether an Extension Header follows. The Payload Length field no longer includes the length of the IP header, and the Type of Service field now is referred to as the Traffic Class field.

One new field has been added: the Flow Label field. This field allows groups of packets that belong to the same flow (i.e., share the same source and destination) to be identified so that all packets can be processed together, reducing network overhead. Its primary function is to improve real-time traffic handling.

Extension Headers

IPv6 has added a collection of Extension Headers to the protocol model. They are listed below and *must* be ordered as shown.

- Hop-by-Hop Options header
- Routing header
- Fragment header
- Authentication header
- Encapsulating Security Payload header

These headers are processed only by the destination device.

The Fragment header allows end devices to fragment packets as required to satisfy maximum transmission unit (MTU) size limitations, and the Authentication and ESP headers provide IPSec authentication for the IPv6 packet.

Addressing

IPv6 addresses are now 16 bytes (128 bits) long rather than 4 bytes (32 bits); that means that additional address space must be allocated and devices transporting these packets must be able to handle the greatly expanded address size. A number of other changes have taken place as well. For example, there is no longer a dedicated broadcast address. Instead, unicast, multicast, and "anycast" addresses have been provisioned.

Figure 3-26
IPv6 packet
format.

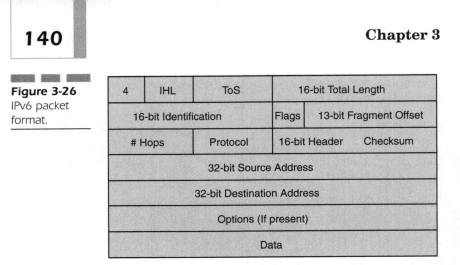

The format of the content has changed as well. IPv6 addresses include a general routing prefix, a subnet ID, and an interface ID. This results in additional complexity but will be handled easily by the resource-rich routers that now constitute the bulk of the network. Finally, the IPv6 address is expressed in hexadecimal, not decimal, so that the old familiar IP address will now look rather odd. The IPv6 packet structure is shown in Figure 3-26.

Transport Layer Protocols

We turn our attention now to layer 4, the Transport Layer. Two key protocols are found at this layer: the *Transmission Control Protocol* and the *User Datagram Protocol*. TCP is an ironclad, absolutely guaranteed service delivery protocol with all the attendant protocol overhead one would expect. UDP is a more "lightweight" protocol that is used for delay-sensitive applications such as VoIP. Its overhead component is relatively light.

In TCP and UDP messages, higher-layer applications are identified by *port identifiers*. The port identifier and the IP address together form a *socket*, and the end-to-end communication between two or more systems is identified by a four-part complex address: the source port, the source address, the destination port, and the destination address. Commonly used port numbers are shown in the table on the next page.

The Transmission Control Protocol

The Transmission Control Protocol provides a connection-oriented communication capability across the end-to-end network. It stipulates rule

Port Number	Protocol	Service	Port Number	Protocol	Service
7	TCP	echo	80	TCP	http
9	TCP	discard	110	TCP	pop3
19	TCP	charge	119	TCP	nntp
20	TCP	ftp-control	123	UDP	ntp
21	TCP	ftp-data	137	UDP	netbios-ns
23	TCP	telnet	138	UDP	netbios-dgm
25	TCP	smtp	139	TCP	netbios-ssn
37	UDP	time	143	TCP	imap
43	TCP	whois	161	UDP	snmp
53	TCP/UDP	dns	162	UDP	snmp-trap
67	UDP	bootps	179	TCP	bgp
68	UDP	bootpc	443	TCP	https
69	UDP	tftp	520	UDP	rip
79	TCP	finger	33434	UDP	traceroute

sets for message formats, establishing virtual circuit establishment and termination, data sequencing, flow control, and error correction. Most applications designed to operate within the TCP/IP suite use TCP's reliable, guaranteed delivery services.

In TCP, the transmitted data entity is referred to as a *segment* because TCP does not operate in message mode: It simply transmits blocks of data from a sender and a receiver. The fields that make up the segment (Figure 3-27) are described below.

The *Source Port* and the *Destination Port* identify the originating and terminating connection points of the end-to-end connection as well as the higher-layer application. The *Sequence Number* identifies this particular segment's first byte in the byte stream and, since the sequence number refers to a byte count rather than to a segment, the sequence numbers in sequential TCP segments are not numbered sequentially.

The *Acknowledgment Number* is used by the sender to acknowledge to the transmitter that it has received the transmitted data. In practice, the field identifies the sequence number of the next byte that it expects from

Figure 3-27
The TCP
header.

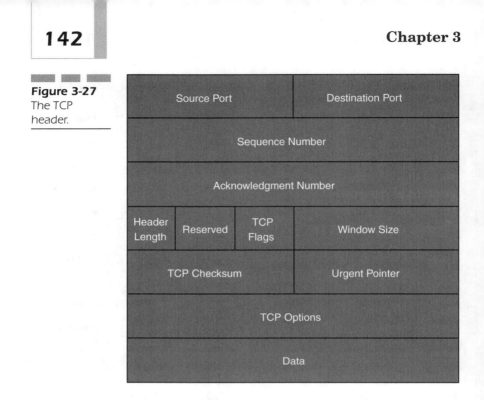

the receiver. *The Data Offset Field* identifies the first byte in this particular segment; in effect, it indicates the segment header length.

TCP relies on a collection of *Control Flags* that do in fact control certain characteristics of the virtual connection. They include an *Urgent Pointer Field Significant* (URG), which indicates that the current segment contains high-priority data and that the Urgent Pointer field value is valid; an *Acknowledgment Field Significant* (ACK), which indicates that the value contained in the Acknowledgment Number field is valid; a *Push Function* (PSH) flag, which is used by the transmitting application to force TCP to transmit data immediately that it currently has buffered, without waiting for the buffer to fill; a *Reset Connection* (RST) *Flag*, which is used to terminate an end-to-end TCP connection immediately; a *Synchronize Sequence Numbers* (SYN) *Flag*, which is used to establish a connection and indicate that the segments carry the proper initial sequence number; and a *Finish* (FIN) *Flag*, which is set to request a normal termination of a TCP connection in whatever direction the segment is traveling.

The *Window Field* is used for flow control management. It contains the value of the permitted *receive window size*, the number of transmitted bytes the sender of the segment is willing to accept from the receiver. The *Checksum Field* offers bit-level error detection for the entire segment, including both the header and the transmitted data.

The *Urgent Pointer Field* is used for the management of high-priority traffic as identified by a higher-layer application. If so marked, the segment typically is allowed to bypass normal TCP buffering.

The last field is the *Options Field*. At the time of the initial connection establishment this field is used to negotiate functions such as maximum segment size and *Selective Acknowledgment* (SACK).

The User Datagram Protocol

Unlike TCP, which guarantees end-to-end delivery of the transmitted message, the User Datagram Protocol provides connectionless service. Although "connectionless" often implies "unreliable," that is a bit of a misnomer. For applications that require nothing more than a simple query and response, UDP is ideal because it involves minimal protocol overhead. UDP's primary responsibility is to add a port number to the IP address to create a socket for the application. The fields of a UDP message (Figure 3-28) are described below.

The *Source Port* identifies the UDP port used by the sender of the datagram, and the *Destination Port* identifies the port used by the datagram receiver. The *Length Field* indicates the overall length of the UDP datagram.

The *Checksum* provides the same primitive bit error detection of the header and transported data that we saw with TCP.

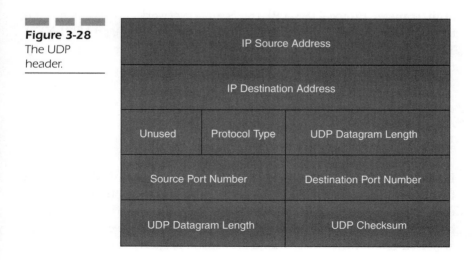

Figure 3-28
The UDP
header.

The Internet Control Message Protocol

The Internet Control Message Protocol is used as a diagnostic tool in IP networks to notify a sender that something unusual happened during transmission. It offers a healthy repertoire of messages, including *Destination Unreachable*, which indicates that delivery is not possible because the destination host cannot be reached; *Echo* and *Echo Reply*, which are used to check whether hosts are available; *Parameter Problem*, which is used to indicate that a router encountered a header problem; *Redirect*, which is used to make the sending system aware that packets should be forwarded to another address; *Source Quench*, which is used to indicate that a router is experiencing congestion and is about to begin discarding datagrams; *TTL Exceeded*, which indicates that a received datagram has been discarded because the TTL field reached 0; and *Timestamp* and *Timestamp Reply*, which are similar to Echo messages except that they time-stamp the message, giving systems the ability to measure how much time is required for remote systems to buffer and process datagrams.

The Application Layer

The TCP/IP application layer protocols support the actual applications and utilities that make the Internet useful. They include the BGP, the DNS, the File Transfer Protocol (FTP), the HTTP, the OSPF, the Packet Internetwork Groper (Ping), the Post Office Protocol (POP), the Simple Mail Transfer Protocol (SMTP), the Simple Network Management Protocol (SNMP), the Secure Sockets Layer Protocol (SSLP), and TELNET. This is a small sample of the many applications that are supported by the TCP/IP application layer.

A Close Relative: Multiprotocol Label Switching

In establishing connections over an IP network, it is critical to manage traffic queues to ensure the proper treatment of packets that come from delay-sensitive services such as voice and video. To do this, packets must be differentiable, that is, identifiable, so that they can be classified properly. Routers in turn must be able to respond properly to delay-sensitive traffic by implementing queue management processes. This requires that routers establish both normal and high-priority queues and handle the traffic found in high-priority routing queues at a speed greater than the arrival rate of the traffic.

Multiprotocol Label Switching (MPLS), which rapidly is becoming one of the mainstays of the next-generation network (and therefore a central component of IMS), delivers QoS by establishing virtual circuits known as *Label Switched Paths* (LSPs), which in turn are built around traffic-specific QoS requirements. An MPLS network such as the one shown in Figure 3-29 has *Label Switch Routers* (LSRs) at the core of the network and *Label Edge Routers* (LERs) at the edge. It is the responsibility of the LERs to set QoS requirements and pass them on to the LSRs responsible for ensuring that the required levels of QoS are achieved. Thus, a router can establish LSPs with explicit QoS capabilities and route packets to those LSPs as required, guaranteeing the delay that a particular flow encounters on an end-to-end basis. It's interesting to note that some industry analysts have compared MPLS LSPs to the trunks established in the voice environment.

MPLS uses a two-part process for traffic differentiation and routing. First, it divides the packets into Forwarding Equivalence Classes (FECs) based on their quality of service requirements, and then it maps the FECs to their next hop point. This process is performed at the point of ingress at the edge of the network. Each FEC is given a fixed-length "label" that accompanies each packet from hop to hop; at each router, the FEC label is examined and used to route the packet to the next hop point, where it is assigned a new label.

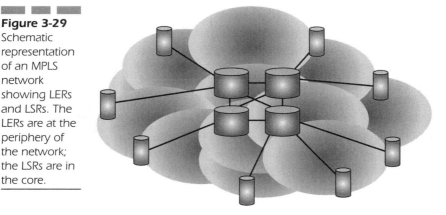

Figure 3-29
Schematic representation of an MPLS network showing LERs and LSRs. The LERs are at the periphery of the network; the LSRs are in the core.

MPLS is a "shim" protocol that works closely with IP to help it deliver on QoS guarantees. Its implementation allows for the eventual dismissal of ATM as a required layer in the multimedia network protocol stack. It offers a promising solution, but its universal deployment is still a ways off. However, it is growing in popularity and rapidly becoming the preferred core routing technique in wide area IP networks.

Voice over Internet Protocol

As IMS becomes a reality and customers find themselves dealing with a network that has the ability to adapt itself to their individual communications requirements, VoIP will emerge as one of the formative components in this evolution. VoIP has the inherent ability to reduce the total cost of ownership of the network and enhance its overall effectiveness.

In the PSTN, the analog voice signal is sampled by the digital network and converted to a digital bit stream. The signal can be compressed if desired, but either way the signal is transported through the network in digital format. In a PBX environment, the process is identical, with a few minor changes; the PBX is simply a remote switch connected to the PSTN via high-bandwidth facilities.

In the IP voice network, the data signal must be packetized for transmission, as shown in Figure 3-30. It is important to note the key differ-

Figure 3-30
Circuit-to-packet conversion.

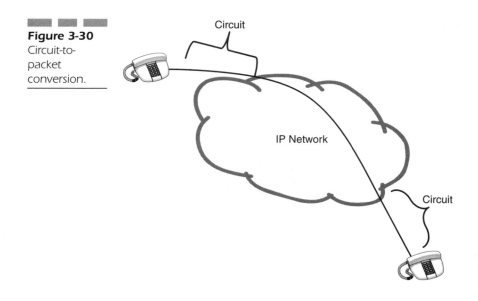

ence between traditional PBXs and IP systems: Older PBX systems rely on proprietary signaling protocols, whereas IP PBXs employ internationally standardized signaling schemes.

VoIP Anatomy

The major components of the PSTN are the user access device (phone or PC), the local loop leading to the local switch or PBX, a corollary toll switch array, and a separate signaling network. A VoIP network provides the same type of functionality (call establishment, maintenance, takedown, and associated accounting functions), but over a very different architecture. Although the devices in both networks have corollary relationships to each other, there is one component in VoIP networks that is not found in the PSTN: a gateway device that bridges the gap between the PSTN and the VoIP infrastructure.

To establish a connection, the phone system must act on the setup signals received from the calling device. Typically, this is done by using software that manages the call setup process and the conversion that must take place between the standard International Telecommunication Union (ITU) E.164 address (the 1-plus 10-digit telephone number) used in the PSTN and the IP addresses used in VoIP networks.

The key components of a converged IP-based voice network are the call-processing server, usually an IP-enabled PBX; one or more media gateways, sometimes called gatekeepers; an IP network over which calls will be placed; and endpoint devices that provide user functionality. We will describe each of these in turn (Figure 3-31).

The SoftSwitch

The SoftSwitch handles multiple tasks: recognition of an off-hook condition, dial tone instigation, call routing, and call tear-down. These functions are performed as part of the interaction that goes on between a telephone and a call server, functions that naturally would be performed by a traditional PBX.

SoftSwitch technology is designed to support next-generation networks that rely on packet-based voice, data, and video communications technologies and can interface with a variety of transport technologies, including copper, wireless, and fiber. One goal of the SoftSwitch concept

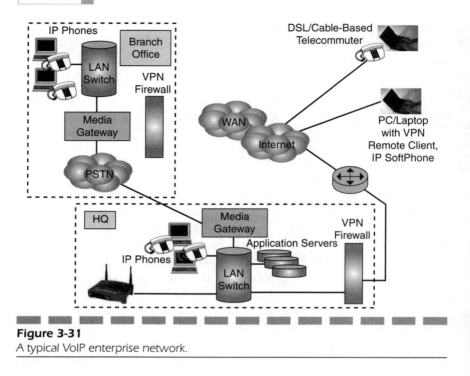

Figure 3-31
A typical VoIP enterprise network.

is to separate network hardware functionally from network software. In traditional circuit-switched networks, hardware and software are dependent on one another, resulting in what many believe is an unnecessarily inextricable relationship. Circuit-switched networks rely on dedicated facilities and are designed primarily for delay-sensitive voice communications. The goal of SoftSwitch is to bring about dissolution of this interdependent relationship where appropriate.

As the overall network has evolved, the SoftSwitch has changed as well, particularly given the vast range of transported data types with which it must deal. As more networks use IP as their fundamental protocol, VoIP services become viable as an alternative to circuit-switched voice.

There is more to SoftSwitch, however, than redesigning the functional components of the network. Another goal is to put in place an "open service creation development environment" so that application developers can offer products to the market that can be implemented across an entire network. Part of this evolution will include the development of call control models that seamlessly support data, voice, and multimedia services; this, of course, is a tenet of IMS. The result of widespread SoftSwitch deployment will be a switching model that is free of the restrictions that plague circuit switches, such as intelligent network triggers, application invocation mechanisms, and complex service logic.

This functional distribution will result in faster and more targeted feature development and delivery and significantly lower service delivery costs. SoftSwitches will be architecturally simpler, operationally efficient, and less expensive to operate and maintain than their circuit-switched predecessors.

A number of corporations have focused their efforts on the development of SoftSwitch products. Both Lucent and Nortel announced SoftSwitch products as early as 1999, in the form of the 7R/E (Lucent) and the Succession (Nortel). After the collapse of the telecom bubble they were all but forgotten, largely because the market wasn't ready to bridge the gap between the circuit-switched Bellheads and the IP bitweenies. The good news is that with industry recovery there has come renewed interest in SoftSwitch technology, and both companies have come back into the fray with Succession (Nortel) and iMerge (Lucent). Today the market again is growing, this time ferociously. Companies such as Taqua Systems are beginning the process of reinvigorating the SoftSwitch marketplace. A key sector is the small rural telephone company. These providers are ideal SoftSwitch targets because they can take advantage of the incremental deployment nature of the SoftSwitch and because they are one of the few segments that have money earmarked for capital growth.

SoftSwitch originally was intended as a local switch replacement technology to facilitate circuit-to-packet migration. When SoftSwitch originally was rolled out, the economy was in turmoil and progress has not been as aggressive as the sector would have liked. In truth, SoftSwitches have been used to replace lines, not wholesale switches. Although the incumbents are not buying, they are shopping with requests for proposals (RFPs) and requests for quotes (RFQs)—a good indicator of later movement. To date, the main applications SoftSwitch solutions have addressed are enterprise applications such as PBX management, IP Centrex, VoIP, and wireless LANs.

The Call-Processing Server

The call-processing server, often a specially designed IP-based PBX, provides central management for VoIP calls. The call-processing server performs signaling and supervision for functions such as conferencing, transfer of calls from one server to another, and supplementary capabilities such as music on hold. VoIP relies on a client-server architecture under which the call-processing server (PBX) is the server and user devices are the clients. All traffic flows in a peer-to-peer fashion from terminal device to terminal device. The terminals manage traffic flow, and the call-processing servers interact with the network to negotiate the service parameters needed to satisfy QoS requirements. One advantage of these networks over the PSTN is that the call processor is typically a software module that runs on one or more dedicated servers and therefore offers tremendous flexibility and enhanced redundancy.

The Gateway

We haven't yet discussed the interface between the IP voice network and the PSTN. This function is performed by the gateway, which is made up of three components: the line or trunk interface to traditional PSTN devices, IP interfaces for communication with VoIP networks, and a "gateway" function between the two that communicates with the SoftSwitch or call server to perform call setup functions. In many cases the gateway and SoftSwitch/call server functions are a single device that provides logically distinct functions.

Gateways and Gatekeepers

Because of the ongoing need for connectivity between the PSTN and the emerging IP voice network, some network element must be responsible for converting between the analog and digital streams that flow between the networks if traffic is to be shared between them seamlessly and transparently. This device is the *gateway* and, in addition to its responsibilities for protocol conversion, it collects and reports on network usage, performs echo cancellation, carries out silence suppression if necessary, and compresses transmitted voice signals.

For all intents and purposes, the gateway is the origination point for voice traffic. In fact, an IP voice conversation typically is made up of an IP session that is transported inside a stream of Real-Time Protocol (RTP) packets carried over UDP, all under the control of the gateway.

It is important to note that gateways and gatekeepers historically have been classified as two different devices performing two different responsibilities. The gateway has always been the device that performs the protocol conversion between the two networks, and the gatekeeper's functions include bandwidth management, call admission, and call control, clearly responsibilities that a controlling gatekeeper would perform. As VoIP has evolved, however, the functions traditionally carried out by the gatekeeper have been absorbed by the gateway, with both sets of functions now being performed by the single device.

Gateways include a variety of responsibilities that bridge the capability gap between the IP and PSTN environments. In some cases the gateway is a stand-alone rack-mounted device that is hidden away in a closet; in other cases it may be a dedicated PC that is set aside to run VoIP software and augmented with additional memory and a very fast processor. The functions a gateway performs include management of access gateways, which connect a legacy PBX to the VoIP network; management of trunk gateways, which interconnect the PSTN to the VoIP network; management of local or residential gateways, which are nothing more than access points for VoIP networks so that DSL, cable modems, and broadband wireless access services can reach the VoIP environment; and management of media gateways, which offer interfaces to the VoIP network for a digital PBX or "soft" (software-based) PBX.

User Devices

Whereas the SoftSwitch takes care of switching and call management functions, the gateway performs the "protocol conversion" between the PSTN and IP, the gatekeeper oversees functional access to the network, and the end-user handsets provide overall functionality. Modern gateways can support standard analog devices, but most new VoIP installations are designed exclusively to manage IP phones. They come in two forms: a physical device that sits on the desktop and plugs into the Ethernet LAN and a logical softphone that runs on the desktop or laptop as an application. A softphone is nothing more than a software application that runs on a PC. It typically is designed to support mobile users who do not want to carry a telephone in addition to a laptop computer. The features are the same as those found on a typical enterprise telephone, and the application commonly runs in the background on the desktop so that it can be accessed at will and callers can reach the user on demand. Either way, the IP phone serves not only as the user access device but also as the gateway, bridging the gap between the

PSTN and IP worlds. *Telephone* therefore may be something of a misnomer; the device a user employs to access the network may be a physical IP telephone or may be a softphone running in a desktop or laptop PC.

VoIP telephones, regardless of whether they are physical or logical devices, are assigned an IP address for the subnet on which they are installed. They therefore rely on the TCP/IP suite for functionality but also may rely on other protocols for directory, instant messenger/SMS (Short Message System), or screen-sharing applications. These devices typically rely on DHCP to autoconfigure their relationship with the network. The Dynamic Host Configuration Protocol (DHCP) gives network administrators the ability to manage and automate the assignment of IP addresses centrally in a managed network. When an enterprise connects its users to the Internet, an IP address must be assigned to each machine. Before the arrival of DHCP, the IP address for each machine had to be entered manually and, if machines were moved from one location to another in a different part of the network, a new IP address had to be assigned; this was the famous MAC problem.

DHCP relies on a "leasing" technique that assigns a specific amount of time for which a given IP address can be used "legally" by a computer. The lease time varies with the nature of the Internet connection at a particular location and can be renewed automatically if desired. On college campuses or in business parks that rely on "hoteling," where users change their physical locations on a regular but often random basis, DHCP is a powerful addition, since it avoids the need for human intervention as people move from location to location. DHCP is a highly desirable and efficient addition to the network manager's tool kit. By using very short leases, DHCP can dynamically reconfigure a network in which there are more computers than there are available IP addresses.

DHCP also supports static addresses for computers serving as Web servers, which by design need a permanent IP address.

In practice, the DHCP server tells the phone where to find the configuration server, which typically is collocated with or resident in the call-processing server.

The IP phones that are in common use today are extraordinarily flexible and support a wide range of software customization capabilities. Keep in mind that the phone is the user's "window on the services world." It is essential that the view be as broad as possible.

■ Service Delivery in the IP World

How does the VoIP architecture work to provide calling services? The answer is simple: It delivers services in much the same way the PSTN does. The major components of the converged VoIP network—the SoftSwitch, the media server, the gateways and gatekeepers, and the IP telephones—intercommunicate with one another to perform call setup. When the phone goes off-hook, it transmits a state change message to the SoftSwitch, which then communicates with the phone to collect the dialed digits (the address), select a route for the call, enter the appropriate state information into a table, and proceed with the steps necessary to set up the actual call. The SoftSwitch easily converts back and forth between the two native address modes and establishes the call as requested by the caller. Once the call is established, the SoftSwitch bows out of the equation, its job done—for the moment.

Assuming that the call is placed to an off-net number (outside the enterprise IP network), the gateway performs the appropriate conversion of the IP packets to make them palatable to the PSTN. If, however, the call is on-net and is to be routed to another IP phone, no circuit-to-packet conversion is required, although the packets may be handled by more than one SoftSwitch.

How is a telephone call carried across an IP network when it originates on the PSTN? In much the same way a call traverses the PSTN. A customer begins the call, often using a traditional telephone. The call is carried across the PSTN to an IP telephony gateway, which is nothing more than a special-purpose router designed to interface between the PSTN and a packet-based IP network. As soon as the gateway receives the call, it interrogates an associated gatekeeper device, which provides information about billing, authorization, authentication, and call routing. As soon as the gatekeeper has delivered the information to the gateway, the gateway transmits the call across the IP network to another gateway, which hands the call off to the local PSTN at the receiving end, completing the call.

Let's address an important misconception. At the risk of sounding as if I'm dipping into Greek logic, let me say, "All Internet telephony is VoIP, but all VoIP is not Internet telephony." Let me explain. It is quite possible today to make telephone calls across the Internet by using such services as Skype and Vonage, which by definition are IP-based calls simply because IP is the fundamental operational protocol of the Internet. However, IP-based calls can be made without involving the Internet at all. For example, a corporation may interconnect multiple locations by using dedicated private-line facilities and may transport IP-based phone calls across that dedicated network facility. This is clearly VoIP, but it is *not* Internet telephony. There's a big difference.

VoIP Implementation

IP voice has become a reasonable technological alternative to traditional PCM voice. VoIP gateways are in the late stages of development and offer high levels of reliability, features, and manageability. As a result, service providers that want to deploy VoIP services have several options. One is to accept the current state of the technology and deploy it today while waiting for enhanced versions to arrive, knowing that, although the product may not be 100% carrier-grade, it certainly is an acceptable solution.

A second option is a variation of the first: Implement the technology that is available today but make no guarantees of service quality. This approach is being used in Western Europe and some parts of the United States as a way to provide low-cost long-distance service. The service is actually quite good. Although it is not "toll-quality," it is inexpensive. Since most telephony users have become accustomed to the lower than toll quality of cellular service, as we discussed earlier in this book, they are less inclined to be annoyed by VoIP service that offers quality that is inferior to what they might expect. What does "lower QoS" actually mean? For the most part it means that audio levels may be lower than expected or that there occasionally may be echo on the line similar to what we used to experience when making international calls that involved a satellite hop. In other cases dropouts may occur, although that is rare.

Needless to say, this works in the favor of the VoIP service provider. Furthermore, the companies deploying the service often have no complex billing infrastructure to support because they rely on prepaid billing models; thus, they can keep their costs low.

VoIP is here to stay and is a serious contender for voice services in both the residence and enterprise markets. The dollars don't lie: Domestic revenues for VoIP will grow exponentially between 2004 and 2009, from $600 million in early 2005 to $3 billion.

From a customer's perspective, the principal advantages of VoIP include consolidated voice, data and multimedia transport, elimination of parallel systems, the ability to exercise PSTN fallback if the IP network becomes overly congested, and reduction of long-distance voice and facsimile costs.

For an ISP or CLEC, the advantages are different but no less dramatic, including efficient use of network investments due to traffic consolidation, new revenue sources from existing clients because of demand for service-oriented applications that benefit from being offered over an IP infrastructure, and the option of transaction-based billing. These features collectively can be reduced to the general category of customer service, on which service providers such as ISPs and CLECs should focus. The challenge they face will be to prove that the service quality they provide over their IP networks will be identical to that provided over traditional circuit-switched technology.

Major carriers are voting on IP with their wallets, a sure sign of confidence in the technology. As the IMS model becomes more prevalent and as enterprise and residence customers come to expect more from the network as the network demonstrates its ability to *offer* more, VoIP will become an even more highly demanded service.

The key to IP's success in the voice provisioning arena lies with its "invisibility." If this is done correctly, service providers can add IP to their networks, maintaining service quality while dramatically improving their overall efficiency. IP voice (not to be confused with Internet voice) will be implemented by carriers and corporations as a way to reduce costs and move to a multiservice network fabric. Virtually all major equipment manufacturers, including notables such as Lucent, Nortel, and Cisco, have added SS7 and IP voice capability to their router products and access devices, recognizing that their primary customers are looking for IP solutions. They have recognized that there are interdependencies among SS7, SIP, H.323, and other signaling protocols and have embraced them.

The Origins of IMS

IMS was born in the wonderful chaotic world of the Third Generation Partnership Project (3GPP). As we have seen, IMS and the standards it is based on offer the potential for a customer- and service provider–friendly installation that offers real-time packet-based services that will preserve the utilization of existing network infrastructure and signaling and put in place a mechanism for networkwide and customerwide usage-based billing. IMS will provide the underpinnings for the identification of new sources of revenue, using traffic examination capabilities such as deep packet inspection of protocols, Uniform Resource Identifiers, and content management.

IMS originally was designed in response to the burgeoning mobile telephony domain. As cellular networks grew more complex and usage climbed, demand for enhanced services and more efficient handling of calls rose in lockstep. Based on the long-held telephone company observation "If it ain't broke, don't fix it," IMS is designed to take advantage of preexisting technology bases. The benefits of legacy signaling capabilities (SS7, SIP) and long-standing, highly functional billing models are recognized and supported by the 3GPP and, because they publicly support these existing functions, IMS attracted the early attention of traditional wireline operators as well as a significant number of standards bodies. Those bodies include the ITU, the European Telecommunications Standards Institute (ETSI), and the U.S.-based Alliance for Telecommunications Industry Solutions (ATIS), among others. Cable operators are equally intrigued, a fact that should come as no surprise since they control an immense percentage of broadband in the United States and were the first in the greater industry to roll out both triple- and quadruple-play service offers. The recently announced PacketCable initiative from CableLabs and the DOCSIS 3.0 standards are in strong agreement with the IMS philosophy. Furthermore, the WiMAX Forum, the powerful industry group led by Intel that supports broadband wireless rollouts, has been approached repeatedly through its Network Working Group by various industry players that want IMS to be included as part of its final reference architecture.

The equipment manufacturers have joined the fray, as we'll see later in the book, offering comprehensive strategies and equipment (often more strategy than equipment) designed to address IMS demand as it becomes more prominent. Companies with significant IMS plays include Lucent, Nortel, Ericsson, Alcatel, and Nokia. Although the announced products are all over the map in terms of availability and rollout plans, there is no question that *all* major manufacturers have jumped on the IMS bandwagon.

IMS and Third-Generation Systems: The Relationship

In June 2005, I attended SuperComm in Chicago, the last SuperComm ever held. Whenever I attend major trade events, I always try to guess what the major themes will be before I wander onto the show floor. For this show I guessed that the themes would be IMS, WiMAX, and VoIP. I was correct: It seemed that every booth either had a product directly related to one or more of those three or made a product that indirectly supported the technologies that *directly* supported IMS, WiMAX, or VoIP.

As I listened to the "buzz" on the floor, I began to make out a common thread. Quite a few people were wandering the show floor, looking for the booth where they could buy IMS. That was interesting, since IMS is still very much a philosophy or approach to the market; hard products are for the most part embryonic. Clearly, there is a great deal of confusion in the marketplace about exactly what IMS is and where it fits in the constantly shape-shifting services pantheon.

Because it was conceived of within the 3GPP domain and originally was designed to address the emerging and evolving needs of third-generation wireless users, it is far better understood there than anywhere else. One thing IMS is *not* is a complete, well-defined system that offers fully converged multimedia access and transport. In reality IMS is one piece of that capability. The complete system (Figure 3-32) is the 3GPP's vision of the role of IMS in the third-generation wireless world. The entire 3G system, of which IMS is a component, has five major elements: an IMS-based core with an SIP/SDP control plane, a media- and signaling-specific conversion layer that surrounds the core, a set of dedicated applications offered by the service provider and a rule set that defines the relationship between customers and those applications, a billing and OSS/BSS layer that handles the plethora of administrative (OAM&P) tasks required to keep the system operating and profitable, and a collection of tools and procedures designed to perform systems management, operations, and network administration tasks.

So what *is* IMS?

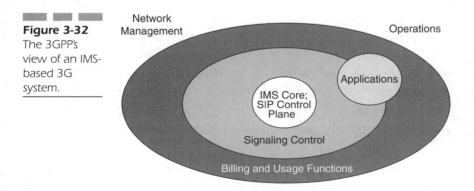

Figure 3-32
The 3GPP's view of an IMS-based 3G system.

IMS Anatomy

The "functional philosophy" behind IMS is very different from that of its predecessors. Whereas in traditional networks, service delivery and the devices that make it possible are viewed as a somewhat monolithic process, in IMS the devices are seen more as a collection of functions (again, separating the function from the device) and the various functions are related to one another through a collection of reference points, similar to the way in which ISDN was designed. A great deal of work has been performed by the 3GPP to identify and publish the specifics of both functions and reference points. Although some of them are clearly understood, others remain elusive. The Universal Mobile Telephony System (UMTS), the natural outgrowth of the battle for dominance between GSM and CDMA, will include additional details in future standards releases.

As with ISDN, IMS reference points are used to identify and describe the traffic that flows between a pair of functional resources, often down to the protocol level. They go beyond that detail, however, detailing how resources are to be used as well as the relationships that must exist between endpoint devices or processes and the various resources present in the network. This concept is not unusual in the telephony world; again, the P, Q, R, S, T, and U reference points that are so well defined for ISDN are examples of their use to identify functional "network regions" rather than more specific and therefore necessarily limiting interfaces.

As we noted earlier, IMS is still in a somewhat embryonic state. Nailing down a complete and clear picture of IMS is a bit like grabbing smoke. Reference diagrams such as the one shown in Figure 3-33 have been developed. Although they go a long way toward explaining the logical interactions and functional requirements within an IMS system, they are still high-level and perhaps incomplete. Until further definition occurs, and in the interest of getting to the market quickly, most analysts agree that manufacturers will roll out IMS products that are multifunctional to ensure "base coverage." The gateways and feature servers embedded in the IMS network undoubtedly will offer multiple capabilities to ensure that they provide the required functionality early on and will be streamlined and made more functionally specific as the concept evolves.

IMS Functions

Let's take a few minutes to describe the components shown in Figure 3-34. The Call Session Control Function (CSCF) that lies at the physical

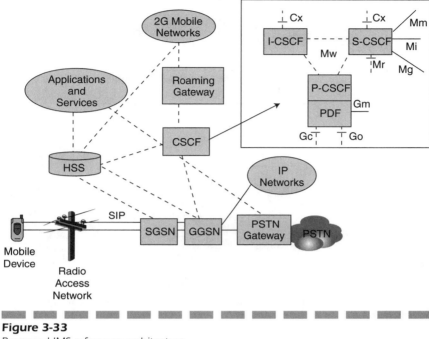

Figure 3-33
Proposed IMS reference architecture.

heart of the network is not there by accident. It is the heart and soul of IMS and is subdivided into three responsibility areas: interrogation, serving, and proxy session control. Under the IMS concept, every signaling event that is generated by a user is first sent to the Proxy CSCF (P-CSCF) regardless of the actual signaling event. Signaling events could include things such as a request to initiate a call session, the activation of a requested feature, network resource allocation, and a request for services from another application. The P-CSCF is the first contact made within the core of the IMS network by the user device.

When SIP messages arrive from an interrogating user device, the P-CSCF forwards them to the Interrogating Call Session Control Function (I-CSCF) or, alternatively, the Serving Call Session Control Function (S-CSCF). The I-CSCF serves as a single point of contact within a service provider's network for local subscribers (i.e., subscribers who are home-hosted on that network) and roaming customers to register for service. As soon as the I-CSCF registers a user, the S-CSCF takes over and manages the session, providing access to all requested or subscribed services.

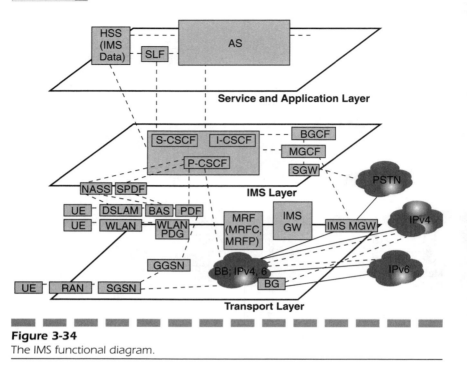

Figure 3-34
The IMS functional diagram.

It is important to note that in most cases the I-CSCF behaves like an SIP proxy in spite of the fact that its primary role in IMS is to offer a service location capability. It is also important to realize that there may be multiple I-CSCFs within a service provider's network that are responsible for functions such as registration, which is the process of assigning an S-CSCF for SIP registration; session flow management, which is used to route an SIP request to the S-CSCF that has been received from a different network or to route SIP requests between users on different S-CSCFs; creation of usage data in the form of Call Detail Records (CDRs) that track billing and revenue-generating resource utilization; and serving as a "pay no attention to that man behind the curtain" I-CSCF that hides the topology, configuration, capability, and capacity of the network from outside prying eyes, a function commonly known as the *Topology Hiding Internetwork Gateway* (THIG).

In effect, the S-CSCF is an SIP server that performs session-by-session engagement control for network service subscribers. It manages interaction with network-based databases such as the Home Subscriber Server (HSS) for support of mobile users and Access, Authorization, and Accounting (AAA) servers for security control. As a SIP proxy server, it passes traffic generated by a roaming user (i.e., a user who is connected to a network that is not her or his home network) to the HSS that is hosted in her or his Home Public Land Mobile Network (HPLMN), where the subscriber's profile is held and where confirmation of "billability" is performed.

As soon as the S-CSCF has performed its responsibilities to validate the user who is requesting services, the request can be passed on to the appropriate application servers and gateways that are required to comply with the requested session. If the request is destined for a different network, other signaling may have to be performed up to and including protocol conversions to deal with disparate media types among different network regimes.

Central to the smooth operation of an IMS environment is the Proxy CSCF and, over the few years of its existence, its responsibilities have morphed. Originally, the P-CSCF had responsibility for the Policy Decision Function (PDF), which accumulates, stores, manages, and refers to archived usage policies to make decisions related to requests for IP resource allocation. After a great deal of discussion among IMS policy makers, the PDF was removed from the purview of the P-CSCF as a way to make it more accessible to wireless LANs and other access networks. Because of their "gatekeeper" role and the fact that they are ideally positioned to collect usage data, P-CSCFs generate billing records that can be accumulated and transferred to a centralized Charging Gateway Function (CGF) before the generation of user invoices.

In essence, then, the IMS functions and reference points described earlier are designed to provide interdevice signaling and monitor the availability and disposition of network-based features and services. These features and services are not created or delivered by IMS; IMS simply serves as the "facilitative agent," making it possible for the underlying network to deliver them as required.

How did this innovation come about? What were the causative factors that drove IMS into existence? Read on.

The History of IMS

The concept of IMS has been bandied about for years under various names, but it wasn't until 1998 that true IMS began to take shape. That occurred when specifications were being developed for UMTS-based third-generation mobile systems. After bouncing along for a few years, IMS was formally accepted as a component of the UMTS 3G system definition at the June 1998 3GPP Meeting in Düsseldorf, Germany. Wireless systems were still in a state of foment at that time (not that they aren't still), analog and second-generation TDMA systems were being phased out slowly, and the so-called two-and-a-half G (2.5G) Generalized Packet Radio System (GPRS) systems were being deployed with relatively low data rates, offering rudimentary Internet access to roaming users (better not be in a hurry). Wideband CDMA (W-CDMA) was introduced at roughly the same time, increasing data throughput from 56 Kbps to as much as 384 Kbps.

Contrary to what might be concluded, that meeting did not yield any specifics as to IMS functions. It did, however, raise industry awareness and initiated the IMS specification process, an activity that got the attention of the incumbent telephone companies for several reasons. First, it "put meat on the bones" of their nascent desires to ally themselves with the Internet as an alternative service delivery vehicle; second, it provided the seminal impetus required to move them away from commodity status by aligning network access and transport with a model for content delivery. IMS, it seemed, might be the appropriate strategy for saving their technological bacon.

Time marched on and, in 2003, the first complete draft IMS specifications were released by the 3GPP as part of UMTS Release 5. These documents were complete only in the sense that they supported the ultimate goal of delivering functional third-generation service to the marketplace, a goal that had attracted heightened attention after its failure years earlier during the bubble years when everybody had spectrum to burn but no one had broadband wireless applications that could use it. UMTS Release 5 spoke favorably about the growing and functionally important relationship between IMS, SIP, and end-to-end quality of service as part of the next-generation full-service IP network. It also added detail to the voice services that ultimately would be delivered over IP.

There was a fly in the ointment, however. Existing radio access networks (RANs) were not considered particularly efficient, and transmission of IP packets over them was poor at best because of the high packet overhead required to combine the wireless and packet environments. In some cases the header data was more voluminous than the actual user data, making for a less than elegant network model.

UMTS Release 5 addressed QoS and billing in a rudimentary way by suggesting the use of IMS as a model for a control infrastructure for UMTS packet. The idea was to identify new applications using the

GPRS or UMTS network and perform control and billing services at that point. UMTS Release 5 stipulated that SIP would be used for call control and offered Service Based Local Policy (SBLP). SBLP is a familiar construct for telephony operators; it authorizes QoS requests and defines policies to be enforced by the bearer service network elements. The release also suggested logical placement of common billing and QoS functions within the network.

The last suggestion made by UMTS Release 5, and certainly the most controversial (and ignored), was its mandate to use IPv6. The "suggestion" met with yawns, and equipment manufacturers continue to implement by using IPv4. They all keep an eye on version 6 but do not feel a compelling reason to move ahead with it at this time.

Since that initial effort in 2003 IMS development has continued apace. Equipment manufacturers and service providers alike are investing tremendous energy and innovative activity into the IMS service definition exercise. Some of them add solid functionality to the ongoing IMS effort and are accepted immediately into the change request (CR) process; others are defeated or postponed because they are deemed to be too early for the current stage of IMS process definition.

The staged migration plan implemented by the UMTS standards organizations is a slow, deliberate process by design. By attacking the functional issues in manageable pieces, the organization can address logically the multitude of issues that arise with each change, ensuring reasonable success once the deployment of true UMTS-based 3G systems begins. Figure 3-35 illustrates the release history for UMTS and the point at which IMS first came on the scene.

Stumbling Blocks

The degree to which service providers' perspectives have affected the overall IMS rollout strategy is interesting. Part of 2003's Release 6 was a provision for IMS-based delivery of Instant Messaging and Presence (IMPRES) applications. In that year, however, awareness of the Millennial Generation and its network utilization preferences had not occurred, and service providers did not see either of these applications as worthwhile revenue generators. As a result of the service providers' seeming disdain for IMPRES applications, the IMS specifications once again were modified late that year to include Push-to-Talk over Cellular (PoC) as their initial defining application. Because of Nextel's (now Sprint) success with push-to-talk and the fact that it was an application that tele-

Figure 3-35

UMTS release
history.

Release 97 (1997): Often referred to as 2.5G, this release introduced GPRS for data delivery over existing 2G GSM networks.

Release 99 (1999, UMTS R3 3GPP): Initial release of the (3G) UMTS standard, which included a provision for acceptance of W-CDMA.

UMTS Release 4 (2001): Divided the overall system into a circuit-switched domain and a packet-switched domain.

UMTS Release 5 (March 2003): A seminal event inasmuch as this was the initial IMS release. It proposed IMS as the packet domain control structure, using SIP for call control. It also mandated IPv6, which largely has been ignored by vendors and service providers. This release also introduced the concept of end-to-end QoS and the now widely recognized Service-Related Local Policy (SRLP) designed to facilitate the introduction of new services over the GPRS/UMTS bearer service.

UMTS Release 6 (December 2004 to March 2005): This release addressed a handful of outstanding IMS issues that were left over from Release 5.0, such as SRLP-based QoS improvements and the disintegration of the PDF and P-CSCF functions for QoS policy control. The release also provided support for IMS Access Independence, Instant Messaging and Presence, push-to-talk over cellular service, wireless LAN integration, multimedia messaging services, and enhancements for SIP and multicast and broadcast service. It also introduced consideration for event-based charging.

UMTS Release 7: Started in the middle of 2005, Release 7 focuses on remaining issues not addressed in Release 6 and tackles a definition for fixed broadband access over IMS. It also speaks to QoS policy issues, voice handoff between circuit switching, wireless LANs, and the delivery of end-to-end QoS. At the time of this writing the work is still under way. Although this already is an ambitious list, it undoubtedly will grow as IMS continues to be defined.

phone people could understand (voice), it was initially far more widely accepted than the IMPRES concepts.

Unfortunately, as elegant and sexy as the PoC concept was, it had serious problems. Because of the way PoC calls were handled in the network, they required multiple round-trip transmissions to complete the push-to-talk function. These calls incurred long delays and therefore were deemed unsatisfactory in terms of their QoS capabilities. In spite of all the work, Nextel still had the better service.

An Interim Solution

After a great deal of haranguing and discussion, all indications are that for the time being, IMS will be used specifically for transmission of Web data and session signaling in concert with traditional circuit-switched voice. IMS Release 6 will address trials and lab deployments of the capability; live deployments with real customers most likely will be based on the multifunction devices we described earlier that incorporate multiple simultaneous IMS capabilities to ensure that all demands are met with a single device rollout. This undoubtedly will continue through Release 7.

That being said, some vendors have forged agreements with service providers for early-release IMS deployments. In mid-October 2005, Cingular Wireless announced its intention to select Lucent Technologies' IMS solutions as part of its overall strategy for the delivery of advanced personalized and multimedia services to its wireless subscribers. Cingular already is well into the deployment of a regionwide 3G network, and its choice of IMS in the core will facilitate that company's intention to deliver a triple- or even quadruple-play of voice, video, data, and wireless services in addition to offering full connectivity with the existing wireline network. Lucent's IMS product falls within a product collection known as the Accelerate Next Generation Communications Solutions Portfolio; Cingular's implementation will be served largely from that portfolio. Accelerate includes Lucent's Session Manager, Feature Server, Unified Subscriber Data Server, Network Controller, Network Gateway, Communication Manager, Active Phonebook, and MiLife Application Server, all of which interoperate to provide a complete suite of multiservice functionality that aligns rather elegantly with the overall IMS concept.

As we will discuss later in this book, Lucent has received high marks from analysts who see its IMS strategy as very strong and forward-looking. The relationship with Cingular is a good one and will serve as a bellwether for the industry's rollout of IMS.

Cingular is not alone in its intention to use Lucent's IMS products. Shortly after its announcement, Cingular's parent company announced that it too will use Lucent's IMS platform for its next-generation network rollout.

Lucent has cause to feel good about its IMS strategy. In addition to getting fair remarks from the analyst community for its overall IMS strategy, it is also fully involved in the real world with more than three dozen trials under way with wireless, wireline, and converged (hybrid) service providers all over the world. These trials are designed to use some or all of the critical components of the company's IMS portfolio, and the results to date have been positive. Other vendors are equally involved, and there is unquestionably widespread support for IMS at this early stage.

One area all vendors must manage is the perception that because IMS has numerous components, it is more complex than a traditional network. Although it is a complex construct, it is no more complex than other deployed infrastructures and may in fact be less complex than some. All involved parties—standards bodies, government agencies, regulatory organizations, manufacturers, and service providers—are working closely with one another to reduce the perception that IMS is inordinately complex. The 3GPP also has had a strong hand in the process and has undertaken responsibility for the commercial introduction of true third-generation networks that offer legacy voice services in addition to broadband mobile data services.

Other standards bodies and industry groups have come to the table, including 3GPP2, the Open Mobile Alliance (OMA), the previously mentioned IETF, and ETSI's Telecoms and Internet Converged Services and Protocols for Advanced Networks (TISPAN) subcommittee. Although standards bodies often are seen as stumbling blocks to progress because of their necessarily cautious progress, in the case of IMS and its corollary technologies they continue to offer highly valuable assistance in the overall effort to move IMS from concept to commercially deployed products.

What is IMS, really? It is a foundation on which a service delivery environment can be built for the creation and delivery of voice, video, data, and other multimedia services. With IMS, these services can be converged and delivered to subscribers on demand, however and whenever they like, serving as lifestyle enablers. Imagine a technology innovation designed from day 1 to enhance a desirable lifestyle rather than to be accommodated by it. When the database and management capabilities of IMS are combined with traditional services such as SS7 and SIP data, SMS and IM buddy lists, location data, presence information, purchase histories, and subscriber preferences and profiles, new combinations of services can be created on demand that adapt instantaneously to user behaviors and profiles. SMS could be interlaced with voice and video services, all IP-based, to deliver multiparty videoconferencing for individuals or for use in schools.

IMS invoked by network operators and equipment suppliers lies in the future, but the answer continues to evolve and change as more players involve themselves with it and other technologies are added to the overall IMS vision. Functionally designed to converge voice and data services with end-to-end QoS over a packet-based infrastructure and to combine wireline and wireless infrastructures logically under a shared set of end-to-end signaling and billing capabilities, IMS has a role in the evolving network definition that is relatively clear. That role continues to grow more complex, however, as time passes and it is more clearly understood. Recently, a collection of mobile providers interested in expanding their purview to include alternative data technologies has begun to petition for the inclusion of both WiFi and WiMAX in the IMS vision. To round out the table banging, cable television providers are beginning to clamor for inclusion alongside traditional wireline providers to avoid being left out of the game.

A Brief Aside: IMS and the Next-Generation Network

The Next-Generation (or in some countries the New-Generation) Network (NGN) is a concept that has been banging around the service provider domain for years and is just now coming to fruition. It is driven by a set of enterprise, consumer, government, and investor requirements and purports to reframe network service delivery in accordance with IMS's vision of a user-centric network.

Not surprisingly, enterprise and residence customers exhibit an ongoing demand for integrated data, voice, and video; support for any service, anywhere, with high speeds and media flexibility; on-demand circuit, bandwidth, and service provisioning; support for highly flexible virtual private networks; security, storage, and application-layer routing; and the ability to integrate network (telecom) and information (IT) systems easily and seamlessly.

Consumer and government groups have a related but different set of requirements. They include broadband access to every home; business-capable telecommuting services; reasonable prices for bundled data, voice, and video services; access to firewall and intrusion protection services; availability of on-demand video; and access to and support for high-speed peer-to-peer networking and applications.

Finally, there is the investment community, which must fund the whole thing. Not surprisingly, it wants increased revenue, enhanced profitability, larger served areas, and enhanced productivity.

Service providers have their own set of challenges. They currently must deliver data, voice, and video services over expensive, service-specific, largely stand-alone networks that are incapable of delivering the flexible, integrated services that the market demands. They realize that they must offer a wide range of access methods and protocols that better fit the needs of differentiated profitable services and must build IP and MPLS networks that rely on fairly complex redundant architectures.

In essence, then, the future network can satisfy all these disparate groups if it offers the following:

- The mobility of wireless
- The reliability of the PSTN
- The universality of the Internet
- The security and service isolation capability of a private line
- The flexibility of IP and MPLS to support integrated data, voice, and video services
- The high bandwidth of optical networks
- The operational efficiency of a common, consistent infrastructure

As the NGN concept continues to develop, three overarching characteristics emerge: *infrastructure convergence*, which is simply the convergence of multiple service-specific networks onto a common MPLS core through Multiservice Edge (MSE) routers that deliver layer 2 and layer 3 virtual private network (VPN) services; *service convergence*, the convergence of data, voice, and video services onto flexible and ubiquitous IP and MPLS networks; and *network simplification*, which is the elimination of complex tiered architectures and redundancy to create more scalable, reliable, and manageable networks that rely on POP architectures.

Numerous organizations have contributed to the definition of NGN, including the ITU. They have a remarkably simple view of it that aligns nicely with the IMS vision, as illustrated in the following quotes:

"Nothing should be done in the network that can be efficiently done in an end system."

"An NGN is a packet-based network able to provide telecommunications services and able to make use of multiple broadband, QoS-enabled transport technologies in which service-related functions are independent from underlying transport-related technologies."

The architecture of the NGN (Figure 3-36) is quite straightforward. As the diagram illustrates, the NGN is designed to take into account the disparate nature of the modern telecom network and "harmonize" the disparities among the various components while hiding the complexity from the user. Although the NGN vision differs slightly from that of IMS, the

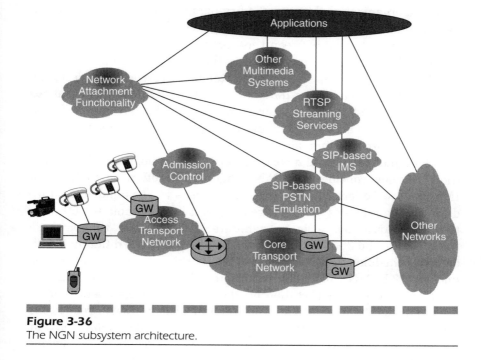

Figure 3-36
The NGN subsystem architecture.

results are the same. Furthermore, even though the groups responsible for the two efforts only partially overlap, their goals seem to be somewhat the same although there is a slight degree of friction between them. For example, there is wide support for IMS's concept of billing and control NGN. However, something as simple as a naming convention can bring things to a halt. The ITU is working hard on the development and rollout of NGN and at the same time is committed to enrolling IMS in the overall concept of ETSI's Telecoms and Internet Converged Services and Protocols for Advanced Networks. Its efforts consist of terminology modifications and architectural shifts in addition to adjustment and alignment of the two organizations' migration strategies.

IMS is one component of the ITU's NGN strategy, focusing as it does on bringing convergence, signaling, multimedia, and billing to the overall NGN effort. Other international efforts are ongoing as well. In March 2005, the ATIS hosted an IMS workshop in Herndon that attracted 170 participants, over double the previous year's attendance. The primary goal of the meeting was to discuss the appropriate use of IMS within TISPAN's efforts. Although little in the way of substantive work was completed, a great deal of attention was paid to the identification of technical and organizational issues, the firming up of collaboration opportunities, and discussions of mutual working methodologies.

The principal issue between the 3GPP and ETSI's TISPAN is that many 3GPP companies, most notably the GSM mobile operators, see TISPAN as the wireline providers' attempt to rescue their declining business model by adopting IMS and forcing the 3GPP to make changes to it to accommodate their requirements. Although there has been conflict between the groups, their relationship has improved significantly in recent months. Mutual agreement has been reached on the idea that the 3GPP has and should have control of IMS development efforts, and the 3GPP now considers TISPAN's ongoing IMS effort part of its own IMS Release 7 effort. Specific TISPAN requests will be handled as standard change requests, an arrangement that is acceptable to both parties. TISPAN's desire is to generate specifications that include references to the 3GPP's IMS activities. Because of the different development schedules the groups have been working under, however, it is unclear if TISPAN will be able to keep up with the current schedule.

There is also an expectation on the part of ITU members that by using IMS as the foundation for NGN, they ultimately will reduce the number of IMS implementations (the nice thing about standards is that there are so many to choose from). There is a perception—somewhat justified—that the 3GPP often divides its efforts among multiple projects, limiting its overall effectiveness. Although neither of the two organizations has ever won a prize for the rapid development of standards, there is hope that the cooperation between the two groups will lead to accelerated IMS development, since some of the internecine rivalry seems to have been eliminated. At the very least the industry probably will see a single architecture and migration path to facilitate service providers' entry into the IMS game in spite of infrastructure differences.

What is this IMS thing, anyway, and how does it work? Let's take a look at its anatomy and makeup before we go any farther.

IMS Basics

IMS is an open and standards-based networking and service delivery architecture that falls into the realm of the Next-Generation Network. It represents a multimedia architecture for both wireline and wireless IP-based services. Using a version of SIP that has been blessed by the 3GPP, it gives traditional service providers the ability to offer a new range of multimedia services in a converged delivery model.

The goal of IMS is to provide a set of services that combine the best of what is available from the legacy telephone network and the best of what the Internet has to offer. Furthermore, it will facilitate the delivery of services to users regardless of location, the device being used, or access modality. Because it is modular and designed to adapt to environmental changes (market demand, technology shifts, etc.), service providers can rest assured that it will adapt to their changing requirements as the need arises.

IMS depends on open standard protocols from the IP suite, and that guarantees its universal applicability within the realm of global data networks. Because it was created by and for the mobile services world, it seamlessly combines the best of the Internet with the best of cellular telephony to bring the two domains together.

As we will discuss in some detail later, IMS was conceived by the 3GPP. Its primary charge historically has been the development of standards for third-generation mobile telephony systems, with a focus on W-CDMA. Other standards development agencies, including TISPAN, also have been involved, the common theme being their mutual desire to create standards for wireline-wireless convergence.

IMS first appeared on the scene in the 3GPP's Release 5 standard, which stipulated the rule set for migration from second-generation to third-generation wireless systems. At that time UMTS was emerging as a driving force for the harmonization of GSM and CDMA networks, and multimedia applications were driving interest in SIP-based systems, particularly as Next-Generation Networks began to appear. Release 6 added interoperability with wireless LANs; both releases were backward-compatible with legacy GSM and GPRS networks.

Meanwhile, a different organization came into the picture. 3GPP2 arrived on the scene with its CDMA2000 Multimedia Domain (MMD), based on 3GPP IMS, which added CDMA2000 to the global mix of supported standards. Release 7 incorporated the requirements of wireline networks, completing the convergence circle between fixed and wireless. Shortly thereafter a migration plan appeared for evolution from IPv4 to IPv6. Although it has not been adhered to, the strategy is in place.

IMS in a Nutshell

Perhaps the most fundamental and far-reaching characteristic of IMS is that it is designed to work with literally any network: UMTS, GPRS,

Wireless LAN (WLAN), WiMAX, WiFi, DSL, CDMA2000, and cable. In fact, it works quite well with legacy (as in nonpacket) circuit-switched telephone networks by interfacing with them through a gateway conversion device. Because of the open protocol independency around which the system is designed, access networks with different characteristics can interoperate seamlessly. In operation, interfaces between the service layer and the network control layer permit sessions from disparate networks to share resources and deliver applications to the customer from any of the networks. As a result of the interworking between wireless and wireline networks, users can roam freely among member networks, using whatever applications they are subscribed to regardless of the network to which they are connected.

Service delivery in IMS is remarkably straightforward, and the modular design of the architecture (refer back to Figure 3-36) supports the addition of capabilities such as PoC, videoconferencing, multiplayer gaming, screen sharing, VoIP, and any other IP-based services that can be controlled by SIP.

Building IMS: An Architectural Overview

IMS relies on a core capability set for its basic functions. The IP Multimedia Core Network Subsystem contains multiple functional elements interconnected by standard, well-accepted interfaces. One distinction must be made here: A *function* is not a piece of hardware; it is indeed a function and can be placed logically anywhere in the network that makes the most sense from a performance point of view. In fact, functions can have multiple appearances if the requirements of the network make it reasonable to design it that way.

IMS Access

Because IP is the fundamental access protocol in IMS, the customer can connect to the network in a variety of ways. IMS-capable devices can register with the network immediately regardless of the network to which they are connecting. Although the standards stipulate SIP and IPv6, most implementers are building workarounds for the IPv6 requirement in light of the ongoing popularity of Version 4.

Fixed-access devices such as Ethernet LANs, broadband cable modems and DSL, wireless systems such as GSM, GPRS, CDMA2000, W-CDMA, WiMAX, and WiFi, also can connect to the network in a seamless fashion. As we described earlier, legacy systems such as PSTN phones and some VoIP systems will connect to the IMS network through a protocol converter, typically referred to as a gateway.

The Power of Information: Databases

Two primary network-based databases empower IMS: the Home Subscriber Server (HSS) and the Subscriber Location Function (SLF).

The HSS hosts the bulk of the user information required for the network to function properly. It provides information support for all IMS functions related to call setup and session establishment. Among other things, it contains services subscription information (sometimes referred to as user profiles) and provides the data required to authenticate and authorize user access to services. Based on database entries that identify what services the user is accessing and what network he or she currently is connected to, the HSS also supports user location. Similar to the Home Location Register or Visitor Location Register in mobile systems, it performs numerous critical functions.

The SLF comes into play any time multiple HSSs are invoked for a particular user's network-based activities, for example, when a user is roaming out of the home area and using services from a different network. Both HLF and HSS rely on DIAMETER[2] for AAA-like functions.

Into the Network

The heart and soul of the IMS network is a motley collection of sloppily named servers that work in concert to perform a broad collection of functions. Collectively, these servers are known as the CSCF; their primary function is to receive, analyze, process, and respond to SIP signaling

---

[2] The name DIAMETER is a play on words from the original AAA protocol called RADIUS.

packets that arrive in the IMS network. Below, we describe each of these servers and their functions in detail.

The P-CSCF

The first CSCF server we'll discuss is the Proxy CSCF, which is the initial network entry point for a SIP device (a terminal, for example). It can be located in various places, including within the home network or within the network to which a visiting device is temporarily connected. In most cases the P-CSCF is in the visited network if the visited network is completely IMS-compliant; if not, it is "discovered," typically with DHCP, and used in the home, IMS-compliant network.

The P-CSCF does not change during the lifetime of a registration session and typically is assigned to the terminal during initial registration. It intercepts all signaling messages and interprets them, using information gathered to authenticate the user and establish an IPSec relationship between the network and the IMS-compliant terminal. This reduces the potential for security breaches such as spoofing opportunities and denial-of-service attacks. Because of the proxy role of the P-CSCF, other nodes assume that if it has "vetted" the inbound IMS terminal, they can trust it as well, eliminating the need for additional authentication procedures if users move from network to network.

Another valuable function performed by the P-CSCF is SIP message compression. Since the volume of SIP messaging can be quite high and therefore can consume significant bandwidth, this capability is valuable, particularly over bandwidth-constrained wireless facilities.

QoS selection and management is another function the P-CSCF can handle as part of its policy enforcement process. Within this responsibility domain it has the ability to enforce application and network usage policies, authorize access to network resources, manage QoS, facilitate lawful intercept under the Communications Assistance for Law Enforcement Act (CALEA), and perform very granular bandwidth assignment and management. In some cases the Policy Decision Function is not housed in the P-CSCF; it also can be enabled at a Session Border Controller, another likely point of entry for IMS terminals that wish to connect to the network.

Finally, the Proxy CSCF has the ability to collect usage data that is required for billing functions. When enabled, the P-CSCF collects this data and forwards it to a device tasked with collecting billing data.

The S-CSCF

The Serving CSCF is a SIP server that is found in the user's home network domain. It serves as the central node within the signaling plane and as a session controller. Using DIAMETER, it interfaces to the HSS for the primary purpose of gaining access to user service profiles. It does not store anything locally but instead relies on the distributed nature of the network databases and the ability to reach them to facilitate its need to upload and download user profile information. The S-CSCF also manages the process of logically binding the user's location (typically the IP address of the user's terminal) to the SIP address, thereby performing SIP registrations. Like the P-CSCF, the S-CSCF reviews all signaling messages and therefore can select the most appropriate application server the user should be connected to on the basis of the functional requirements. Similarly, the S-CSCF performs network routing functions using internationally standardized protocols (ENUM, for example). Unfortunately it's not an acronym... and occasionally does network policy enforcement on an administration-by-administration basis.

The Interrogating CSCF

Like most networks, IMS networks are divided into administrative "regions" or domains to facilitate effective network management. The I-CSCF typically is found at the edge of an IMS administrative domain and is identified by an IP address found in the domain's DNS. This facilitates the ability of remotely located servers to find it. These remote systems might include a P-CSCF in a temporarily visited domain or an S-CSCF in a foreign network domain.

In practice, the I-CSCF connects to the HSS to download the user's profile data, relying on DIAMETER for that purpose. The SIP request then is routed to the appropriately assigned S-CSCF.

By encrypting components of the SIP message, the I-CSCF can disguise itself as a "stealth proxy," hiding the details of the internal network from prying eyes. When the I-CSCF performs this function, it sometimes is referred to as a Topology-Hiding Interface Gateway.

Application Servers

IMS would not add much to the evolving network without application servers. Their responsibility, simply stated, is to host and make available the applications that users want to have access to from their various devices. These servers use SIP to connect to the S-CSCF; consequently, it is a relatively straightforward process for service providers and third-party application developers to create, integrate, make available, and bill for their services when those services become available within IMS.

Remember that one of the elegant characteristics of IMS is the ability of users to gain access to applications regardless of where they are hosted. Application servers can reside in any network; if they are in the user's home network, they can interrogate the HSS via a DIAMETER interface (if the server is an SIP application server or OSA-SCS application server). A SIP application server is an application server that runs in native IMS mode. An OSA-SCS is an Open Service Access–Service Capability Server that uses Parlay to interface with OSA application servers. Alternatively, the HSS can be accessed via a Mobile Application Part (MAP) server, which is used for IM-SSF (IP Multimedia Service Switching Function), which interfaces with Customized Applications for Mobile Networks Enhanced Logic (CAMEL) application servers using the CAMEL Application Part (CAP).

Media Servers

The media server is the IMS component that makes service providers smile because it sources content for which users are obliged to pay premium prices. Key to the functionality of the media server is a logical component known as the Media Resource Function, which serves as the source point for content within the user's home network. It is used to perform speech recognition, speech-to-text conversion, recorded announcements, coder-decoder (CODEC) transcoding, and multimedia conferencing.

Each media resource function has two principal components: a Media Resource Function Controller (MRFC) and a Media Resource Function Processor (MRFP). The MRFC acts as a SIP signaling proxy to the S-CSCF and controls the MFRC processor via an H.248 interface. The MRFP is responsible for enabling all media-related functions.

The Breakout Gateway Control Function

If IMS does nothing else, it attempts to slake the industry's thirst for new acronyms. Here's yet another one: The Breakout Gateway Control

Function (BGCF) has a very specific function that is called into play whenever an IMS-based device attempts to call a telephone connected to the legacy PSTN. It is functionally a SIP server that performs routing functions based on standard telephone numbers. Needless to say, it will be critically important in the initial phases of IMS deployment but will fade in importance as IMS is deployed more widely.

The PSTN Gateway

The PSTN gateway, sometimes called a circuit-switched gateway, does precisely what its name implies: It interfaces between an IMS network and a legacy circuit-switched network. Circuit-switched networks often signal by using ISDN protocols such as ISDN User Part (ISUP) or Bearer-Independent Call Control (BICC) over Message Transfer Part (MTP) protocols. IMS, in contrast, relies on SIP. For content control, legacy networks use the time-tested Pulse Code Modulation (PCM) scheme, whereas IMS relies on the Real-Time Transport Protocol (RTP).

RTP is a UDP-based application that typically is implemented in the media gateways; the protocol is used to deliver the voice traffic. The protocol's greatest contribution to an IP session is that it has the ability to monitor and manage timing, signal loss detection, data security, content delivery, and perpetuation of encoding schemes. An RTP session is identified by two IP addresses (the endpoint device addresses) and, even though RTP rides on a connectionless UDP network, it supports a sequencing system that allows the detection of missing packets.

RTP is designed to manage the control requirements of real-time communication. Its structure is straightforward; its message format (Figure 3-37) includes a Sequence Number field that is incremented for each RTP packet and a Time-Stamp field that records the sampling rate and the resultant message playback rate.

One problem that RTP handles elegantly is packet loss. Rather than "extrapolate" by repeating the contents of a previous packet, it does something different. To achieve high levels of QoS in the received audio signal, the sampling rate of the voice signal must be increased, and that leads to smaller packets. The smaller packets take less time to process than do larger packets, but they create a different problem. Although the sampled content gets smaller, the header of each packet does not, leading to a strange form of data packet in which the header size approaches the size of the payload. RTP overcomes this inefficiency through a technique called *header compression*.

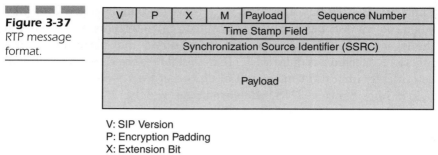

Figure 3-37
RTP message
format.

V: SIP Version
P: Encryption Padding
X: Extension Bit
M: More
Payload: Encoding methodology for video, other content
Sequence Number: Packet sequence number
Time Stamp: Compression algorithm-dependent
SSRC: Randomly assigned; identifies source

The RTP header compression technique has two stages. In the first stage the system takes note of fields in the packet headers that do not change over the life of a flow. In the second stage the system takes note of the fact that there are few flows at the "edge of the network" so that such information can be conveyed over the first hop by a single packet, after which the flows are identified by a short "connection identifier" that identifies the full state of the packet so that the first hop router can reconstruct the full packet. In RTP, certain fields change only a small amount from packet to packet, which means that the nonchanging information can be sent once and stored and then reused for multiple packets related to the same flow. If the router resets, the route changes, or the end system alters its state dramatically, an invalid checksum will be calculated, resulting in a reset of the stored state and an exchange of the full packet information necessary to recreate the current state. In the right circumstances, RTP can result in a 10-fold reduction in protocol overhead.

The Signaling Gateway

The signaling gateway interfaces with the signaling system associated with the legacy circuit-switched network. In practice it converts between circuit-switched signaling protocols such as MTP and IP network-based protocols such as Stream Control Transmission Protocol (SCTP). This allows ISUP messages to be passed effectively and seamlessly between the Media Gateway Controller Function (MGCF) and the wireline network. The MGCF performs call control protocol conversion between the

SIP and ISUP worlds. Using SCTP, it interfaces with the Media Gateway to control the resources in its purview. The Media Gateway performs the protocol conversion between RTP and PCM as well as providing "harmonization" between disparate CODECs in situations in which they do not interface directly with one another.

Payment and Billing Options in IMS

In the world of service delivery there are two recognized options for billing. *Recurrent billing*, sometimes called offline billing, generally is used for customers who receive a bill every month for whatever services were used in the previous billing period. *Transaction-based billing*, sometimes called online billing or credit-based billing, is used for prepaid customers who want to be billed for the services they use on a transaction-by-transaction basis. It is possible to use both in the same session; for example, a customer may pay on a monthly basis for voice but may want to be billed for the transaction when he or she downloads a movie or invokes an enhanced service.

In recurrent charge billing situations, all the IMS network components—the various CSCFs, the BGCF, the Media Resource Control Function (MRCF), the MGCF, and the application servers—collect usage and account information and then send that information to the Charging Collector Function (CCF), which constructs a Charging Data Record and sends it to the billing system, which in turn generates an invoice for the customer. In IMS each established session is assigned what is known as an IMS Charging Identity (ICID) that uniquely identifies each session. Additionally, an Inter-Operator Identifier (IOI) identifies the source and destination networks for purposes of billing and service identification. This is also important for the roaming user: Because different network domains have their own billing systems, it is important that they exchange usage data to ensure that roaming details can be exchanged for proper billing.

In transaction-based billing situations, the Serving CSCF communicates with a Session Charging Function (SCF), which looks to the network like a SIP Application Server. If the customer runs out of available credit during the session, the SCF has the ability to order the S-CSCF to terminate the session for "insufficient funds." Like other communications functions within the IMS realm, DIAMETER protocols govern all AAA activities. An Event Charging Function (ECF) collects data about transactions from the application servers.

One option for transaction-based billing is called Immediate Event Charging (IEC) or Immediate Transaction Charging (ITC). When invoked, IEC deducts credit from the customer's account, after which it gives the service delivery function (the application server, for example) permission to deliver the requested service. One option that can be invoked is called Event Charging with Unit Reservation, under which the ECF reserves a preestablished number of credits in the customer's account, after which it authorizes the requested service. When the delivered service is complete, the number of credits used is deducted from the account and the record of the reserved credits is deleted.

■■■ IMS Pros and Cons: A Summary

Clearly, IMS offers significant advantages to content providers, service providers, and customers alike. These advantages accrue in a number of areas, including basic functional advantages, cost advantages, and service delivery advantages.

The advantages of IMS are powerful and compelling. First and foremost, services can be deployed faster and more cost-effectively than ever before because of the broadly accepted and standardized architecture of IMS. Second, the network is completely independent of access technology, erasing the line between wireline and wireless infrastructures and service delivery "areas." Third, because of the elimination of the arbitrary line between wireline and wireless, the ability to migrate applications between the two domains becomes much simpler, and mobility can be incorporated into existing applications, expanding their reach beyond traditional wireline bounds. Fourth, the need to develop customized, small-market, high-cost applications becomes irrelevant and unnecessary, and that leads to lower capital and operating expenses.

The applications are much more powerful in their own right. The ability to add on-demand videoconferencing and presence capabilities, in addition to SMS and instant messaging, is made much more responsive by IMS simply because the information about each user is hosted in a single repository, making the discovery and response processes much more effective. Finally, voice becomes a major advantage because it now can be offered in combination with other applications, proving the adage that the whole is greater than the sum of the parts.

Many pundits argue that IMS offers little additional value because of the presence of "free" voice such as Skype. Although Skype and its peers offer a good service, there is no question that IMS has significant advantages over the so-called free services.

First of all, IMS places a high priority on quality of service, something the Internet does not have the ability to do regardless of how good its applications are. Because the Internet is something of a "no-man's-land" in terms of overall management (*everybody* manages it and *nobody* manages it), there is little predictability about the quality of any session. It isn't that an Internet session will be bad; it's that there's no way of knowing how jitter, delay, and packet loss will affect an individual session.

The second advantage that IMS has is data collection and billing support. Free VoIP services do not and cannot offer this, whereas IMS not only can collect the data, it can offer a variety of billing options to the user. Service providers can take advantage of this by offering premium services (a higher price for better QoS) or offering value-added services such as downloadable content, which they can bill for separately.

Third on the list of perceived advantages of IMS is the ability to create new from old, that is, to converge multiple services into a new collected capability either by combining existing telco applications or by combining telco applications with new third-party applications. This is where clever thinking will have its greatest impact: By designing applications that address specific customer requirements through interaction, service providers will always be a step ahead of the game instead of the other way around.

There are, of course, concerns and challenges with IMS. First of all, it falls into the "be careful what you wish for; you might get it" category. Under IMS, service providers will find themselves in complete control of content for the first time ever; that means they will be controlling the element of service provisioning that customers want the most. Customers rarely care about which network their content is being delivered over; they do, however, care about the content itself. This is a serious responsibility for the service provider and requires significant advance planning.

Second, the money changers need to be satisfied. Inasmuch as IMS is a new concept, its value remains largely unquantified in terms of real dollars. Its benefits and value therefore need to be explored further and established. Related to this is the fact that IMS is not really a new network per se but rather a reinvention of existing networks. Consequently, there is no real history on the books about the relative success of the IMS model; it will have to be proved in action.

Third, a few technical considerations will create heartburn. First, IMS relies on the 3GPP version of SIP, which raises a warning flag: It *must* interoperate seamlessly with the IETF standard version of SIP.

Do any of these issues raise show-stopper concerns? There is no question that some of these are serious issues, but in the grand scheme of things none of them are strategically important. They certainly have tactical and perhaps even operational weight, but they will be ironed out in the near to medium term.

Controlling the Impact of Culture Clashes

Because IMS represents such a departure from the norm for network architecture, service providers must take care to reduce the impact of the "technological culture clashes" that inevitably will result from its introduction. The wireline and wireless worlds, for example, differ in a number of substantive ways. In the wireline world, the service provider has very little control over the device the customer chooses to connect to the network. In wireless environments, however, the service provider has *direct* control over the devices used because of the access technologies deployed (CDMA versus GSM, for example). Other than government emission requirements and electrical compliance with network standards, wireline devices offer diverse functions and are not power-limited, whereas wireless devices have relatively limited functions and suffer from noise, range, and power limitations.

Another way in which the two worlds differ is in the arena of user identification and services delivery. In the GSM wireless world the Smart Card (SIM) has become the norm for identification of the user, service assignment, billing initiation, roaming permissions, and service flexibility (users can move the card from device to device as they wish, taking their service preferences with them). There is no analog in the wireline world.

Equally important are regulatory differences between the two service domains, minimal QoS constraints, SLA considerations, network management issues, and security concerns.

The *good* news is that many of these differences already have been addressed by industry groups that have made it their mission to resolve the disparities between the two "halves" of the emerging IMS network.

Most of the original IMS work has been done by the 3GPP and its corollary organizations, and so it is fairly clear which network elements will have to undergo changes to accommodate the shift. They include modifications to the Media Gateway Control Function, the HSS, the Serving CSCF, the Proxy CSCF, the Subscription Locator Function, the Interconnection Border Control Function, and a collection of specific billing and ancillary accounting functions. The Media Resource Function Controller, the Media Resource Function Processor, and the Interrogating CSCF remain unchanged from the original 3GPP design at the time of this writing, although they too could evolve as service providers as manufacturers learn more about the behavior of the network and the demands of the customer base. Inevitably, new change requests will drive the demand for additional modifications, which the various involved standards bodies and service providers will have to adapt to and which will drive manufacturers to incorporate changes rapidly into their IMS-specific equipment prototypes.

Service specifics, many of them driven by regulatory and legal compliance, also must be taken into consideration. For example, the Communications Assistance for Law Enforcement Act requires that certain minimum requirements be met for legal wiretap capabilities under Homeland Security Rules. Regulatory requirements related to E911 emergency services calling and universal services must be adhered to under the law. Although the 3GPP version of IMS and the emerging ETSI TISPAN version claim to be moving closer together, there are still substantial differences that require constant vigilance on the part of IMS developers and services architects.

At the time of this writing TISPAN is completing its IMS Release 1. It originally was scheduled for the middle of 2005, but it is not in dire jeopardy. Release 2 is scheduled for completion at the end of 2007, and Release 3 is scheduled for release at the end of 2009. Release 1 defines a Network Attachment Subsystem (NASS) that supports nomadic roaming with a focus on support of multimedia content delivered over DSL access technologies. The NASS function can be distributed, shared across both the home and visited networks. Its functions include IP address provisioning, user authentication, access authorization based on the user's network profile, access network configuration based on the user's profile, and granular location management for the correct handling of emergency calls.

Release 2, scheduled for availability at the end of 2007, will focus on network resource optimization using customer profiles. It also may include the ability to perform predictive service use based on the development of service usage profiles.

Release 3, currently scheduled for availability in 2009, is scheduled to address issues such as more extensive roaming and support for higher-bandwidth access modalities such as WiMAX, fiber, and Very High-Speed Digital Subscriber Line (VDSL).

As we said earlier, the 3GPP and ETSI TISPAN organizations are working to reconcile their different approaches to IMS architecture, but they tend to approach the challenge from different angles, leading to different design philosophies. TISPAN tends to operate in "top-down mode," beginning with services identification and then moving into the underlying infrastructure required to deliver them. 3GPP, in contrast, is more technology-centric, beginning most of its work inside the bowels of the network and later worrying about services. Although this situation is by no means irreconcilable, it is significant enough to slow the wheels of meaningful progress.

The fact that the networks involved are so substantively different is a matter of some concern, if for no other reason than the difficulty of coordinating the efforts of all interested parties toward some kind of marginally unilateral decision about the architecture and capabilities of IMS's ultimate shape and form.

IMS is not cheap. It is a complex and costly evolutionary gamble, and like its embryonic predecessor, convergence, is designed to accrue more value to the service provider than to the user. However, if the service provider world can manage to put on its customer hatslong enough to appreciate the sublime value IMS brings to the customer at large, it will be able to develop a compelling argument for IMS's value. If it cannot, it will be creating the next ISDN: a technology that spends its days looking for a problem to fix.

IMS
Regulatory
Issues

Throughout this book we have observed repeatedly that the technology within IMS is not new but instead represents a new approach to service delivery. We also have observed that regulation is about regulating the user's experience and ensuring service availability, not about regulating the underlying technology. It therefore is important to spend some time addressing the regulatory changes that will come about as a result of the success of IMS in the marketplace.

The U.S. Regulatory Environment

Perhaps the single most important characteristic of the U.S. regulatory environment is the fact that the Federal Communications Commission (FCC) has written into its regulatory laws a clear set of distinctions between what it refers to as "telecommunications services" and what it refers to as "information services." Telecommunications services consist of traditional telephony and other regulated services, typically delivered by an ILEC or a competitive provider. These services include voice and all the supporting applications and services that round out the offering of the typical telephone company: repair, operator services, and so on. These services are bound by certain minimum service-level criteria and by requirements that ensure that legal wiretap and intercept can be performed, universal service be facilitated, and communications in support of emergency services (Enhanced 911, commonly known as E911) be made available.

Information services, in contrast, are those typically delivered by a cable or Internet services provider. They include applications and services such as Internet access and content downloads and content delivery—movies delivered by a cable provider, for example.

What has clouded the waters recently is the entry of information services providers into telephony. Cable operators, for example, that want to cash in on the perceived high demand for triple-play packages now offer VoIP as the third leg of their stool along with high-speed Internet access and content. Since they already are regulated as information services providers and since the Internet is perceived to be a hands-off environment (most regulators correctly see the Internet as something of an innovation engine and are therefore reluctant to do anything that would stifle the creativity and innovation that come out of it), cable providers' voice service offerings currently are looked at askance as regulators wrestle with the issues of regulatory parity. Telephone companies cry foul over the fact that regulators have failed to reregulate cable providers as telecom providers since they are after all offering voice service; cable companies thumb their noses at the telephone companies, claiming that VoIP is merely another form of content and should not be regulated separately.

At issue here is the fact that neither cable providers nor pure VoIP providers are required by law to comply with telephony service mandates in the same way that incumbent providers and CLECs are. For example, traditional carriers are bound by rigorous E911 mandates that require that the service be available everywhere, with strict penalties for noncompliance. Information services providers, in contrast, have no such mandate; Vonage, for example, one of the best known VoIP providers, makes E911 available, *but only if the subscriber tells Vonage where he or she is at any point in time so that Vonage can ensure the ability to dispatch emergency help when required*.

Late in 2003, when the furor over VoIP was at an all-time high, the FCC conducted a VoIP forum followed by a rigorous investigation into telecom versus information services regulation. The investigation was kicked off in March 2004. Those events followed on the heels of attempts by state-based regulatory bodies to impose traditional telephony regulation on providers of VoIP services. In October 2003, in a case involving the Minnesota Communications Commission, a federal court ruled conclusively that VoIP is an information service. The battle continues to rage, fueled by strong and often conflicting emotions on both sides of the services aisle.

From the FCC's point of view, good things have come from this. The most important is the creation of a relatively healthy competitive environment dependent on facilities-based competition rather than on the contrived earlier system of local loop unbundling, which failed to live up to the industry's expectations. Recognition of the fact that the local loop *is* a natural monopoly and the putting in place of regulation that not only recognizes that fact but rewards providers for using alternative access solutions have resulted in a healthier, more vibrant local services industry in which competitive position stems more from creative and innovative business practices than from artificial regulatory requirements that attempt to "create" a competitive marketplace through punitive and unyielding regulatory decisions.

▇ IMS Regulatory Issues

As IMS becomes more fully defined and as its service offerings are better understood, a number of issues are confronting it from a regulatory perspective. The most important of these issues are QoS and public safety (including lawful intercept, E911, and privacy). In the United States recent regulatory decisions based largely on the brief history cited earlier in this book have taken a relatively light approach, allowing the market's preferences to dictate the criteria that define VoIP and other IMS services rather than doing it through well-intentioned but often arbitrary regulatory mandates.

Today all major carriers offer VoIP as a matter of competitive course, and the regulatory arguments continue. In a recent decision the FCC ruled that providers such as Vonage, Skype, and Pulver.com's Free World Dialup would remain classified as information services, keeping them free from the regulatory requirements imposed on traditional carriers. However, this ultimately will change. As VoIP becomes more widespread and demands for it grow, the "be careful what you wish for; you might get it" rule will begin to apply. IMS and its VoIP component will find themselves bound by the same regulatory requirements that burden legacy carriers, including support for emergency services, legal intercept and wiretap, international numbering plans, local number portability, mandated cost control, QoS, presence and caller location identification, user and data privacy, network interoperability, network integrity, and wireless spectrum considerations. These requirements will bleed over into competitive aspects of service delivery, including the imposition of standards and norms to guarantee ongoing competition, to ensure that technologies are at their best deployment level within the network and drive seamless interoperability and connectivity among disparate carriers.

Ultimately, telecom regulation (including regulation of both information services and telecommunications services) is driven by several service-oriented mandates.

The first of these mandates—and this by no means is unique to the United States or to the FCC—is customer protection and oversight. Regulatory agencies must maintain a balance between the decisions they make that are for the public good (and often are perceived to be punitive) and the demands placed on them by manufacturers that have agendas that go beyond the public good—not "evil" necessarily, but driven by Wall Street. Ultimately, regulators have as their primary responsibility the goal of improving the overall state of the public's welfare through the judicious application of regulatory law.

The second issue is transparency and regulatory independence. In most developed nations the regulator is an independent body that bases its decisions on its own analysis of the market without the stringent oversight and undue influence of the government. The FCC, for example, has no financial stake in the market it regulates; it has no vested interest. Furthermore, service providers and manufacturers alike—the regulated companies—are public corporations that are subject to the whims of the market for their success or failure. Investors vote with their wallets, and so it is incumbent on these companies to perform successfully or they will not receive investment funds. Since investors are typically far more effective users of new technologies than are the companies they invest in, they also tend to read the market more effectively and make investments in it accordingly. Investments drive innovation, and so prudent regulators do everything they can to put into place regulatory infrastructures that do not get in the way of these companies' innovation efforts.

The final characteristic of regulatory "stability" is reliance on public comment before final rule making. Forward-thinking regulatory bodies, when considering a regulatory decision that will have a far-reaching impact, typically solicit the public for input before coming to a final decision, often through a public forum. In the case of the FCC this is performed via what is known as a Notice of Proposed Rule-Making (NPRM), which notifies the public of a pending decision and solicits from it input and insight.

This process works well, largely because the pace of change within the market and the technologies it depends on is accelerating constantly, making it virtually impossible for any single agency to keep abreast of the flood of changes on a daily basis. Key to this sense of urgency is the perceived impact of broadband deployment. It is well known that month over month, a broadband user generates on average 13 times the traffic that a dial-up user generates, leading to high levels of network usage and attendant investment in that usage. It also is known that universally deployed broadband has a powerful economic impact as well, rising into levels of economic advantage that lie in the tens of billions of dollars and creating tens of thousands of jobs annually. Regulators therefore take their mandate seriously, knowing that responsible decisions made today will have long-term and powerful economic impacts tomorrow.

Taking into account all that is under way at the moment with the IMS evolution, regulators perceive that there is something of a digital migration that is changing the perceived rules of the regulatory and services road. The result is a need for a profound change in regulatory policy as it relates to technology and competition. For the most part regulators perceive this shift—and the impact of IMS in particular—as a process that will provide untold new benefits to consumers, largely because of the capabilities of broadband technology and the signaling functions that are inherent in IMS networks.

Legacy networks delivered limited applications to customers over a narrowband facility based on a one-to-one relationship between the underlying network technology and the delivered application. In broadband networks there is an inherent separation between the network and the applications because of the use of IP; the result of this is the ability to deliver multiple applications, often simultaneously, over a single broadband network access infrastructure. One advantage of this simultaneous delivery modality is the ability to create new applications from old, combining the best characteristics of multiple applications to deliver a new converged capability.

So what? As disparate service providers offer parallel broadband networks, a competitive market emerges, not so much between broadband networks as between the services delivered over those networks. This natural competition allows regulators to lighten the regulatory pressures originally put in place to prevent anticompetitive behavior and, since natural competition emerges as a result of broadband deployment, these regulations no longer are required. Instead, regulators can focus their attention on creating a healthy environment for the entry of other access solutions, such as broadband-over-power (BPL), cable, and various forms of wireless technology such as WiMAX.

By facilitating the deployment of multiple network types, regulators have the ability to give greater flexibility to service providers that want to enter the market and offer innovative solutions that inject energy and verve into it. As a result, enterprise and residence customers are more empowered because the pressure of full-on competition causes providers to deliver the services most demanded by consumers. The result is that regulators can take a more hands-off approach to telecom regulation, since their efforts can shift to enforcement of outcomes rather than enforcement of compliance.

Ultimately, telecom regulation in the IMS world comes down to this: Traditional, long-term monopoly-based regulatory policy does not apply, nor does an "all-or-nothing" regulatory approach. The application of case-based granular rules is far more effective than a generalized approach and lends itself to the accomplishment of the basic goals of regulatory law. In telecom these goals are largely social: the provision of universal service, the availability of emergency services, the careful monitoring of and availability of lawful intercept activities, and guaranteed access to telecommunications services for persons with disabilities.

At the same time there is a growing movement to limit issues associated with jurisdictional control. There historically has been a power struggle between the FCC and the state regulatory bodies over issues such as policy enforcement, interpretation of the law, and the levying of fines for failure to comply with regulatory mandates. Although it is critical that the FCC be charged with the establishment of a national set of policies that govern the development and rollout of IMS and other Next-Generation Network technologies, it is equally critical—and is becoming more critical—that the states have a say in the interpretation of the law as it relates to each of their constituencies.

Central Regulatory Trends

Perhaps the most telling trend involves VoIP. In recent months VoIP has become far more "psychically central" in the marketplace than ever before because of its growing influence in the enterprise, the growing volumes of venture money directed toward it, and the number of business moves that have resulted from its rise to success. Witness, for example, the acquisition of Skype by eBay, the customer volume of Vonage, the inclusion of VoIP as a central messaging component in Microsoft's Vista operating system, and the money being spent on VoIP-enabled PBXs and call centers in modern enterprises.

Regulators continue to wrestle with VoIP as they attempt to categorize it. Is it an information service, a telecom service? Cable operators that now offer it as the third leg of their triple-play stool argue that it is an information service; telephone companies, watching themselves undergo the death of a thousand cuts, argue that the service is actually telecom and therefore should be regulated as such. The regulators seem to fall somewhere in the middle, applying a relatively light hand and at the same time setting deadlines for E911 compliance by VoIP providers.

Amid the chaos regulators have for the most part come to a new realization about VoIP. For the longest time they have regulated VoIP as a separate service simply because it is IP-based. In fact, the service is *voice*; the IP part is nothing more than a technology delivery option.

What is happening and will continue to happen is that the regulators of the world will allow the two to coalesce because it makes sense to do so.

There are good reasons for the IP evolution. Although the belief that VoIP is always cheaper than a traditional circuit-switched call is largely a fallacy, there is no question that IP-based services are far more efficient in terms of the utilization of network resources. In a circuit-switched call network, resources are reserved for the duration of the call by a single pair of calling parties. In IP-based calls, in contrast, physical network resources are shared in a round-robin fashion, resulting in far more cost-effective network utilization patterns. Services such as Vonage, Skype, and Pulver's Free World Dial-Up operate in a peer-to-peer fashion, managing databases of end-user customers and allowing the magic of Internet routing to facilitate connections between endpoints.

Things get muddy somewhere in the center of the cloud. Whereas the pure VoIP providers continue to sprout like crabgrass, the traditional players continue to deliver millions of calls over the circuit-switched network. Somewhere in the middle the two meet, and hybrid calls result, further confusing the mandate of the regulator. Consider the following situation: A VoIP call originates on a broadband DSL connection but terminates on a traditional circuit-switched connection. Is it an information or telecom service? How should carriers be required to compensate one another for the call? In the traditional world, when a long-distance company terminates a call on a local provider's network, it is required to pay the local carrier an intercarrier compensation fee for the privilege of terminating the call. How does that work in the Internet domain? The problem is that existing regulations do not address this mixed environment, particularly as they relate to an Internet call that terminates on a traditional network connection.

On February 12, 2004, the FCC released an NPRM designed to study the impact and management of VoIP. The FCC has used this rule-making procedure to generate and collect data about the impact of VoIP on the public and draw up suggested requirements for evolving the regulator profile to reflect more accurately the demands of the public as they relate to VoIP and the interplay among incumbents and pure VoIP players.

As always, regulators are most concerned about the ability of evolving technologies to support public policy mandates, particularly public safety, which naturally translates into universal availability of E911, among other things.

Payment Models

A second area of focus for the regulatory world is payment schemes. There has always been debate between local providers and long-distance providers about the relative fairness of intercarrier compensation schemes; the addition of VoIP into the mix has made the problem that much worse.

As we alluded to earlier, one of the problem areas surrounding IMS and VoIP is the issue of intercarrier compensation. Under current rules, standard rates for circuit-switched call termination are set to be slightly above cost and include a factor to offset the cost of service provision in high-cost areas: a subsidy of sorts. When a call originates on a broadband connection, service providers do not assess a per-minute charge, one of the bones of contention among the carriers. Furthermore, there is an assumption that there is a cost-based rate in place, typically between 0.1 and 0.25 US cent per minute, for call termination. The problem (okay, one problem) is that different carriers pay different termination rates. Wireline carriers pay one fee, wireless another, VoIP another, and data and paging another. This disparity results in bad feelings and serious concerns about favoritism. Consequently, both regulators and service providers are working to come up with some form of regulatory compliance model that works for all concerned and levels the playing field. The goal is to converge the intercarrier compensation rules so that (1) they are applied fairly across the board and (2) carriers charge the same rate no matter what is being carried, under the belief that "bits is bits." In other word, a packet is a packet is a packet, and the same rules should apply to all.

Finally, carriers and regulators alike would prefer to put in place a system that allows carriers to recover their costs directly from the end customer instead of from each other. However, in a service provisioning environment in which multiple disparate systems (cable, wireless, traditional telephony) provide voice service, this subsidy concept is not equal across the board, and this leads to a slew of concerns among service providers (which currently are burdened with meeting the requirements of subsidy) and regulators (which must apply subsidy law fairly across the board).

A proper policy therefore calls for regulatory action that creates an explicitly detailed subsidy that supports universal service delivery in costly areas of the country. Unless this is done, no progress will be made because those areas *must* be serviced but, at the same time, the cost burden of service delivery must be applied fairly. Today the U.S. Universal

Service Fund is used to defray the cost of operating in hard-to-serve (and therefore expensive) areas by taking funds from legacy wireline carriers and distributing them as appropriate to those costly areas. Most regulatory bodies have as a goal some form of universal service mandate designed to level the competitive playing field as the market becomes increasingly complex and competitive.

The third major trend that has gotten the attention of regulators is the ongoing, inexorable, and painful shift of service demand from the traditional circuit-switched wireline network to the global VoIP network. There are dire predictions regarding the long-term viability of the circuit-switched network, including its demise within the next five years. I think that this is rubbish for all kinds of reasons. For example, what percentage of Internet traffic travels across the wireline network, and what percentage of cellular telephone traffic is carried by the legacy wireline network? The answer: *100%*. The Internet is nothing more than a collection of facilities leased from service providers all over the world (and some private circuits), and the only thing that's wireless in a cellular call is the link between the handset and the cell tower. Somewhere along the line the call enters the legacy telephone network and traverses it until it reaches the distant local loop regardless of whether the called party is a cellular user or a wireline customer. To paraphrase Mark Twain, "Rumors of the network's death are somewhat exaggerated."

Spectrum Management

I often take part in discussions about wireless technology and its regulation. One of the statements I hear during those discussions is "We have to do something soon because we're running out of spectrum."

That comment is patently ridiculous for a very simple reason: *We have all the spectrum there is*. The problem is not that we're running out of spectrum but that we're not managing it particularly well. Vast swaths of it have been set aside by large organizations and government bodies in case they someday discover a need for it.

Because of recent technological changes, regulatory bodies have had to modify their stance on spectrum control and management and on the issue of wireless policy enforcement. For example, cognitive radio has emerged, and it has changed the rules of the game in a dramatic way: Rather than build a multifunction wireless device that necessarily has multiple chipsets for each radio mode (for example, a combination GSM-

CDMA-WiFi device would have three radio chipsets), a cognitive radio chipset modifies itself to accommodate the radio spectrum in which it finds itself. As a user moves from radio area to radio area (from a GSM domain, to a CDMA domain, to a WiFi domain, to a Bluetooth domain, for example), the chipset adapts to the strongest signal type and moves the session from domain to domain. This reduces the cost of the device (a single chipset) and dramatically reduces the physical size, since less internal "real estate" is required. Of course, it necessarily creates an interesting regulatory conundrum since the device is no longer a limited-purpose product, and for the service provider it creates a massive challenge: How do you bill for a service in which the users are bouncing all over the landscape between paid and unpaid spectral domains?

These areas of focus are changing the nature of the regulator's job in a serious and nonnegotiable way. Corporations will find that the best decision they can make will be to engage in what I call a "culture of regulatory compliance," which simply recognizes that regulation is here to stay, that it exists purely for the public good, and that it is an inalienable part of the technology world. The sooner they engage and work with regulators to help them achieve their vision of universal, affordable service for everyone, the sooner those companies will benefit from the changes that are arriving with the implementation of technological innovations such as VoIP and IMS.

The Future of IMS: Key Issues and Scenarios

In this chapter we pull together current thinking about the future of IMS. Inasmuch as it remains a nascent technology and is incomplete in terms of functional definition, scope, cost, rollout strategy, and deployment timeline, questions remain about the "believability" of the "facts" that have been published about IMS. Let me be the first to tell you some of the truths about IMS.

First, it is real, it is important and, with the exception of the World Wide Web it is perhaps the most powerful innovation to hit the industry in the last 50 years.

Second, there is nothing new about the components of IMS. Earlier we observed that customers aren't looking for the next killer app but for the killer way to access the applications they already have. This is what IMS is all about and why it is fundamentally important.

Third, it begins with the wireless world, GSM specifically, and has expanded its purview to include the wireline world, the wireless LAN world, and the broadband wireless domain.

Fourth, IMS is fundamentally dependent on both legacy capabilities and innovative practices, bringing together as it does the traditional wireline environment with its focus on carrier-grade service, the mobile telephony world with its focus on mobility and diverse services, and the IP domain with its basis in ubiquity and universal support.

Fifth, IMS has the widespread support of multiple standards bodies and industry groups, including the ITU, the IETF, the Parlay Group, the Java Alliance, and many service providers, hardware manufacturers, regulatory agencies, and third-party application developers.

That being said, let's dive into what we know about IMS and its prospects for a successful future.

IMS Development

As we discussed in Chapter 3, the Third Generation Partnership Project (3GPP) has guided the development of the global GSM mobile network since early 1999, overseeing its evolution from an environment based on a circuit-switched architecture to an innovative and far-reaching packet-based network. Early on, the operational focus was on the lower layers of the protocol stack, specifically layers 1 through 3: the physical, data link, and network layers that defined the third-generation radio access network. Later, when Release 4 came about, the effort shifted to higher-layer considerations, including the delivery of enhanced services and the creation of the open systems architecture (OSA). This architecture also is known as *Parlay OSA*, named for the Parlay Group, a multivendor consortium that develops open, technology-independent application-programming interfaces for applications that operate across multiple disparate networks. The group combines intelligent network services with IT applications over a secure, billable interface. Parlay application programming interfaces (APIs) facilitate innovation within the enterprise, and their portable, network-independent applications connect IT and telecom, creating new revenue opportunities for service providers, application service vendors, and independent software vendors.

According to the Parlay Group's website, the organization's multipart mission is to define, establish, and support a common specification for industry-standard APIs; facilitate the development of test suites and reference code, using a variety of technologies to create related products and services that operate across wireless, IP, and public-switched telephone networks; provide an environment within which Parlay members can review and approve suggested revisions and enhancements to initial technical specifications; submit recommendations to established agencies with the purpose of accelerating the creation of international standards; and provide a usability and interoperability forum in which users can meet with developers and providers of products and services to identify requirements and ongoing issues.

Later, when the focus shifted to Releases 5 and 6, the inclusion of IP became a mandate, and work evolved to consider the roles of the nascent service and control planes, including the IMS specification.

The 3GPP laid the groundwork for multimedia systems, and other organizations rode its coattails. The 3GPP2 effort, the Open Mobile Alliance, and ETSI focused on the relevance of the organization's Multimedia Domain (MMD) specifications. Since IMS is synonymous with convergence in its support for wireline, wireless, and IP interworking, it continues to be supported by a range of other industry bodies, including ETSI's TISPAN committee.

Fundamental Concepts of IMS

Remember that IMS is designed to specify components and functions that support interworking with SIP-based services. It does *not* dictate new protocols but instead reuses the parts of the preexisting IP suite. This collection includes protocols such as SIP, the SDP, and DIAMETER. As an aside, DIAMETER is an authentication, authorization, and accounting protocol for network access, including mobile IP. The basic idea behind DIAMETER is to provide a protocol that can provide AAA services to emerging access technologies. It is intended to work in both local and roaming environments and offers some advantages over its RADIUS predecessor. It uses reliable transport protocols such as TCP, offers IPSec TLS transport-level security, supports RADIUS in backward-compatible mode, supports larger address space than does RADIUS, operates in peer-to-peer mode rather than a client-server mode, has dynamic peer discovery, supports application layer acknowledgments, supports error notification, and, naturally, provides a rudimentary set of accounting services.

SIP and SDP, in contrast, have been around for quite some time and are closely associated with IP. They are intended to enable the creation of a real-time, peer-to-peer multimedia network architecture.

IMS is designed to merge the Internet, the legacy telecom network, and the IT domain into a single powerful construct for user-oriented communications. It converges fixed and wireless networks and delivers seamless roaming to all devices regardless of access modality. The best part? It ensures what is known as *service transparency*: the idea that services and applications are available regardless of location or the network to which a user is connected at any point in time.

In IMS environments SIP is used most commonly for user registration and session control. As we described earlier, the Call Session Control Function (CSCF) is the core signaling server, acting as both a registrar and a proxy server. The Home Subscriber Server (HSS) is functionally analogous to the well-known Home Location Register seen in traditional mobile environments, offering AAA responsibilities and maintaining centralized subscriber profile data. For AAA, the CSCF relies on DIAMETER for user authorization and access to subscriber profiles located within the HSS.

The IMS standards specify (not surprisingly) open interfaces for access control, session management, mobility management, service control, and billing functions. They also recommend deployment over a carrier-class SIP network, largely because of the lower complexity and cost associated with the legacy circuit-switched network and the inexorable evolution of major networks to IP.

IMS also stipulates an SIP-based common interface known as the IMS Service Control (ISC) interface. ISC provides a seamless interface that allows applications hosted by Parlay/OSA, SIP, and CAMEL application servers to interface with the IMS core. CAMEL represents a set of GSM-derived standards that operate over a GSM core network. They allow a service provider to define services that go beyond the limited services available through native GSM. The CAMEL architecture is based on intelligent network (IN) standards and uses the CAP protocol. It is particularly effective for the design and deployment of mobile applications that are to be shared across multiple networks in an IMS environment.

The primary integration effort that occurs between IMS application servers and the IMS core is via the Serving Call Session Control Function (S-CSCF) described in an earlier chapter.

Deployment Realities

One of the major challenges facing IMS deployment to the mobile device is the management of spectrum for VoIP delivered to a roaming device. Most of the deployed spectrum already is in use by other 3G and GSM networks, and the investment in it is quite high, sometimes prohibitively so. Redeployment of some or all of that spectrum for IMS applications to the mobile device therefore is not particularly likely in the near term. Service providers therefore will look for solutions that bridge the gap between legacy and IMS environments as a way to overcome this challenge.

Another key consideration is the need to resolve the signaling disparity between traditional SS7 network signaling and IP-based SIP signaling. One way to achieve this is with a technique that has been used with significant (though early) success: the deployment of converged service gateways that provide interoperability between SS7 and the nascent IMS signaling environment that is based on SIP and DIAMETER. Because of current marketplace uncertainty and the fact that providers will want to hedge their bets until the market's direction is known clearly, IMS signaling environments most likely will support a range of application protocols and application extensions designed to deal with the reality of multiple vendors in the space.

One of the architectural advantages of the Parlay/OSA gateway is its ability to connect to both the IMS and the 2G environment, serving in effect as a gateway device between them. As such, it can bridge the gap between the legacy PSTN world and the emerging IMS environment, creating a world where applications can operate across both "platforms." For example, traditional legacy voice can be moved to IMS by installing it on an SIP application server.

Execution Environments

An execution environment is simply the platform on which applications and services are presented or delivered to the market. Parlay/OSA is an example, but there are others, including the Java 2 Execution Environment (J2EE) and the Java Advanced Intelligent Network Java Language Execution Environment (JAIN SLEE), both of which are widely available. Although all these platforms have loyal followers, it is unclear whether one of them will prevail over the others. Given the emerging demands of the market, mobile carriers will have to put in place the facility for moving services from one execution environment to another rather than reinvent the service logic for each disparate environment.

Service Demands

Naturally, IMS's demands for service will vary with the execution environment, network limitations, and application requirements. Some environments will require low bandwidth, and others will require more rigorous access to data or enterprise applications and network resources. None of these execution environments is capable of handling the varying demands of different application scenarios; that means that multiple environments unquestionably will be a reality. Although multiple execution environments certainly will coexist from a network perspective, only one service creation environment must be visible from a user perspective. To that end, services should be able to be created one time and reused across the different platforms, seamlessly and without regard for infrastructure differences.

Parlay X Web Services and the Service-Oriented Architecture

SIP is unquestionably the preferred execution domain for most emerging environments and, though it is quite capable, its extension for IMS service creation is complex, and in fact it is referred to occasionally as Signaling System Eight, a fact to which the company of that name probably takes exception.

In IT, service-oriented architecture (SOA) often is implemented over traditional technologies such as SOAP, Web Services Definition Language (WSDL), and XML. In keeping with its drive to push the limits of services interfaces, the Parlay Group has created Parlay X, a collection of Web service interfaces designed to communicate effectively with traditional telecom environments.

Parlay X defines a set of telecommunications-oriented services that have been incorporated into 3GPP Release 6. Parlay X creates an interoperability link for service providers that is based on the SOA relied on by service providers. It bridges the gap between traditional environments and IMS, making it easier to incorporate the efforts of developers. Other organizations, such as the Open Mobile Alliance (OMA), also are developing interfaces that address specific telecom functions. More are likely to follow as the two domains grow closer.

As we observed earlier, a critical requirement of these interfaces is support for transparent and seamless connectivity between the legacy wired network and the wireless networks and, by extension, logical interoperability (i.e., service sharing) between service providers.

▇▇▇ Service Dependencies

IMS services, which typically are resident on application servers, include short messaging, third-party add-on, incoming call notification, multimedia messaging service, account payment, account management, device status, device location (presence), call handling, conferencing, and individual subscriber address list management.

Equally valuable is the fact that a growing collection of third-party developers will offer an expanding range of new services that are based on existing services and applications. Designed to realize the true promise of IMS, they will be based on combinations of applications such as telepresence, QoS selection, custom charging and billing, and location-based services. These new product sets will enable the delivery of enhanced services such as seamless customized billing across multiple networks regardless of where the user is connected (recall the examples we described earlier in the book), customizable services packages that span the voice-video-data-wireless continuum, converged fixed and mobile service packages, user-aware—and user-adapted—network services, enterprise packages adapted specifically to their varied tariff and rate plans requirements, and special consideration for complex and heterogeneous access modalities including (again, remember the discussion earlier in the book) wireless LANs, Bluetooth, WiMAX, and other options.

Perception Management: IMS Migration

"Be careful what you wish for; you might get it" is a common aphorism in the technology world, and IMS is certainly not immune from the impact of overstated capabilities. The danger of an innovation as remarkable as IMS lies not so much in its perceived lack of capabilities as in the fact that it is misunderstood. IMS adds very little in the way of new capability; instead, it creates new and exciting ways to *deliver* capability to a broader and more demanding family of users. Although all the components of IMS already exist and the relationships between them are in a late state of evolution, full-blown rollout and services deployment are still quite a ways in the future. Since service providers most likely will deploy overlay networks as part of their IMS deployment strategies, cost considerations will hold sway and be major influencers until adequate infrastructure and services are in place to ensure the cost effectiveness of the widespread rollout, particularly in the mobile arena. In the legacy wireline environment the migration to IP will continue apace, not as quickly as many would like but certainly at a measurable rate. In lockstep with IP deployment will be the slow but deliberate deployment of broadband access, another necessary component of a successful IMS push.

Both wireless and wireline strategists must caution their service provider employers to be patient with their individual rollouts because in the near term IMS will be a chaotic environment of constantly changing technology components, and any attempt to keep up will result in a great deal of wasted effort. Waiting until substantive changes have been made and then implementing them in the aggregate probably will be the most effective deployment strategy. Given the fact that many of the services and applications will be developed and sold by third-party providers, a whole new way of thinking about strategic relationships will have to be crafted by incumbent providers.

 Convergence, Thy Name Is IMS

In the IMS world convergence has multiple related meanings. First, it addresses the convergence of the mobile, fixed line, and broadband service domains. Second, it lends itself to the convergence of circuit-switched, packet-switched, and wireless technologies, all of which must be served by the IMS vision. Third, it addresses the very real need for players in the IMS game to play by the "*some* of the money or *none* of the money" rules, since no company today has the wherewithal to "do it all" for the customer. Alliances, partnerships, and other strategic relationships will become the norm rather than the exception in the service delivery world. Fourth, it speaks to the fact that the money will accrue to the company or companies with the best service delivery vision and execution, which means converged capabilities, strategies, and vision.

One of the biggest challenges facing traditional players is this need to work closely with companies that could be perceived as competitors. Third-party application and services developers will become part of the overall delivery strategy, and traditional service providers will have to develop nontraditional behaviors, integrating their own offerings with those of third-party players to create the famous "whole that's greater than the sum of the parts."

Think about the companies that have been most successful in recent years and why. Microsoft, Dell, eBay, and Cisco all have formed alliances with other players, and the results are clear. Legacy companies, which have a history of monopoly presence in the market, are often hard-pressed to enter into relationships with third-party players for the simple reason that they don't know how to treat the partner company in the relationship. The answer is quite simple: The partners should be treated the same way the company would treat a customer. This should not be a major issue for service providers: Numerous industry analyst reports predict that if IMS succeeds as it is expected to, 30% to 40% of service providers' revenues will come from third-party players by 2010. That's the kind of number that makes companies pay attention.

IMS Timeline...for Now

Service providers are faced with a quandary as they move forward with their IMS deployments. The first issue is financial. They have *massive* investments in plant and equipment and are therefore loath to make a long-term decision that will result in the need to abandon that investment, given that much of it is only partially depreciated. Consequently, they are looking for any opportunity to use network infrastructure that is already in place.

Second, as demand grows for additional capabilities, they are taking the steps necessary to move into the realm of the next-generation network discussed earlier.

Third, they see competition looming, some of it anticipated and some of it not, and are gearing up to face off against the forces of evil as they enter the market with innovative behavior, low-cost networks, and deep, rich service offerings.

Fourth, they are engaged in the proverbial "fixing the train while it's rolling down the track" problem. In response to both the promise of IMS and the demands of the ever more sophisticated market, they must seamlessly, transparently, and cost-effectively cause fixed-wireless-IP to happen.

According to industry reports, most service providers in most regions are engaged in the Request for Information (RFI) and Request for Proposal (RFP) parts of the IMS system selection process for the network infrastructure component of IMS deployment. In terms of SIP-based network deployment, North America is currently the leader, particularly in terms of IMS strategy. Many companies in the region have indicated their intent or made early IMS equipment purchases with plans for installation in 2006 and 2007. They're not alone, however; most analysts believe that all the world's developed markets will have IMS core networks in place to some degree by midyear 2006.

The Asia-Pacific region is equally aggressive, with service providers in Korea and Japan planning service rollouts during the first half of 2006. The Caribbean and Latin America region is somewhat behind the other two, with deployment plans scheduled for mid-2007. Africa is diverse, with major markets (South Africa) planning NGN and IMS rollouts in late 2006 to mid-2007.

The bulk of the providers that are in the IMS selection and planning process are concentrating almost exclusively on the network infrastructure aspects of IMS. Although they certainly intend to (and must) address the application set that provides IMS functionality, they have chosen for the most part to delay that decision. Better the enemy you know than the enemy you don't, apparently.

◼︎◼︎◼︎ A Linchpin Component: Network Signaling

If it ain't broke, don't fix it. The telephony network's SS7 signaling system has been around for nearly 20 years and most likely will remain in place for another 15, with a few caveats. In addition to the wireline network, SS7 is used in 3G networks, and so there is no compelling reason for it to disappear. Furthermore, it is SS7 that facilitates interoperability functions (call control, roaming, messaging) between the PSTN and the older 2G networks that are still around.

◼︎◼︎◼︎ Predictions and Prognostications

Although SS7 will not be carted off to the Smithsonian any time soon, its influence will begin to wane as the new network takes root. SS7, which is a narrow-band (56 Kbps) architecture, most likely will evolve over the next three to five years to SIGTRAN. SIGTRAN is a protocol under which SS7 signaling messages can be transported within an IP network using SCTP.

The result of this partial migration should be obvious: It preserves the use of SS7 (and the substantial investment in it) while moving closer to the all-IP dream. Again, based on analysts' reports, signaling traffic should be roughly 50% IP by 2010. Going beyond 50% will be difficult because of preexisting conditions and requirements. One of these conditions and perhaps the biggest show-stopper of all is the perception that IP is not adequately secure to move something as critical as network signaling to a network that is based 100% on the protocol. Second, mobile devices will be required to move from the circuit-switched network to high-speed wireless networks such as High-Speed Packet Downlink Packet Access (HSDPA), which in turn will drive most other devices to IP.

◼︎◼︎◼︎ The Players in the IMS Game

Most of the IMS product announcements have come from the expected players: major manufacturers such as Lucent, Nortel, Ericsson, Alcatel, and Siemens. However, a number of other players, many of them SoftSwitch manufacturers, have announced their intent to enter the fray. They include Motorola with its IMS server and IBM with its Network Directory Server.

On the software side, the list is equally long, with companies selling everything from platform solutions to signaling to middleware. These companies include AePona with its OSA/Parlay and ParlayX Gateway products, Appium with its applications platform, BEA Systems with its converged OSS offer and WebLogic Service Delivery Platform, HP with its ISM Integration Framework, IBM with its Network Transformation Solutions family, jNetX with its family of middleware solutions, Kabira with its Real-Time SLEE platform, Leapstone with its Communications Convergence Engine, Microsoft with its Connected Services Framework, Portal with its fully convergent Revenue Management Platform, and Telcordia with its IMS Online Charging System. These are major companies with strong products, and they are positioning themselves to enter the market as IMS matures.

Ultimately, because of its universal appeal, IMS will become so company- and product-rich and so widely deployed that it will move to commodity status. As that happens, the industry's focus will move from the hardware platforms, facilitative software, and middleware to the upper-layer services that drive real differentiable revenue. The ultimate result of that movement will be an evolution in the nature of the relationships among companies that drive the IMS services vision.

Toward a New Business Model

An interesting trend in the IMS market is the clash between the traditional way of doing business and a new model that relies, for lack of a better term, on a different type of "vendor trust."

Historically, service providers always purchased major platform installations from large, trusted vendors with which they had long-standing relationships. These companies are often in a position to offer vendor financing, guarantee ironclad service level agreements, and subject themselves to binding liability clauses. I had a conversation with a contract manager from a large service provider who made an interesting observation that took a bit of thought to understand. She said,

"There are lots of small vendors out there that make top-notch products, sometimes better and more innovative than those produced by the big industry players. However, we rarely buy from them because I have a policy that says, 'We won't buy from a vendor if we represent more than 20% of its revenue.' I can't afford to take a chance: If we buy from them, come to depend on them for service and support, and then we have a bad year and can't spend with them as we have historically, I run the risk of pushing them out of business simply because they rely on us for such a large part of their earnings. If my actions cause them to go away, I can't rely on them for support, in which case I've shot myself in the foot. So it doesn't matter how good they are: If the relationship is that much of a David and Goliath imbalance, I won't enter it regardless of how good their products are. It's sad, but it's reality."

The trend of buying from large providers undoubtedly will continue in the IMS realm, but there probably will be a bit of a twist. Service providers trust the companies they know because there is a great deal riding on the relationship with regard to survivability and support. However, because of capability limitations, many of those long-standing suppliers will be forced to buy from third-party contractors to supplement their own product sets; the result of this will be the natural emergence of a hybrid solution model. This will become a major advantage in the medium to long term. Like most layered systems, IMS views the applications and services layer as being at the top of the protocol model; this means that service providers will be able to select from a mix-and-match menu to create the best possible solutions for themselves. Because they will build their IMS environments on a standards-based platform, they also will have the option of writing their own applications if they desire, injecting an unprecedented level of flexibility into the system.

Some of the money or none of the money.

IMS Downsides and Liabilities

It would be irresponsible to write a book about something as new and innovative as IMS without addressing its downsides as well as praising its contributions. Like all technology innovations that depart from the norm (and IMS certainly does that), IMS is potentially a severely disruptive event in the continuum of telecommunications development. It disrupts the rules of engagement, changes the way customers interact with the network, ruins existing billing models, and drives a fundamental change in the long-standing traditional relationship between suppliers and buyers.

All these things are good and important. They change the business for the better as long as the business pays attention to them and adjust accordingly. Consider the following quotes:

> Destroy your business—change or die. When the rate of change inside the company is exceeded by the rate of change outside, the end is near.
>
> —J. Welch

> To meet the demands of the fast-changing competitive scene, we must simply learn to love change as much as we hated it in the past.
>
> —Tom Peters

> In the end there will be just two kinds of firms: those that disrupt their markets and those that don't survive the assault.
>
> —Richard D'Aveni

The people who uttered those words know what they're talking about. IMS is a change agent, and its influence will be felt for years. However, it isn't all wine and roses. There are both clear and unclear issues, challenges and misperceptions that surround the deployment of IMS, some of which can be ignored and others of which must be considered. I've listed some of them below; others will surface as the system moves toward widespread deployment.

Perhaps the most critical issue is the fact that IMS's scope of responsibilities and application sets have not been defined clearly. As in any industry, there are competitive forces at work and, if the IMS standards development bodies and systems contributors fail to move quickly to "bound the system," someone else will step in and do it for them. This could result in IMS being sidelined in favor of another solution or could retard its development inasmuch as such a move would inject uncertainty into the market and potentially disrupt the flow of venture money that IMS currently receives.

Another consideration is the myth, legend, and hype that surrounds IMS. I said this before, and I'll say it again: IMS is not a panacea for all that ails the telecommunications and IT worlds. It is not a universal solution for all things, nor will it be a complete replacement for the existing technology bases that currently provide services. As important as defining the scope of IMS is, it is equally important for developers and industry players to state clearly what it is *not*.

Related to this issue is a serious concern about the interaction between IMS and preexisting systems. Because there is so much misinformation (or lack of information) about IMS, the definition of *system interfaces* remains largely unaddressed. Because IMS is really a "system of systems," the internal interfaces are as important as are those that connect IMS to the legacy systems of the outside world. This is another opening for alternative development efforts to hold sway if it is not dealt with quickly and effectively by accepted standards and development bodies.

Another impediment is the fact that service providers may underestimate the potential returns from an IMS implementation. One must recognize that IMS is first and foremost an architecture, not a product. As such, it constitutes a list of "guidelines" for implementing a far-reaching philosophy of service and application delivery. The calculation of financial returns from an IMS deployment must go far beyond the perceived value of the infrastructure components and include the third-party software that resides in the system, the difficult-to-calculate value of converged applications, and the equally ephemeral value of IMS's ability to accelerate time to market for new service introduction.

One danger with IMS is the potential that it could fall into what I call the 3G trap. When third-generation wireless systems first hit the market in the late 1990s, the trade journals brimmed with advertisements that heralded the service providers' new ability to deliver 2 Mbps to a customer's mobile device. The problem was that although the network was capable of delivering massive mobile bandwidth, there were no applications available that could take advantage of it. As a result, 3G became a technology looking for a problem to fix. Service providers invested billions of dollars in spectrum and network overlays only to discover that their efforts and expenditures were for naught. Only today are applications emerging that can take advantage of 3G capabilities.

On the subject of trust once again, a cultural shift will have to take place within the service provider community. These companies have never mastered the "art" of building business relations with other companies as part of the revenue-sharing culture that is becoming so prevalent today because until recently they never needed to. They often have been full-service shops capable of satisfying customer service demands with their own resources. Today, all too often, they enter relationships with other companies with the intent of controlling the partner. That's not a partnership, nor is it an alliance.

The strength of IMS lies in the fact that a power shift takes place during which control of application availability migrates from the service to the user, taking full advantage of the customizable nature of IMS and its modular makeup. This is yet another definition of convergence under the IMS umbrella: It is very likely that *all* service providers will not offer *all* services. However, all services will be available from the "technological organism" that will result from IMS's widespread deployment. As companies begin to interconnect and offer their services as part of a converged system (Figure 5-1), the statement claiming that the whole is greater than the sum of the parts will become a powerful reality. Suddenly customers will be able to buy any service they want from their own service provider even though a particular service may not be hosted by that provider.

This brings up another serious potential weakness in the IMS deployment fabric. Imagine the scenario under which customers "mix and match" their service complement in a situation in which they own half the services and the other half are delivered over their network but owned and hosted by other providers. How will billing be done for such an arrangement? What happens when there is a glitch in the network that prevents customer access over the provider's network to a remotely hosted application? What will the revenue-sharing model look like?

I have long maintained that one of the biggest untapped opportunities for service providers today is their largely underutilized network management and operations support systems. These complex applications collect and archive massive volumes of information about the state of the network, drilling down into the well-known fault, configuration, accounting, performance, and security (FCAPS) management domains. All five of these become fundamental to the success of IMS in the converged net-

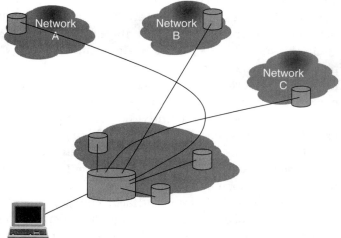

Figure 5-1
Imagine the complications that arise when applications hosted on different networks are delivered to a user via his own service provider's network in an IMS environment!

work; without any one of them the other four cannot be completely useful. Today these systems are used primarily to monitor and manage the network with an inward-looking eye.

Many measures of service, such as QoS and the various factors that lend themselves to the tenets of service-level agreements (SLAs), are based on network performance *as seen through the eyes of the service provider*. Proclaiming to the customer that the network offers five nines of reliability has little meaning to the customer, because if the network is unavailable when the customer *really* needs it, the five nines are meaningless. A far more meaningful measure might be something that assesses the degree to which network services make a difference to the customer's business processes. The point is that service providers will have to assess their role as *service providers*, perhaps redefining the nature of service in this new role that they must take on. Failure to do so will result in an open door for alternative providers to offer something that resembles IMS and its remarkable capabilities, leaving the service provider network to become what it already is in danger of becoming: a transport network only.

Admonitions

In addition to the obvious challenges of implementing a new system in the face of strong incumbency, dealing with the CAPEX and OPEX involved in the transition/migration, forming previously untested business relationships with other companies, and learning a whole new set of definitions of convergence, service providers will have to manage customer expectations to a degree that they never have done before. Earlier in the book we talked about Google, Skype, Yahoo!, and Vonage offering free or low-cost voice, video, and e-mail services to the masses, and the number of companies doing that grows every day. Consequently, many subscribers will expect free service from their service providers. This is an interesting problem that deserves some discussion.

Today users boot up their computers, start working, and occasionally make phone calls to friends and colleagues with Skype as they marvel about how good it is for a free service. But is it really free? Does my ISP give me free Internet access every month because I'm such a nice guy? Did Cisco send me the router and hubs in my office for nothing because it likes me? I think not. What's happening is a "piece-of-the-spend" challenge. The money is being spent by the same customers, but the lines of demarcation that define the various recipients of the money are being gerrymandered by a slew of new rules of engagement.

I am waiting for the first service provider that offers free voice service to the customer, saying something like this: "Sure, I'll give you free service. Here's how it works. You pay me $80 per month. For that I'll give you high-speed Internet access and 10 movie downloads, and I'll throw in local and long-distance voice for free."

It clearly isn't free. The cost of the service is bundled into the fee of $80 per month. However, by creating the perception that the customer is going to get something for nothing, the service provider makes that customer sticky and has the opportunity to sell him or her a complete package of services.

This also speaks to the need to engage in cross-company selling. If a customer wants access to a service that is not hosted locally, the service provider must make that service available to the customer or risk losing the customer to a competitor. Again, forging these "cross-border treaties" with other providers is a powerful construct provided that the usage, provisioning, and billing algorithms can be worked out.

Finally, the implementation must demonstrate long-term viability. Using the same logic stated earlier in the book, IMS should do for the service provider what any new technology does for a customer: lower its CAPEX and OPEX costs, raise its overall revenues, improve or stabilize its competitive position, and mitigate whatever downside risk the service provider faces while operating in an increasingly competitive market. In all this discussion about IMS and its intent, isn't that precisely what we've been talking about?

■ Unintended Consequences

Physicists observe that for every action there is an equal and opposite reaction. When planning and implementing IMS in the network, service providers must be careful to avoid what I call the "Jurassic Park effect." This effect echoes Jeff Goldblum's concerns about the place in the first movie. Recall that when the park's curator queries him about his reservations, observing that "they spared no expense—they built dinosaurs," Goldblum responds, "Yes, yes—yes—but you see, you spent so much time and money proving that you *could*, you forgot to ask whether you *should*." (We know they shouldn't have because there are *two* sequels.)

A significant number of IMS's advantages accrue only to subscribers who wish to take advantage of them. Simply stated, many customers will have no need for videoconferencing, multimedia messaging, presence management applications, or even SMS. The value they bring to the party will be minimal, and so there will be a requirement for a healthy upsell and awareness campaign or a financial plan that takes into account the revenue hemorrhage that will result from nonuse. Related to this is the cost of replacement or retirement of the legacy infrastructure. The "if it ain't broke, don't fix it" brigade will resist IMS's entry, as will providers that face oblivion from its arrival: mobile content providers, for example. Furthermore, as the system reaches critical mass, is tested, and goes online, a migration strategy will have to be put in place to move legacy customers onto the new infrastructure with little if any impact on their day-to-day activities. This falls into the same category as perception management, only in this case the reputation of the company is at stake.

Service providers cannot afford to perform this all-important step poorly. In fact, it is critical that as service providers begin the deployment process, they stage a campaign designed to highlight the unique capabilities of their deployment. Because of the strong mutual support between existing telco capabilities and the new functions IMS brings to the table, service providers easily can describe applications that are not available elsewhere, including the "free" services available via the Internet. Some of these services are AAA, custom billing, custom QoS management, and location-based services. Furthermore, traditional service providers have a long-standing legacy of customer service whose value cannot be overstated.

▰▰▰ The Big Enchilada: Billing Models

Many customers like the idea of a flat-rate billing model. In other words, they work out an agreement with the service provider under which they pay a single amount month over month, for which they receive an agreed level of service. This is common, for example, in mobile telephony. However, a growing population of users has expressed interest in and a desire for transaction-based billing and for prepaid models.

In the world of the service provider the billing model becomes complicated because in many cases billing for disparate services is accomplished via multiple unrelated billing systems. For example, many wireless service providers have both a prepaid billing system and their standard postpaid system because that's the way the system evolved: in services silos. Under the IMS architecture multiple systems can be combined into a single platform that bills each customer on the basis of his or her known preferences and preestablished profile. The result of this is a dramatically reduced OPEX associated with the process of collecting, validating, and billing each customer and potentially greatly increased revenue as the system identifies new upsell opportunities because of the data collected on each customer's usage patterns.

Equally compelling is the ability to bring new services fluidly and accurately to market at minimal cost. Since IMS supports online billing, algorithms will be put in place that immediately connect the charging model for a particular new service with the application itself. If a customer engages with the new service, billing will be immediate, accurate, and effortless.

Summary

IMS faces a number of challenges but none that it is incapable of dealing with over time. Perhaps most challenging is the fact that IMS changes everything: It thumbs its nose at existing service, architecture, customer relationship, and billing paradigms and then proves that they are not the only way to do things by proposing new business models, behavior models, economic models, and relationship models. This is a time for bravery in the industry.

Whenever change occurs in an industry, two types of companies emerge: those which have the wherewithal to shape their industry and those which hold back and adapt to the changes brought about by the shapers doing what they do best. Shapers are important players in the IMS game because they are not afraid to go out on a limb and tell the world what it will look like and how customers will behave in the future. However, it takes bravery to accept such a risk, and so they don't do it without first doing their homework. Of course, there's nothing wrong with being an adapter: Some of the most successful companies in the world are successful purely because they allowed the shapers to do their thing and then carved out a niche in the market and served it better than anyone else could. To a very large extent, Microsoft is a very successful adapter.

CHAPTER **6**

Conclusion

We've spent a couple hundred pages talking about the driving forces behind IMS, but far more important, a large part of the book dealt with the social, economic, regulatory, and competitive forces that give a compelling argument for its success. Over the next five years the industry will continue to stabilize and become increasingly economically viable. At the same time, the Millennials will come into their own, maturing in the workplace and moving into middle management positions where they will exert extraordinary decision-making power as employees, customers, and competitors. Their demands from the network are very different from those of earlier generations of users, who expected staid, stable service delivered largely through some kind of physical conductor. The Millennials eschew tethered services, preferring the spontaneity of anytime, anywhere service to whatever roaming device they are using at that moment. Enterprises are beginning to jump on that bandwagon, recognizing that under the "time is money but speed is profit" mantra every second counts and that the ability to deliver competitive position-affecting content on demand, as required, can mean the difference between success and failure in business.

The IMS naysayers continue to speak out against its potential success, claiming that the technological changes it espouses are far too expensive, the business-related cultural shifts are far too difficult, and the value of its enhanced service offerings is far too ephemeral and ill defined. But IMS is not an *if* technology; it is a *when* technology. In spite of the dire predictions from industry pundits, the traditional legacy wireline network is not in danger of disappearing; it is far too important as a core transport mechanism for that to happen. It is, however, in danger of marginalization, of being sidelined as a commodity incapable of delivering additional revenue. This cannot be allowed to happen because there is too much at risk. Given the increasing focus on wireless and wireline as simply "access" and the desire to have content available in any form at any time, IMS seems to represent the best hope of satisfying that demand and ensuring the survival—and indeed the flourishing—of the legacy carriers.

That said, let's be realistic. Numerous standards bodies are at work on disparate versions of IMS, and their strong efforts must be reconciled to ensure market acceptance. Network architecture standards must be agreed on, service standards established, regulations written, and equipment guidelines created if IMS is to become a widespread reality that transforms the telecommunications service delivery environment. That transformation will occur for one specific reason: the market's desire for a network environment that makes interaction with telecommunications services completely seamless.

When IMS makes possible the reality of a user-aware network and begins to offer services on the user's terms rather than on those of the network provider, *magic will happen*. At that point a compelling investment opportunity will appear, and revenue will begin to flow at an unprecedented level. I observed earlier in the book that I believe that we are on the beginning curve of the next great bubble. IMS is the driver, and everyone—service provider, systems manufacturer, component manufacturer, content provider, and customer—will win.

Common
Industry
Acronyms

AAL   ATM Adaptation Layer

AARP   AppleTalk Address Resolution Protocol

ABM   Asynchronous Balanced Mode

ABR   Available Bit Rate

AC   Alternating Current

ACD   Automatic Call Distribution

ACELP   Algebraic Code-Excited Linear Prediction

ACF   Advanced Communication Function

ACK   Acknowledgment

ACM   Address Complete Message

ACSE   Association Control Service Element

ACTLU   Activate Logical Unit

ACTPU   Activate Physical Unit

ADCCP   Advanced Data Communications Control Procedures

ADM   Add/Drop Multiplexer

ADPCM   Adaptive Differential Pulse Code Modulation

ADSL   Asymmetric Digital Subscriber Line

AFI   Application Family Identifier (RFID)

AFI   Authority and Format Identifier

AI   Application Identifier

AIN   Advanced Intelligent Network

AIS   Alarm Indication Signal

ALU   Arithmetic Logic Unit

AM   Administrative Module (Lucent 5ESS)

AM   Amplitude Modulation

AMI   Alternate Mark Inversion

AMP   Administrative Module Processor

AMPS   Advanced Mobile Phone System

ANI   Automatic Number Identification (SS7)

ANSI   American National Standards Institute

APD   Avalanche Photodiode

API   Application Programming Interface

APPC   Advanced Program-to-Program Communication

APPN   Advanced Peer-to-Peer Networking

APS   Automatic Protection Switching

ARE   All Routes Explorer (source route bridging)

ARM   Asynchronous Response Mode

ARP   Address Resolution Protocol (IETF)

ARPA   Advanced Research Projects Agency

ARPANET   Advanced Research Projects Agency Network

ARPU   Average Revenue Per User

ARQ   Automatic Repeat Request

ASCII   American Standard Code for Information Interchange

ASI   Alternate Space Inversion

ASIC   Application Specific Integrated Circuit

ASK   Amplitude Shift Keying

ASN   Abstract Syntax Notation

ASP   Application Service Provider

AT&T   American Telephone and Telegraph

ATDM   Asynchronous Time Division Multiplexing

ATM   Asynchronous Transfer Mode

ATM   Automatic Teller Machine

ATMF   ATM Forum

ATQA   Answer to Request A (RFID)

ATQB   Answer to Request B (RFID)

ATS   Answer to Select (RFID)

ATTRIB   Attribute (RFID)

AU   Administrative Unit (SDH)

AUG   Administrative Unit Group (SDH)

AWG   American Wire Gauge

B2B   Business to Business

B2C   Business to Consumer

B8ZS   Binary 8 Zero Substitution

BANCS   Bell Administrative Network Communications System

BBN   Bolt, Beranak, and Newman

BBS   Bulletin Board Service

Bc   Committed Burst Size

BCC   Blocked Calls Cleared

BCC   Block check character

BCD   Blocked Calls Delayed

BCDIC   Binary Coded Decimal Interchange Code

Be   Excess Burst Size

BECN   Backward Explicit Congestion Notification

BER   Bit Error Rate

BERT   Bit Error Rate Test

BGCF   Breakout Gateway Control Function

BGP   Border Gateway Protocol (IETF)

BIB   Backward Indicator Bit (SS7)

BICC   Bearer Independent Call Control

B-ICI   Broadband Intercarrier Interface

BIOS   Basic Input/Output System

BIP   Bit Interleaved Parity

B-ISDN   Broadband Integrated Services Digital Network

BISYNC   Binary Synchronous Communications Protocol

BITNET   Because It's Time Network

BITS   Building Integrated Timing Supply

BLSR   Bidirectional Line Switched Ring

BOC   Bell Operating Company

BPRZ   Bipolar Return to Zero

Bps   Bits Per Second

BRI   Basic Rate Interface

BRITE   Basic Rate Interface Transmission Equipment

BSC   Binary Synchronous Communications

BSN   Backward Sequence Number (SS7)

BSRF   Bell System Reference Frequency

BTAM   Basic Telecommunications Access Method

BUS   Broadcast Unknown Server

C/R   Command/Response

CAD   Computer-aided design

CAE   Computer-Aided Engineering

CAGR   Compound Annual Growth Rate

CAM   Computer-Aided Manufacturing

CAMEL   Customized Applications for Mobile Networks Enhanced Logic

CAP   CAMEL Application Part

CAP   Carrierless Amplitude/Phase Modulation

CAP   Competitive Access Provider

CAPEX   Capital Expense

CAPEX   Capital Expenditure

CARICOM   Caribbean Community and Common Market

CASE   Common Application Service Element

CASE   Computer-Aided Software Engineering

CASPIAN   Consumers Against Privacy Invasion and Numbering (RFID)

CAT   Computer-Aided Tomography

CATIA   Computer-Assisted Three-Dimensional Interactive Application

CATV   Community Antenna Television

CBEMA   Computer and Business Equipment Manufacturers Association

CBR   Constant Bit Rate

CBT   Computer-Based Training

CC   Cluster Controller

CCIR   International Radio Consultative Committee

CCIS   Common Channel Interoffice Signaling

CCITT   International Telegraph and Telephone Consultative Committee

CCS   Common Channel Signaling

CCS   Hundred Call Seconds per Hour

CD   Collision Detection

CD   Compact Disc

CDC   Control Data Corporation

CDMA   Code Division Multiple Access

CDPD   Cellular Digital Packet Data

CD-ROM   Compact Disc-Read Only Memory

CDVT   Cell Delay Variation Tolerance

CEI   Comparably Efficient Interconnection

CEPT   Conference of European Postal and Telecommunications Administrations

CERN   European Council for Nuclear Research

CERT   Computer Emergency Response Team

CES   Circuit Emulation Service

CEV   Controlled Environmental Vault

CGI   Common Gateway Interface (Internet)

CHAP   Challenge Handshake Authentication Protocol

CHL   Chain Home Low RADAR

CICS   Customer Information Control System

CICS/VS   Customer Information Control System/Virtual Storage

CID   Card Identifier (RFID)

CIDR   Classless Interdomain Routing (IETF)

CIF   Cells in Frames

CIR   Committed Information Rate

CISC   Complex Instruction Set Computer

CIX   Commercial Internet Exchange

CLASS   Custom Local Area Signaling Services (Bellcore)

CLEC   Competitive Local Exchange Carrier

CLLM   Consolidated Link Layer Management

CLNP   Connectionless Network Protocol

CLNS   Connectionless Network Service

CLP   Cell Loss Priority

CM   Communications Module (Lucent 5ESS)

CMIP   Common Management Information Protocol

CMISE   Common Management Information Service Element

CMOL   CMIP over LLC

CMOS   Complementary Metal Oxide Semiconductor

CMOT   CMIP over TCP/IP

CMP   Communications Module Processor

CNE   Certified NetWare Engineer

CNM   Customer Network Management

CNR   Carrier-to-Noise Ratio

CO   Central Office

CoCOM   Coordinating Committee on Export Controls

CODEC   Coder-Decoder

COMC   Communications Controller

CONS   Connection-Oriented Network Service

CORBA   Common Object Request Brokered Architecture

COS   Class of Service (APPN)

COS   Corporation for Open Systems

CPE   Customer Premises Equipment

CPU   Central Processing Unit

CR   Change Request

CRC   Cyclic Redundancy Check

CRM   Customer Relationship Management

CRT   Cathode Ray Tube

CRV   Call Reference Value

CS   Convergence Sublayer

CSA   Carrier Serving Area

CSCF   Call Session Control Function

CSMA   Carrier Sense Multiple Access

CSMA/CA   Carrier Sense Multiple Access with Collision Avoidance

CSMA/CD   Carrier Sense Multiple Access with Collision Detection

CSU   Channel Service Unit

CTI   Computer Telephony Integration

CTIA   Cellular Telecommunications Industry Association

CTS   Clear to Send

CU   Control Unit

CVSD   Continuously Variable Slope Delta Modulation

CWDM   Coarse Wavelength Division Multiplexing

D/A   Digital to Analog

DA   Destination Address

DAC   Dual Attachment Concentrator (FDDI)

DACS   Digital Access and Cross-Connect System

DARPA   Defense Advanced Research Projects Agency

DAS   Dual Attachment Station (FDDI)

DAS   Direct Attached Storage

DASD   Direct Access Storage Device

DB   Decibel

DBS   Direct Broadcast Satellite

DC   Direct Current

DCC   Data Communications Channel (SONET)

DCE   Data Circuit-Terminating Equipment

DCN   Data Communications Network

DCS   Digital Cross-Connect System

DCT   Discrete Cosine Transform

DDCMP   Digital Data Communications Management Protocol (DNA)

DDD   Direct Distance Dialing

DDP   Datagram Delivery Protocol

DDS   DATAPHONE Digital Service (sometimes Digital Data Service)

DDS   Digital Data Service

DE   Discard Eligibility (LAPF)

DECT   Digital European Cordless Telephone

DES   Data Encryption Standard (NIST)

DID   Direct Inward Dialing

DIP   Dual Inline Package

DLC   Digital Loop Carrier

DLCI   Data Link Connection Identifier

DLE   Data Link Escape

DLSw   Data Link Switching

DM   Delta Modulation

DM   Disconnected Mode

DM   Data Mining

DMA   Direct Memory Access (computers)

DMAC   Direct Memory Access Control

DME   Distributed Management Environment

DMS   Digital Multiplex Switch

DMT   Discrete Multitone

DNA   Digital Network Architecture

DNIC   Data Network Identification Code (X.121)

DNIS   Dialed Number Identification Service

DNS   Domain Name Service

DNS   Domain Name System (IETF)

DOD   Direct Outward Dialing

DOD   Department of Defense

DOJ   Department of Justice

DOV   Data Over Voice

DPSK   Differential Phase Shift Keying

DQDB   Distributed Queue Dual Bus

DR   Data Rate Send (RFID)

DRAM   Dynamic Random-Access Memory

DS   Data Rate Send (RFID)

DSAP   Destination Service Access Point

DSF   Dispersion-Shifted Fiber

DSI   Digital Speech Interpolation

DSL   Digital Subscriber Line

DSLAM   Digital Subscriber Line Access Multiplexer

DSP   Digital Signal Processing

DSR   Data Set Ready

DSS   Digital Satellite System

DSS   Digital Subscriber Signaling System

DSSS   Direct Sequence Spread Spectrum

DSU   Data Service Unit

DTE   Data Terminal Equipment

DTMF   Dual Tone Multifrequency

DTR   Data Terminal Ready

DVRN   Dense Virtual Routed Networking (Crescent)

DWDM   Dense Wavelength Division Multiplexing

DXI   Data Exchange Interface

E/O   Electrical to Optical

EAN   European Article Numbering System

EBCDIC   Extended Binary Coded Decimal Interchange Code

EBITDA   Earnings Before Interest, Tax, Depreciation, and Amortization

ECMA   European Computer Manufacturer Association

ECN   Explicit Congestion Notification

ECSA   Exchange Carriers Standards Association

EDFA   Erbium-Doped Fiber Amplifier

EDI   Electronic Data Interchange

EDIBANX   EDI Bank Alliance Network Exchange

EDIFACT   Electronic Data Interchange for Administration,
   Commerce, and Trade (ANSI)

EFCI   Explicit Forward Congestion Indicator

EFTA   European Free Trade Association

EGP   Exterior Gateway Protocol (IETF)

EIA   Electronics Industry Association

EIGRP   Enhanced Interior Gateway Routing Protocol

EIR   Excess Information Rate

EMBARC   Electronic Mail Broadcast to a Roaming Computer

EMI   Electromagnetic Interference

EMS   Element Management Dystem

EN   End Node

ENIAC   Electronic Numerical Integrator and Computer

EO   End Office

EOC   Embedded Operations Channel (SONET)

EOT   End of Transmission (BISYNC)

EPC   Electronic Product Code

EPROM   Erasable Programmable Read-Only Memory

EPS   Earnings per Share

ERP   Enterprise Resource Planning

ESCON   Enterprise System Connection (IBM)

ESF   Extended Superframe Format

ESOP   Employee Stock Ownership Plan

ESP   Enhanced Service Provider

ESS   Electronic Switching System

ETSI   European Telecommunications Standards Institute

ETX   End of Text (BISYNC)

EVA   Economic Value Added

EWOS   European Workshop for Open Systems

FACTR   Fujitsu Access and Transport System

FAQs   Frequently Asked Questions

FASB   Financial Accounting Standards Board

FAT   File Allocation Table

FCF   Free Cash Flow

FCS   Frame Check Sequence

FDA   Food and Drug Administration

FDD   Frequency Division Duplex

FDDI   Fiber Distributed Data Interface

FDM   Frequency Division Multiplexing

FDMA   Frequency Division Multiple Access

FDX   Full Duplex

FEBE   Far End Block Error (SONET)

FEC   Forward Error Correction

FEC   Forward Equivalence Class

FECN   Forward Explicit Congestion Notification

FEP   Front-End Processor

FERF   Far End Receive Failure (SONET)

FET   Field Effect Transistor

FHSS   Frequency Hopping Spread Spectrum

FIB   Forward Indicator Bit (SS7)

FIFO   First in First Out

FITL   Fiber in the Loop

FLAG   Fiber Link Across the Globe

FM   Frequency Modulation

FOIRL   Fiber Optic Inter-Repeater Link

FPGA   Field Programmable Gate Array

FR   Frame Relay

FRAD   Frame Relay Access Device

FRBS   Frame Relay Bearer Service

FSDI   Frame Size Device Integer (RFID)

FSK   Frequency Shift Keying

FSN   Forward Sequence Number (SS7)

FTAM   File Transfer, Access, and Management

FTP   File Transfer Protocol (IETF)

FTTC   Fiber to the Curb

FTTH   Fiber to the Home

FUNI   Frame User-to-Network Interface

FWI   Frame Waiting Integer (RFID)

FWM   Four Wave Mixing

GAAP   Generally Accepted Accounting Principles

GATT   General Agreement on Tariffs and Trade

GbE   Gigabit Ethernet

Gbps   Gigabits per Second (billion bits per second)

GDMO   Guidelines for the Development of Managed Objects

GDP   Gross Domestic Product

GEOS   Geosynchronous Earth Orbit Satellite

GFC   Generic Flow Control (ATM)

GFI   General Format Identifier (X.25)

GFP   Generic Framing Procedure

GFP-F   Generic Framing Procedure-Frame-Based

GFP-X   Generic Framing Procedure-Transparent

GGSN   Gateway GPRS Support Node

GMPLS   Generalized MPLS

GOSIP   Government Open Systems Interconnection Profile

GPRS   Generalized Packet Radio System

GPS   Global Positioning System

GRIN   Graded Index (fiber)

GSM   Global System for Mobile Communications

GTIN   Global Trade Item Number

GUI   Graphical User Interface

HDB3   High Density, Bipolar 3 (E-Carrier)

HDLC   High-Level Data Link Control

HDSL   High-Bit-Rate Digital Subscriber Line

HDTV   High-Definition Television

HDX   Half-Duplex

HEC   Header Error Control (ATM)

HFC   Hybrid Fiber/Coax

HFS   Hierarchical File Storage

HIPAA   Health Insurance Portability and Accountability Act

HLR   Home Location Register

HNO   Host Network Operator

HPPI   High-Performance Parallel Interface

HSS   Home Subscriber Server

HSSI   High-Speed Serial Interface (ANSI)

HTML   Hypertext Markup Language

HTTP   Hypertext Transfer Protocol (IETF)

HTU   HDSL Transmission Unit

I   Intrapictures

IAB   Internet Architecture Board (formerly Internet Activities Board)

IACS   Integrated Access and Cross-Connect System

IAD   Integrated Access Device

IAM   Initial Address Message (SS7)

IANA   Internet Address Naming Authority

ICMP   Internet Control Message Protocol (IETF)

I-CSCF   Interrogating Call Session Control Function

IDP   Internet Datagram Protocol

IEC   Interexchange Carrier (also IXC)

IEC   International Electrotechnical Commission

IEEE   Institute of Electrical and Electronics Engineers

IETF   Internet Engineering Task Force

IFRB   International Frequency Registration Board

IGP   Interior Gateway Protocol (IETF)

IGRP   Interior Gateway Routing Protocol

ILEC   Incumbent Local Exchange Carrier

IM   Instant Messenger (AOL)

IML   Initial Microcode Load

IMP   Interface Message Processor (ARPANET)

IMPRES   Instant Messaging and Presence

IMS   IP Multimedia Subsystem

IMS   Information management system

InARP   Inverse Address Resolution Protocol (IETF)

InATMARP   Inverse ATMARP

INMARSAT   International Maritime Satellite Organization

INP   Internet Nodal Processor

InterNIC   Internet Network Information Center

IP   Intellectual Property

IP   Internet Protocol (IETF)

IPO   Initial Product Offering

IPX   Internetwork Packet Exchange (NetWare)

IRU   Indefeasible Rights of Use

IS   Information Systems

ISDN   Integrated Services Digital Network

ISO   International Organization for Standardization

ISO   Information Systems Organization

ISOC   Internet Society

ISP   Internet Service Provider

ISUP   ISDN User Part (SS7)

IT   Information Technology

ITU   International Telecommunication Union

ITU-R   International Telecommunication Union-Radio Communication Sector

IVD   Inside Vapor Deposition

IVR   Interactive Voice Response

IXC   Interexchange Carrier

JAN   Japanese Article Numbering System

JEPI   Joint Electronic Paynets Initiative

JES   Job Entry System

JIT   Just in Time

JPEG   Joint Photographic Experts Group

JTC   Joint Technical Committee

KB   Kilobytes

Kbps   Kilobits per Second (thousand bits per second)

KLTN   Potassium Lithium Tantalate Niobate

KM   Knowledge Management

LAN   Local area Network

LANE   LAN Emulation

LAP   Link Access Procedure (X.25)

LAPB   Link Access Procedure Balanced (X.25)

LAPD   Link Access Procedure for the D-Channel

LAPF   Link Access Procedure to Frame Mode Bearer Services

LAPF-Core   Core Aspects of the Link Access Procedure to Frame Mode Bearer Services

LAPM   Link Access Procedure for Modems

LAPX   Link Access Procedure Half-Duplex

LASER   Light Amplification by the Stimulated Emission of Radiation

LATA   Local Access and Transport Area

LCD   Liquid Crystal Display

LCGN   Logical Channel Group Number

LCM   Line Concentrator Module

LCN   Local Communications Network

LD   Laser Diode

LDAP   Lightweight Directory Access Protocol (X.500)

LEAF®   Large Effective Area Fiber (Corning product)

LEC   Local Exchange Carrier

LED   Light-Emitting Diode

LENS   Lightwave Efficient Network Solution (Centerpoint)

LEOS   Low Earth Orbit Satellite

LER   Label Edge Router

LI   Length Iindicator

LIDB   Line Information Database

LIFO   Last in First Out

LIS   Logical IP Subnet

LLC   Logical Link Control

LMDS   Local Mmultipoint Distribution System

LMI   Local Management Interface

LMOS   Loop Maintenance Operations System

LORAN   Long-Range Radio Navigation

LPC   Linear Predictive Coding

LPP   Lightweight Presentation Protocol

LRC   Longitudinal Redundancy Check (BISYNC)

LS   Link State

LSI   Large-Scale Integration

LSP   Label-Switched Path

LSR   Label-Switched Router

LU   Line Unit

LU   Logical Unit (SNA)

MAC   Media Access Control

MAN   Metropolitan Area Network

MAP   Mobile Application Part

MAP   Manufacturing Automation Protocol

MAU   Medium Attachment Unit (Ethernet)

MAU   Multistation Access Unit (Token Ring)

MB   Megabyte

MBA™   Metro Business Access (Ocular)

Mbps   Megabits per Second (million bits per second)

MD   Message Digest (MD2, MD4, MD5) (IETF)

MDF   Main Distribution Frame

MDU   Multidwelling Unit

MEMS   Micro Electrical Mechanical System

MF   Multifrequency

MFJ   Modified Final Judgment

MHS   Message Handling System (X.400)

MIB   Management information Base

MIC   Medium Interface Connector (FDDI)

MIME   Multipurpose Internet Mail Extension (IETF)

MIPS   Millions of Instructions per Second

MIS   Management Information System

MITI   Ministry of International Trade and Industry (Japan)

MITS   Micro Instrumentation and Telemetry Systems

ML-PPP   Multilink Point-to-Point Protocol

MMDS   Multichannel, Multipoint Distribution System

MMF   Multimode Fiber

MNP   Microcom Networking Protocol

MON   Metropolitan Optical Network

MoU   Memorandum of Understanding

MP   Multilink PPP

MPEG   Motion Picture Experts Group

MPLS   Multiprotocol Label Switching

MPOA   Multiprotocol over ATM

MPÏS   Multiprotocol Lambda Switching

MRFC   Media Resource Function Controller

MRFP   Media Resource Function Processor

MRI   Magnetic Resonance Imaging

MSB   Most Significant Bit

MSC   Mobile Switching Center

MSO   Mobile Switching Office

MSPP   Multi-Service Provisioning Platform

MSVC   Meta-Signaling Virtual Channel

MTA   Major Trading Area

MTBF   Mean Time Between Failures

MTP   Message Transfer Part (SS7)

MTSO   Mobile Telephone Switching Office

MTTR   Mean Time to Repair

MTU   Maximum Transmission Unit

MTU   Multitenant Unit

MVNE   Mobile Virtual Network Enabler

MVNO   Mobile Virtual Network Operator

MVS   Multiple Virtual Storage

NAD   Node Address (RFID)

NAFTA   North American Free Trade Agreement

NAK   Negative Acknowledgment (BISYNC, DDCMP)

NAP   Network Access Point (Internet)

NARUC   National Association of Regulatory Utility Commissioners

NAS   Network Attached Storage

NASA   National Aeronautics and Space Administration

NASDAQ   National Association of Securities Dealers Automated Quotations

NATA   North American Telecommunications Association

NATO   North Atlantic Treaty Organization

NAU   Network Accessible Unit

NCP   Network Control Program

NCSA   National Center for Supercomputer Applications

NCTA   National Cable Television Association

NDIS   Network Driver Interface Specifications

NDSF   Non-Dispersion-Shifted Fiber

NetBEUI   NetBIOS Extended User Interface

NetBIOS   Network Basic Input/Output System

NFS   Network File System (Sun)

NGN   Next-Generation Network

NGOSS   Next-Generation Operations Support System

NIC   Network Interface Card

NII   National Information Infrastructure

NIST   National Institute of Standards and Technology (formerly NBS)

NIU   Network Interface Unit

NLPID   Network Layer Protocol Identifier

NLSP   NetWare Link Services Protocol

NM   Network module

Nm   Nanometer

NMC   Network Management Center

NMS   Network Management System

NMT   Nordic Mobile Telephone

NMVT   Network Management Vector Transport Protocol

NNI   Network Node Interface

NNI   Network-to-Network Interface

NOC   Network Operations Center

NOCC   Network Operations Control Center

NOPAT   Net Operating Profit after Tax

NOS   Network Operating System

NPA   Numbering Plan Area

NREN   National Research and Education Network

NRZ   Non-Return to Zero

NRZI   Non-Return to Zero Inverted

NSA   National Security Agency

NSAP   Network Service Access Point

NSAPA   Network Service Access Point Address

NSF   National Science Foundation

NTSC   National Television Systems Committee

NTT   Nippon Telephone and Telegraph

NVB   Number of Valid Bits (RFID)

NVOD   Near Video on Demand

NZDSF   Non-Zero Dispersion-Shifted Fiber

OADM   Optical Add-Drop Multiplexer

OAM   Operations, Administration, and Maintenance

OAM&P   Operations, Administration, Maintenance, and Provisioning

OAN   Optical Area Network

OBS   Optical burst Switching

OC   Optical Carrier

OEM   Original Equipment Manufacturer

O-E-O   Optical-Electrical-Optical

OLS   Optical Line System (Lucent)

OMAP   Operations, Maintenance, and Administration Part (SS7)

ONA   Open Network Architecture

ONS   Object Name Service

ONU   Optical Network Unit

OOF   Out of Frame

OPEX   Operating Expenses

OS   Operating System

OSA   Open Systems Architecture

OSF   Open Software Foundation

OSI   Open Systems Interconnection (ISO, ITU-T)

OSI RM   Open Systems Interconnection Reference Model

OSPF   Open Shortest Path First (IETF)

OSS   Operation Support Systems

OTDM   Optical Time Division Multiplexing

OTDR   Optical Time-Domain Reflectometer

OUI   Organizationally Unique Identifier (SNAP)

OVD   Outside Vapor Deposition

OXC   Optical Cross-Connect

P/F   Poll/Final (HDLC)

PAD   Packet Assembler/Disassembler (X.25)

PAL   Phase Alternate Line

PAM   Pulse Amplitude Modulation

PANS   Pretty Amazing New Stuff

PBX   Private Branch Exchange

PCB   Protocol Control Byte (RFID)

PCI   Pulse Code Modulation

PCI   Peripheral Component Interface

PCMCIA   Personal Computer Memory Card International Association

PCN   Personal Communications Network

PCS   Personal Communications Services

P-CSCF   Proxy Call Session Control Function

PDA   Personal Digital Assistant

PDF   Policy Decision Function

PDH   Plesiochronous Digital Hierarchy

PDU   Protocol Data Unit

PIN   Positive-Intrinsic-Negative

PING   Packet Internet Groper (TCP/IP)

PKC   Public Key Cryptography

PLCP   Physical Layer Convergence Protocol

PLP   Packet Layer Protocol (X.25)

PM   Phase Modulation

PMD   Physical Medium Dependent (FDDI)

PML   Physical Markup Language

PNNI   Private Network Node Interface (ATM)

PoC   Push-to-Talk over Cellular

PON   Passive Optical Networking

POP   Point of Presence

POSIT   Profiles for Open Systems Interworking Technologies

POSIX   Portable Operating System Interface for UNIX

POTS   Plain Old Telephone Service

PPM   Pulse Position Modulation

PPP   Point-to-Point Protocol (IETF)

PPS   Protocol Parameter Selection (RFID)

PRC   Primary Reference Clock

PRI   Primary Rate Interface

PROFS   Professional Office System

PROM   Programmable Read-Only Memory

PSDN   Packet Switched Data Network

PSK   Phase Shift Keying (RFID)

PSPDN   Packet Switched Public Data Network

PSTN   Public Switched Telephone Network

PTI   Payload Type Identifier (ATM)

PTT   Post, Telephone, and Telegraph

PU   Physical Unit (SNA)

PUC   Public Utility Commission

PUPI   Pseudo-Unique PICC Identifier

PVC   Permanent Virtual Circuit

QAM   Quadrature Amplitude Modulation

Q-bit   Qualified Data Bit (X.25)

QLLC   Qualified Logical Link Control (SNA)

QoS   Quality of Service

QPSK   Quadrature Phase Shift Keying

QPSX   Queued Packet Synchronous Exchange

R&D   Research and Development

RADAR   Radio Detection and Ranging

RADSL   Rate Adaptive Digital Subscriber Line

RAID   Redundant Array of Inexpensive Disks

RAM   Random-Access Memory

RAN   Radio Access Network

RARP   Reverse Address Resolution Protocol (IETF)

RAS   Remote Access Server

RATS   Request for Answer to Select (RFID)

RBOC   Regional Bell Operating Company

READ_DATA   Read Data from Transponder (RFID)

REQA   Request A (RFID)

REQB   Request B (RFID)

REQUEST_SNR   Request Serial Number (RFID)

RF   Radio Frequency

RFC   Request for Comments (IETF)

RFH   Remote Frame Handler (ISDN)

RFI   Radio frequency Interference

RFID   Radio Frequency Identification

RFP   Request for Proposal

RFQ   Request for Quote

RFx   Request for X, where "X" can be Proposal, Quote, Information, Comment, etc.

RHC   Regional Holding Company

RHK   Ryan, Hankin and Kent (Consultancy)

RIP   Routing Information Protocol (IETF)

RISC   Reduced Instruction Set Computer

RJE   Remote Job Entry

RNR   Receive Not Ready (HDLC)

ROA   Return on Assets

ROE   Return on Equity

ROI   Return on Investment

ROM   Read-Only Memory

RO-RO   Roll-On Roll-Off

ROSE   Remote Operation Service Element

RPC   Remote Procedure Call

RPR   Resilient Packet Ring

RR   Receive Ready (HDLC)

RSA   Rivest, Shamir, and Aleman

RTS   Request to Send (EIA-232-E)

RTT   Round-Trip Translation

S/DMS   SONET/Digital Multiplex System

S/N   Signal-to-Noise Ratio

SAA   Systems Application Architecture (IBM)

SAAL   Signaling ATM Adaptation Layer (ATM)

SABM   Set Asynchronous Balanced Mode (HDLC)

SABME   Set Asynchronous Balanced Mode Extended (HDLC)

SAC   Single Attachment Concentrator (FDDI)

SAK   Select Acknowledge (RFID)

SAN   Storage Area Network

SAP   Service Access Point (generic)

SAPI   Service Access Point Identifier (LAPD)

SAR   Segmentation and Reassembly (ATM)

SAS   Single Attachment Station (FDDI)

SASE   Specific Applications Service Element (subset of CASE, Application Layer)

SATAN   System Administrator Tool for Analyzing Networks

SBLP   Service-Based Local Policy

SBS   Stimulated Brillouin Scattering

SCCP   Signaling Connection Control Point (SS7)

SCM   Supply Chain Management

SCP   Service Control Point (SS7)

SCREAM   Scalable Control of a Rearrangeable Extensible Array of Mirrors (Calient)

S-CSCF   Serving Call Session Control Function

SCSI   Small Computer Systems Interface

SCTE   Serial Clock Transmit External (EIA-232-E)

SDH   Synchronous Digital Hierarchy (ITU-T)

SDLC   Synchronous Data Link Control (IBM)

SDS   Scientific Data Systems

SEC   Securities and Exchange Commission

SECAM   Sequential Color with Memory

SELECT   Select Transponder (RFID)

SELECT_ACKNOWLEDGE   Acknowledge Selection (RFID)

SELECT_SNR   Select Serial Number (RFID)

SF   Superframe Format (T-1)

SFGI   Startup Frame Guard Integer (RFID)

SGML   Standard Generalized Markup Language

SGMP   Simple Gateway Management Protocol (IETF)

SGSN   Serving GPRS Support Node

SHDSL   Symmetric HDSL

S-HTTP   Secure HTTP (IETF)

SIF   Signaling Information Field

SIG   Special Interest Group

SIO   Service Information Octet

SIP   Session Initiation Protocol

SIP   Serial Interface Protocol

SIR   Sustained Information Rate (SMDS)

SLA   Service-Level Agreement

SLIP   Serial Line Interface Protocol (IETF)

SM   Switching Module

SMAP   System Management Application Part

SMDS   Switched Multimegabit Data Service

SMF   Single Mode Fiber

SMP   Simple Management Protocol

SMP   Switching Module Processor

SMR   Specialized Mobile Radio

SMS   Standard Management System (SS7)

SMTP   Simple Mail Transfer Protocol (IETF)

SNA   Systems Network Architecture (IBM)

SNAP   Subnetwork Access Protocol

SNI   Subscriber Network Interface (SMDS)

SNMP   Simple Network Management Protocol (IETF)

SNP   Sequence Number Protection

SNR   Serial Number (RFID)

SOAP   Simple Object Access Protocol

SOHO   Small-Office, Home-Office

SONET   Synchronous Optical Network

SPAG   Standards Promotion and Application Group

SPARC   Scalable Performance Architecture

SPE   Synchronous Payload Envelope (SONET)

SPID   Service Profile Identifier (ISDN)

SPM   Self Phase Modulation

SPOC   Single Point of Contact

SPX   Sequenced Packet Exchange (NetWare)

SQL   Structured Query Language

SRB   Source Route Bridging

SRLP   Service-Related Local Policy

SRP   Spatial Reuse Protocol

SRS   Stimulated Raman Scattering

SRT   Source Routing Transparent

SS7   Signaling System Seven

SSCC   Serial Shipping Container Code

SSL   Secure Socket Layer (IETF)

SSP   Service Switching Point (SS7)

SSR   Secondary Surveillance RADAR

SST   Spread Spectrum Transmission

STDM   Statistical Time Division Multiplexing

STM   Synchronous Transfer Mode

STM   Synchronous Transport Module (SDH)

STP   Signal Transfer Point (SS7)

STP   Shielded Twisted Pair

STS   Synchronous Transport Signal (SONET)

STX   Start of Text (BISYNC)

SVC   Signaling Virtual Channel (ATM)

SVC   Switched Virtual Circuit

SXS   Step-by-Step Switching

SYN   Synchronization

SYNTRAN   Synchronous Transmission

TA   Terminal Adapter (ISDN)

TAG   Technical Advisory Group

TASI   Time Assigned Speech Interpolation

TAXI   Transparent Asynchronous Transmitter/Receiver Interface
    (physical layer)

TCAP   Transaction Capabilities Application Part (SS7)

TCM   Time Compression Multiplexing

TCM   Trellis Coding Modulation

TCP   Transmission Control Protocol (IETF)

TDD   Time Division Duplexing

TDM   Time Division Multiplexing

TDMA   Time Division Multiple Access

TDR   Time Domain Reflectometer

TE1   Terminal Equipment Type 1 (ISDN-capable)

TE2   Terminal Equipment Type 2 (non-ISDN-capable)

TEI   Terminal Endpoint Identifier (LAPD)

TELRIC   Total Element Long-Run Incremental Cost

THIG   Topology-Hiding Interface Gateway

TIA   Telecommunications Industry Association

TIRIS   TI RF Identification Systems (Texas Instruments)

TIRKS   Trunk Integrated Record Keeping System

TL1   Transaction Language 1

TLAN   Transparent LAN

TM   Terminal Multiplexer

TMN   Telecommunications Management Network

TMS   Time-Multiplexed Switch

TOH   Transport Overhead (SONET)

TOP   Technical and Office Protocol

TOS   Type of Service (IP)

TP   Twisted Pair

TR   Token Ring

TRA   Traffic Routing Administration

TSI   Time Slot Interchange

TSLRIC   Total Service Long-Run Incremental Cost

TSO   Terminating Screening Office

TSO   Time-Sharing Option (IBM)

TSR   Terminate and Stay Resident

TSS   Telecommunication Standardization Sector (ITU-T)

TST   Time-Space-Time Switching

TSTS   Time-Space-Time-Space Switching

TTL   Time to Live

TU   Tributary Unit (SDH)

TUG   Tributary Unit Group (SDH)

TUP   Telephone User Part (SS7)

UA   Unnumbered Acknowledgment (HDLC)

UART   Universal Asynchronous Receiver Transmitter

UBR   Unspecified Bit Rate (ATM)

UCC   Uniform Code Council

UDI   Unrestricted Digital Information (ISDN)

UDP   User Datagram Protocol (IETF)

UHF   Ultra-High Frequency

UI   Unnumbered Information (HDLC)

UMTS   Universal Mobile Telephony System

UNI   User-to-Network Interface (ATM, FR)

UNIT   Unified Network Interface Technology (Ocular)

UNMA   Unified Network Management Architecture

UNSELECT   Unselect Transponder (RFID)

UPC   Universal Product Code

UPS   Uninterruptible Power Wupply

UPSR   Unidirectional Path Switched Ring

UPT   Universal personal telecommunications

URL   Uniform Resource Locator

USART   Universal Synchronous Asynchronous Receiver Transmitter

USB   Universal Serial Bus

UTC   Coordinated Universal Time

UTP   Unshielded Twisted Pair (physical layer)

UUCP   UNIX-UNIX Copy

VAN   Value-Added Network

VAX   Virtual Address Extension (DEC)

vBNS   Very High Speed Backbone Network Service

VBR   Variable Bit Rate (ATM)

VBR-NRT   Variable Bit Rate-Non-Real-Time (ATM)

VBR-RT   Variable Bit Rate-Real-Time (ATM)

VC   Venture Capital

VC   Virtual Channel (ATM)

VC   Virtual Circuit (PSN)

VC   Virtual Container (SDH)

VCC   Virtual Channel Connection (ATM)

VCI   Virtual Channel Identifier (ATM)

VCSEL   Vertical Cavity Surface Emitting Laser

VDSL   Very High-Speed Digital Subscriber Line

VDSL   Very High Bit Rate Digital Subscriber Line

VERONICA   Very Easy Rodent-Oriented Netwide Index to
   Computerized Archives (Internet)

VGA   Variable Graphics Array

VHF   Very High Frequency

VHS   Video Home System

VID   VLAN ID

VIN   Vehicle Identification Number

VINES   Virtual Networking System (Banyan)

VIP   VINES Internet Protocol

VLAN   Virtual LAN

VLF   Very Low Frequency

VLR   Visitor Location Register (Wireless)

VLSI   Very Large Scale Integration

VM   Virtual Machine (IBM)

VM   Virtual Memory

VMS   Virtual Memory System (DEC)

VOD   Video-on-Demand

VP   Virtual Path

VPC   Virtual Path Connection

VPI   Virtual Path Identifier

VPN   Virtual Private Network

VR   Virtual Reality

VSAT   Very Small Aperture Terminal

VSB   Vestigial Sideband

VSELP   Vector-Sum Excited Linear Prediction

VT   Virtual Tributary

VTAM   Virtual Telecommunications Access Method (SNA)

VTOA   Voice and Telephony over ATM

VTP   Virtual Terminal Protocol (ISO)

WACK   Wait Acknowledgment (BISYNC)

WACS   Wireless Access Communications System

WAIS   Wide Area Information Server (IETF)

WAN   Wide Area Network

WAP   Wireless Application Protocol (Wrong Approach to Portability)

WARC   World Administrative Radio Conference

WATS   Wide Area Telecommunications Service

WDM   Wavelength Division Multiplexing

WIN   Wireless In-Building Network

WISP   Wireless ISP

WTO   World Trade Organization

WWW   World Wide Web (IETF)

WYSIWYG   What You See Is What You Get

xDSL   x-Type Digital Subscriber Line

XID   Exchange Identification (HDLC)

XML   Extensible Markup Language

XNS   Xerox Network Systems

XPM   Cross Phase Modulation

ZBTSI   Zero Byte Time Slot Interchange

ZCS   Zero Code Suppression

APPENDIX **B**

Glossary
of Terms

▰▰ Numerical

3G 3G systems will provide access to a wide range of telecommunication services supported by both fixed telecommunication networks and services specific to mobile users. A range of mobile terminal types will be supported and may be designed for mobile or fixed use. Key features of these systems are compatibility of services, small terminals with worldwide roaming capability, Internet and other multimedia applications, high bandwidth, and a wide range of services and terminals.

4G 4G networks extend 3G network capacity by an order of magnitude, rely entirely on a packet infrastructure, use network elements that are 100% digital, and offer extremely high bandwidth.

▰▰ A

Abend A contraction of the words *abnormal* and *end*; used to describe a computer crash in the mainframe world.

Absorption A form of optical attenuation in which optical energy is converted to an alternative form, often heat. Often caused by impurities in the fiber; hydroxyl absorption is the best-known form.

Acceptance angle The critical angle within which incident light is totally internally reflected inside the core of an optical fiber.

Access The set of technologies employed by a user to reach the network.

Accounts payable Amounts owed to suppliers and vendors for products and/or services that have been delivered on credit. Most accounts payable agreements call for the credit to be reconciled within 30 to 60 days.

Accounts receivable Money that is owed to a corporation.

Add-Drop Multiplexer (ADM) A device used in SONET and SDH systems that has the ability to add and remove signal components without having to demultiplex the entire transmitted transmission stream; this is a significant advantage over legacy multiplexing systems such as DS3.

Aerial plant Transmission equipment (media, amplifiers, splice cases, etc.) that is suspended in the air between poles.

ALOHA The name given to the first local area network, which was designed and implemented in Hawaii and used to interconnect the various campuses of that state's university system.

Alternate Mark Inversion The encoding scheme used in T-1. Every other "1" is inverted in polarity from the "1" that preceded or followed it.

ALU (Arithmetic Logic Unit) The "brain" of a CPU chip.

Amplifier A device that increases the transmitted power of a signal. Amplifiers typically are spaced at carefully selected intervals along a transmission span.

Amplitude modulation A signal-encoding technique in which the amplitude of the carrier is modified according to the behavior of the signal it is transporting.

Amplitude modulation The process of causing an electromagnetic wave to carry information by changing or modulating the amplitude or loudness of the wave.

AMPS (Advanced Mobile Phone Service) The modern analog cellular network.

Analog A signal that continuously varies in time. Functionally, the opposite of digital.

Analog A word that means "constantly varying in time."

Angular misalignment The reason for loss at the fiber ingress point. If the light source is improperly aligned with the fiber's core, some of the incident light will be lost, leading to reduced signal strength.

Armor The rigid protective coating on some fiber cables that protects them from being crushed and being chewed by rodents.

ASCII (American Standards Code for Information Interchange) A 7-bit data-encoding scheme.

ASIC (Application-Specific Integrated Circuit) A specially designed Integrated Circuit (IC) created for a specific application.

Asset What a company owns.

Asynchronous Data that is transmitted between two devices that do not have a common clock source.

Asynchronous Transfer Mode (ATM) A standard for switching and multiplexing that relies on the transport of fixed-size data entities called cells that are 53 octets in length. ATM has gotten a great deal of attention lately because its internal workings allow it to provide quality of service (QoS), a much-demanded option in modern data networks.

ATM (Asynchronous Transfer Mode) One of the family of so-called fast packet technologies characterized by low error rates, high speed, and low cost. ATM is designed to connect seamlessly with SONET and SDH.

ATM Adaptation Layer (AAL) In ATM, the layer responsible for matching the payload being transported to a requested quality of service level by assigning an ALL Type to which the network responds.

Attenuation The reduction in signal strength in optical fiber that results from absorption and scattering effects.

Avalanche photodiode (APD) An optical semiconductor receiver that has the ability to amplify weak received optical signals by "multiplying" the number of received photons to intensify the strength of the received signal. APDs are used in transmission systems in which receiver sensitivity is a critical issue.

Average revenue per user (ARPU) The average amount of revenue generated by each customer; calculated by dividing total revenue by the total number of subscribers.

Axis The center line of an optical fiber.

B

Back scattering The problem that occurs when light is scattered backward into the transmitter of an optical system. This impairment is analogous to the echo that occurs in copper-based systems.

Balance sheet Provides a view of what a company owns (its assets) and what it owes to creditors (its liabilities). The assets always equal the sum of the liabilities and shareholder equity. Liabilities represent obligations the firm has against its own assets. Accounts payable, for example, represent funds that are owed to someone or to another company that is outside the corporation but that are balanced by a service or physical asset that has been provided to the company.

Bandwidth A measure of the number of bits per second that can be transmitted down a channel.

Bandwidth The range of frequencies within which a transmission system operates.

Bar code A machine-scannable product identification label that consists of a pattern of alternating thick and thin lines that uniquely identify the product to which they are affixed.

Baseband In signaling, any technique that uses digital signal representation.

Baud The signaling rate of a transmission system. One of the most misunderstood terms in telecommunications. Often used synonymously with bits per second, baud usually has a very different meaning. Through the use of multibit encoding techniques, a single signal can simultaneously represent multiple bits. Thus, the bit rate can be many times the signaling rate.

Beam splitter An optical device used to direct a single signal in multiple directions through the use of a partially reflective mirror or another optical filter.

BECN (Backward Explicit Congestion Notification) A bit used in frame relay to notify a device that it is transmitting too much information into the network and is therefore in violation of its service agreement with the switch.

Bell System Reference Frequency (BSRF) In the early days of the Bell System, a single timing source in the Midwest provided a timing signal for all central office equipment in the country. This signal, which was delivered from a very expensive cesium clock source, was known as the BSRF. Today GPS is used as the main reference clock source.

Bend radius The maximum degree to which a fiber can be bent before serious signal loss or fiber breakage occur. One of the functional characteristics of most fiber products.

Bending loss Loss that occurs when a fiber is bent far enough that its maximum allowable bend radius is exceeded. In this case, some of the light escapes from the waveguide, resulting in signal degradation.

Bidirectional Refers to a system that is capable of transmitting simultaneously in both directions.

Binary A counting scheme that uses base 2.

Bit rate Bits per second.

Bluetooth An open wireless standard designed to operate at a gross transmission level of 1 Mbps. It is being positioned as a connectivity standard for personal area networks.

Bragg grating A device that relies on the formation of interference patterns to filter specific wavelengths of light from a transmitted signal.

In optical systems, these gratings usually are created by wrapping a grating of the correct size around a piece of fiber that has been made photosensitive. The fiber then is exposed to strong ultraviolet light that passes through the grating, forming areas of high and low refractive indexes. Bragg gratings (or filters, as they often are called) are used for selecting certain wavelengths of a transmitted signal and often are used in optical switches, DWDM systems, and tunable lasers.

Broadband　Historically, any signal that is faster than the ISDN Primary Rate (T1 or E1). Today, it means "big pipe," in other words, a very high transmission speed.

Broadband　In signaling this term means analog; in data transmission it means "big pipe" (high bandwidth).

Buffer　A coating that surrounds optical fiber in a cable and offers protection from water, abrasion, and so on.

Building Integrated Timing Supply (BITS)　The central office device that receives the clock signal from GPS or another source and feeds it to the devices in the office it controls.

Bull's-eye code　The earliest form of bar code, consisting of a series of concentric circles so that the code could be read from any angle.

Bundling　A product sales strategy in which multiple services (voice, video, entertainment, Internet, wireless, etc.) are sold as a converged package and invoiced with a single easy-to-understand bill.

Bus　The parallel cable that interconnects the components of a computer.

Butt splice　A technique in which two fibers are joined end to end by fusing them with heat or optical cement.

C

Cable　An assembly made up of multiple optical or electrical conductors as well as other inclusions, such as strength members, waterproofing materials, and armor.

Cable assembly　A complete optical cable that includes the fiber itself and terminators on each end to make it capable of attaching to a transmission or receiving device.

Cable plant   The entire collection of transmission equipment in a system, including the signal emitters, the transport media, the switching and multiplexing equipment, and the receive devices.

Cable vault   The subterranean room in a central office where cables enter and leave the building.

Call center   A room in which operators receive calls from customers.

Capacitance   An electrical phenomenon by which an electric charge is stored in a circuit.

Capacitive coupling   The transfer of electromagnetic energy from one circuit to another through mutual capacitance, which is the ability of a surface to store an electric charge. Capacitance is simply a measure of the electrical storage capacity between the circuits. Similar to inductive coupling, capacitive coupling can be both intentional and unplanned.

Capital expenditures (CAPEX)   Wealth in the form of money or property, typically accumulated in a business by a person, partnership, or corporation. In most cases capital expenditures can be amortized over a period of several years, most commonly five years.

Capital intensity   A measure that has begun to appear as a valid measure of financial performance for large telecom operators. It is calculated by dividing capital spending (CAPEX) by revenue.

Cash burn   A term that became a part of the common lexicon during the dot-com years. Refers to the rate at which companies consume their available cash.

Cash flow   One of the most common measures of valuation for public and private companies. True cash flow is exactly that: a measure of the cash that flows through a company during a defined period after factoring out all fixed expenses. In many cases cash flow is equated to EBITDA. Usually, it is defined as income after taxes minus preferred dividends plus depreciation and amortization.

CCITT (Consultative Committee on International Telegraphy and Telephony)   Defunct; has been replaced by the ITU-TSS.

CDMA (Code Division Multiple Access)   One of several digital cellular access schemes. Relies on frequency hopping and noise modulation to encode conversations.

Cell   The standard protocol data unit in ATM networks. It consists of a 5-byte header and a 48-octet payload field.

Cell Loss Priority (CLP)   In ATM, a rudimentary single-bit field used to assign priority to transported payloads.

Cell Relay Service (CRS) In ATM, the most primitive service offered by service providers, consisting of only raw bit transport with no assigned AAL types.

Cellular telephony The wireless telephony system characterized by low-power cells, frequency reuse, handoff, and central administration.

Center wavelength The central operating wavelength of a laser used for data transmission.

Central office A building that houses shared telephony equipment such as switches, multiplexers, and cable distribution hardware.

Central office terminal (COT) In loop carrier systems, the device in the central office that provides multiplexing and demultiplexing services. It is connected to the remote terminal.

Chained layers The lower three layers of the OSI model that provide for connectivity.

Chirp A problem that occurs in laser diodes when the center wavelength shifts momentarily during the transmission of a single pulse. Caused by instability of the laser itself.

Chromatic dispersion Because the wavelength of transmitted light determines its propagation speed in an optical fiber, different wavelengths of light travel at different speeds during transmission. As a result, the multiwavelength pulse tends to "spread out" during transmission, causing difficulties for the receive device. Material dispersion, waveguide dispersion, and profile dispersion all contribute to the problem.

CIR (Committed Information Rate) The volume of data a frame relay provider absolutely guarantees it will transport for a customer.

Circuit Emulation Service (CES) In ATM, a service that emulates private line service by modifying (1) the number of cells transmitted per second and (2) the number of bytes of data contained in the payload of each cell.

Cladding The fused silica "coating" that surrounds the core of an optical fiber. It typically has a different index of refraction than does the core, causing light that escapes from the core into the cladding to be refracted back into the core.

CLEC (Competitive Local Exchange Carrier) A small telephone company that competes with the incumbent player in its own marketplace.

Close-coupling smart card A card that is defined by extremely short read ranges; is similar to contact-based smart cards. These devices are designed to be used with an insertion reader, similar to what often is seen in modern hotel room doors.

CMOS (Complementary Metal Oxide Semiconductor) A form of integrated circuit technology that typically is used in low-speed and low-power applications.

Coating The plastic substance that covers the cladding of an optical fiber. Used to prevent damage to the fiber through abrasion.

Coherent Refers to a form of emitted light in which all the rays of the transmitted light align themselves the same transmission axis, resulting in a narrow, tightly focused beam. Lasers emit coherent light.

Compression The process of reducing the size of a transmitted file without losing the integrity of the content by eliminating redundant information before transmitting or storing.

Concatenation A technique used in SONET and SDH in which multiple payloads are "ganged" together to form a superrate frame capable of transporting payloads greater in size than the basic transmission speed of the system. Thus, an OC-12c provides 622.08 Mbps of total bandwidth, as opposed to an OC-12, which also offers 622.08 Mbps, but in increments of OC-1 (51.84 Mbps).

Conditioning The process of "doctoring" a dedicated circuit to eliminate the known and predictable results of distortion.

Congestion The condition that results when traffic arrives faster than it can be processed by a server.

Connectivity The process of providing electrical transport of data.

Connector A device, usually mechanical, used to connect a fiber to a transmit or receive device or to bond two fibers.

Core The central portion of an optical fiber that provides the primary transmission path for an optical signal. It usually has a higher index of refraction than does the cladding.

Core The central high-speed transport region of the network.

Counter-rotating ring A form of transmission system that includes two rings operating in opposite directions. Typically, one ring serves as the active path and the other serves as the protect or backup path.

CPU (Central Processing Unit) The chipset in a computer that provides the intelligence.

CRC (Cyclic Redundancy Check) A mathematical technique for checking the integrity of the bits in a transmitted file.

Critical angle   The angle at which total internal reflection occurs.

Cross-phase modulation (XPM)   A problem that occurs in optical fiber that results from the nonlinear index of refraction of the silica in the fiber. Because the index of refraction varies with the strength of the transmitted signal, some signals interact with each other in destructive ways. Considered to be a fiber nonlinearity.

CSMA/CD (Carrier Sense, Multiple Access with Collision Detection) The medium access scheme used in Ethernet LANs; characterized by an "if it feels, good do it" approach.

Current assets   The assets on the balance sheet that typically are expected to be converted to cash within a year of the publication date of the balance sheet. Typically include line items such as accounts receivable, cash, inventories and supplies, any marketable securities held by the corporation, prepaid expenses, and a variety of other less critical items that typically fall into the other line item.

Current liabilities   Obligations that must be repaid within a year.

Current ratio   Calculated by dividing the current assets for a financial period by the current liabilities for that period. A climbing current ratio might be a good indicator of improving financial performance but also could indicate that warehoused product volumes are climbing.

Customer relationship management (CRM)   A technique for managing the relationship between a service provider and a customer through the discrete management of knowledge about the customer.

Cutoff wavelength   The wavelength below which a single mode fiber ceases to be single mode.

Cylinder   A stack of tracks to which data can be written logically on a hard drive.

▰▰▰ **D**

Dark fiber   Optical fiber that sometimes is leased to a client that is not connected to a transmitter or receiver. In a dark fiber installation, it is the customer's responsibility to terminate the fiber.

Data   Raw, unprocessed 0s and 1s.

Data communications   The science of moving data between two or more communicating devices.

Data mining   A technique in which enterprises extract information about customers' behavior by analyzing data contained in their stored transaction records.

Datagram   The service provided by a connectionless network. Often said to be unreliable, this service makes no guarantees with regard to latency or sequentiality.

DCE (Data Circuit Terminating Equipment)   A modem or other device that delineates the end of the service provider's circuit.

DE (Discard Eligibility Bit)   A primitive single-bit technique for prioritizing traffic that is to be transmitted.

Debt to equity ratio   Calculated by dividing the total debt for a particular fiscal year by the total shareholder equity for the same financial period.

Decibel (dB)   A logarithmic measure of the strength of a transmitted signal. Because it is a logarithmic measure, a 20-dB loss indicates that the received signal is one one-hundredth its original strength.

Dense Wavelength Division Multiplexing (DWDM)   A form of frequency division multiplexing in which multiple wavelengths of light are transmitted across the same optical fiber. These systems typically operate in the so-called L-Band (1625 nm) and have channels that are spaced 50 to 100 GHz apart. Newly announced products may reduce this spacing dramatically.

Detector   An optical receive device that converts an optical signal to an electrical signal so that it can be handed off to a switch, router, multiplexer, or other electrical transmission device. These devices are usually either Negative-Positive-Negative (NPN) or Avalanche Photodiodes (APDs).

Diameter mismatch loss   Loss that occurs when the diameter of a light emitter and the diameter of the ingress fiber's core are dramatically different.

Dichroic filter   A filter that transmits light in a wavelength-specific fashion, reflecting nonselected wavelengths.

Dielectric   Refers to a substance that is nonconducting.

Diffraction grating   A grid of closely spaced lines that are used to direct specific wavelengths of light selectively as required.

Digital   Refers to a signal characterized by discrete states. The opposite of analog.

Digital   Literally, "discrete."

Digital Hierarchy   In North America, the multiplexing hierarchy that allows 64-Kbps DS-0 signals to be combined to form DS-3 signals for high bit rate transport.

Digital Subscriber Line Access Multiplexer (DSLAM)   The multiplexer in the central office that receives voice and data signals on separate channels, relaying voice to the local switch and data to a router elsewhere in the office.

Diode   A semiconductor device that allows current to flow only in a single direction.

Direct attached storage (DAS)   A storage option in which the storage media (hard drives, CDs, etc.) are either integral to the server (internally mounted) or directly connected to one of the servers.

Dispersion   The spreading a light signal over time that results from modal or chromatic inefficiencies in the fiber.

Dispersion compensating fiber (DCF)   A segment of fiber that exhibits the dispersion effect opposite to that of the fiber to which it is coupled. Used to counteract the dispersion of the other fiber.

Dispersion-shifted fiber (DSF)   A form of optical fiber that is designed to exhibit zero dispersion within the C-Band (1550 nm). Does not work well for DWDM because of Four Wave Mixing problems; Non-Zero Dispersion Shifted Fiber is used instead.

Distortion   A known and measurable (and therefore correctable) impairment on transmission facilities.

Dopant   A substance used to lower the refractive index of the silica used in optical fiber.

DS-0 (digital signal level 0)   A 64-Kbps signal.

DS-1 (digital signal level 1)   A 1.544-Mbps signal.

DS-2 (digital signal level 2)   A 6.312-Mbps signal.

DS3   A 44.736-Mbps signal format found in the North American Digital Hierarchy.

DSL (Digital Subscriber Line)   A technique for transporting high-speed digital data across the analog local loop while in some cases transporting voice simultaneously.

DTE (Data Terminal Equipment)   User equipment that is connected to a DCE.

DTMF (Dual-Tone, Multi-Frequency)   The set of tones used in modern phones to signal dialed digits to the switch. Each button triggers a pair of tones.

Duopoly   The current regulatory model for cellular systems. Two providers are assigned to each market. One is the wireline provider (typically the local ILEC), and the other is an independent provider.

DWDM (Dense Wavelength Division Multiplexing)   A form of frequency division multiplexing that allows multiple optical signals to be transported simultaneously across a single fiber.

E

E1   The 2.048-Mbps transmission standard used in Europe and some other parts of the world. It is analogous to the North American T1.

Earnings before interest, tax, depreciation, and amortization (EBITDA)   Sometimes called operating cash flow; used to evaluate a firm's operating profitability before subtracting nonoperating expenses such as interest and other core "nonbusiness" expenses and noncash charges. Long ago, cable companies and other highly capital-intensive industries substituted EBITDA for traditional cash flow as a *temporary* measure of financial performance without adding in the cost of building new infrastructure. Because it excluded all interest due on borrowed capital as well as the inevitable depreciation of assets, EBITDA was seen as a temporary better gauge of potential future performance.

Earnings per share (EPS)   Calculated by dividing annual earnings by the total number of outstanding shares.

EBCDIC (Extended Binary Coded Decimal Interchange Code)   An 8-bit data-encoding scheme.

Edge   The periphery of the network where aggregation, QoS, and IP implementation take place. Also where most of the intelligence in the network resides.

EDGE (Enhanced Data for Global Evolution)   A 384-Kbps enhancement to GSM.

Edge-emitting diode   A diode that emits light from the edge of the device rather than the surface, resulting in a more coherent and directed beam of light.

Effective-area The cross section of a single-mode fiber that carries the optical signal.

EIR (Excess Information Rate) The amount of data that is being transmitted by a user above the CIR in frame relay.

Encryption The process of modifying a text or image file to prevent unauthorized users from viewing the content.

End-to-end layers The upper four layers of the OSI model that provide interoperability.

Enterprise resource planning (ERP) A technique for managing customer interactions through data mining, knowledge management, and customer relationship management (CRM).

Erbium-Doped Fiber Amplifier (EDFA) A form of optical amplifier that uses the element erbium to bring about the amplification process. Erbium has the quality that when struck by light operating at 980 nm, it emits photons in the 1550-nm range, providing agnostic amplification for signals operating in the same transmission window.

ESF (Extended Superframe) The framing technique used in modern T-carrier systems that provides a dedicated data channel for nonintrusive testing of customer facilities.

Ethernet A LAN product developed by Xerox that relies on a CSMA/CD medium access scheme.

Evanescent wave Light that travels down the inner layer of the cladding instead of down the fiber core.

Extrinsic loss Loss that occurs at splice points in an optical fiber.

Eye pattern A measure of the degree to which bit errors are occurring in optical transmission systems. The width of the "eyes" (eye patterns look like figure eights lying on their sides) indicates the relative bit error rate.

F

Facilities-based A regulatory term that refers to the requirement that CLECs own their own physical facilities instead of relying on those of the ILEC for service delivery.

Facility A circuit.

Faraday effect Sometimes called the magneto-optical effect; describes the degree to which some materials can cause the polarization angle of incident light to change when placed within a magnetic field that is parallel to the propagation direction.

Fast Ethernet A version of Ethernet that operates at 100 Mbps.

Fast packet Refers to technologies characterized by low error rates, high speed, and low cost.

FDMA (Frequency Division Multiple Access) The access technique used in analog AMPS cellular systems.

FEC (Forward Error Correction) An error correction technique that sends enough additional overhead information along with the transmitted data so that a receiver not only can detect an error but actually can fix it without requesting a resend.

FECN (Forward Explicit Congestion Notification) A bit in the header of a frame relay frame that can be used to notify a distant switch that the frame experienced severe congestion on its way to the destination.

Ferrule A rigid or semirigid tube that surrounds optical fibers and protects them.

Fiber grating A segment of photosensitive optical fiber that has been treated with ultraviolet light to create a refractive index within the fiber that varies periodically along its length. It operates analogously to a fiber grating and is used to select specific wavelengths of light for transmission.

Fiber to the Curb (FTTC) A transmission architecture for service delivery in which a fiber is installed in a neighborhood and terminated at a junction box. From there, coaxial cable or twisted-pair cable can be cross-connected from the O-E converter to the customer premises. If coaxial is used, the system is called Hybrid Fiber Coax (HFC); twisted-pair-based systems are called Switched Digital Video (SDV).

Fiber to the Home (FTTH) Similar to FTTC except it FTTH extends the optical fiber all the way to the customer's premises.

Fibre Channel A set of standards for a serial I/O bus that supports a range of port speeds, including 133 Mbps, 266 Mbps, 530 Mbps, 1 Gbps, and, soon, 4 Gbps. The standard supports point-to-point connections, switched topologies, and arbitrated loop architecture.

Financial Accounting Standards Board (FASB) The officially recognized entity that establishes standards for accounting organizations to ensure commonality among countries and international accounting organizations.

Four Wave Mixing (FWM) The nastiest of the so-called fiber nonlinearities. Commonly seen in DWDM systems; occurs when the closely spaced channels mix and generate the equivalent of optical sidebands. The number of these sidebands can be expressed by the equation $\frac{1}{2}(n^3 - n^2)$, where n is the number of original channels in the system. Thus, a 16-channel DWDM system potentially will generate 1920 interfering sidebands.

Frame   A variable-size data transport entity.

Frame relay   One of the family of so-called fast packet technologies characterized by low error rates, high speed, and low cost.

Frame Relay Bearer Service (FRBS)   In ATM, a service that allows relay frame to be transported across an ATM network.

Freespace optics   A metro transport technique that uses a narrow unlicensed optical beam to transport high-speed data.

Frequency-agile   Refers to the ability of a receiving or transmitting device to change its frequency to take advantage of alternative channels.

Frequency-division multiplexing   The process of assigning specific frequencies to specific users.

Frequency modulation   The process of causing an electromagnetic wave to carry information by changing or modulating the frequency of the wave.

Fresnel loss   The loss that occurs at the interface between the head of the fiber and the light source to which it is attached. At air-glass interfaces the loss usually equates to about 4%.

Full-duplex   Two-way simultaneous transmission.

Fused fiber   A group of fibers that are fused together so that they remain in alignment. Often used in one-to-many distribution systems for the propagation of a single signal to multiple destinations. Fused fiber devices play a key role in passive optical networking (PON).

Fusion splice   A splice made by melting the ends of the fibers together.

G

Generally Accepted Accounting Principles (GAAP)   The commonly recognized accounting practices that ensure financial accounting standardization across multiple global entities.

Generic Flow Control (GFC)   In ATM, the first field in the cell header. It is largely unused except when it is overwritten in NNI cells, in which case it becomes additional space for virtual path addressing.

GEOS (Geosynchronous Earth Orbit Satellite) A family of satellites that orbit above the equator at an altitude of 22,300 miles and provide data and voice transport services.

Gigabit Ethernet A version of Ethernet that operates at 1000 Mbps.

Global Positioning System (GPS) The array of satellites used for radiolocation around the world. In the telephony world, GPS satellites provide an accurate timing signal for synchronizing office equipment.

Go-Back-N A technique for error correction that causes all frames of data to be transmitted again, starting with the errored frame.

Gozinta "Goes into."

Gozouta "Goes out of."

GPRS (General Packet Radio Service) An add-on for GSM networks that is not having a great deal of success in the market yet.

Graded index fiber (GRIN) A type of fiber in which the refractive index changes gradually between the central axis of the fiber and the outer layer instead of abruptly at the core-cladding interface.

Groom and fill Similar to add-drop; refers to the ability to add (fill) and drop (groom) payload components at intermediate locations along a network path.

Gross domestic product (GDP) The total market value of all the goods and services produced by a nation during a specific period.

GSM (Global System for Mobile Communications) The wireless access standard used in many parts of the world; offers two-way paging, short messaging, and two-way radio in addition to cellular telephony.

GUI (Graphical User Interface) The computer interface characterized by the "click, move, drop" method of file management.

▦ H

Half-duplex Two-way transmission, but in only one direction at a time.

Haptics The science of providing tactile feedback to a user electronically. Often used in high-end virtual reality systems.

Headend The signal origination point in a cable system.

Header In ATM, the first five bytes of the cell. Contains information used by the network to route the cell to its ultimate destination. Fields in the cell header include Generic Flow Control, Virtual Path Identifier, Virtual Channel Identifier, Payload Type Identifier, Cell Loss Priority, and Header Error Correction.

Header Error Correction (HEC) In ATM, the header field used to recover from bit errors in the header data.

Hertz (Hz) A measure of cycles per second in transmission systems.

Hop count A measure of the number of machines a message or packet has to pass through between the source and the destination. Often used as a diagnostic tool.

Hybrid fiber coax A transmission system architecture in which a fiber feeder penetrates a service area and then is cross-connected to coaxial cable feeders into the customer's premises.

Hybrid Loop An access facility that uses more than one medium, for example, Hybrid-Fiber Coax (HFC) or hybrids of fiber and copper twisted pair.

▉ I

ILEC (Incumbent Local Exchange Carrier) An RBOC.

Income statement Used to report a corporation's revenues, expenses, and net income (profit) for a particular defined time period. Sometimes called a profit and loss (P&L) statement or statement of operations. Charts a company's performance over a period of time. The results most often are reported as earnings per share and diluted earnings per share. Earnings per share is defined as the proportion of the firm's net income that can be accounted for on a per-share basis of outstanding common stock. It is calculated by subtracting preferred dividends from net income and dividing the result by the number of common shares that are outstanding. Diluted earnings per share takes into account earned or fully vested stock options that have not been exercised by their owner and shares that would be created from the conversion of convertible securities into stock.

Indefeasible Rights of Use (IRU) A long-term capacity lease of a cable. IRUs are identified by channels and available bandwidth and typically are granted for long periods.

Index of refraction   A measure of the ratio between the velocity of light in a vacuum and the velocity of the same light in an optical fiber. The refractive index is always greater than 1 and is denoted n.

Inductance   The property of an electric circuit by which an electromotive force is induced in it by a variation of current flowing through the circuit.

Inductive coupling   The transfer of electromagnetic energy from one circuit to another as a result of the mutual *inductance* between the circuits. May be intentional, as in an impedance matcher that matches the impedance of a transmitter or a receiver to an antenna to guarantee maximum power transfer, or may be unplanned, as in the power line inductive coupling that occasionally takes place in telephone lines, often referred to as crosstalk or hum.

Information   Data that has been converted to a manipulable form.

Infrared (IR)   The region of the spectrum within which most optical transmission systems operate; between 700 nm and 0.1 mm.

Injection laser   A semiconductor laser.

Inside plant   Telephony equipment that is outside the central office.

Intermodulation   A fiber nonlinearity that is similar to four-wave mixing, in which the power-dependent refractive index of the transmission medium allows signals to mix and create destructive sidebands.

Interoperability   Characterized by the ability to share information logically between two communicating devices and be able to read and understand the data of the other.

Interoperability   In SONET and SDH, the ability of devices from different manufacturers to send and receive information to and from each other successfully.

Intrinsic loss   Loss that occurs as the result of physical differences in two fibers being spliced.

ISDN (Integrated Services Digital Network)   A digital local loop technology that offers moderately high bit rates to customers.

Isochronous   A term used in timing systems to indicate that there is constant delay across a network.

ISP (Internet Service Provider)   A company that offers Internet access.

ITU (International Telecommunications Union)   A division of the United Nations that is responsible for managing the telecom standards development and maintenance processes.

ITU-TSS (ITU Telecommunications Standardization Sector)   The ITU organization responsible for telecommunications standards development.

J

Jacket   The protective outer coating of an optical fiber cable. The jacket may be polyethylene, Kevlar, or metal.

JPEG (Joint Photographic Experts Group)   A standards body tasked with developing standards for the compression of still images.

Jumper   An optical cable assembly, usually fairly short, that terminates on both ends with connectors.

K

Knowledge   Information that has been acted on and modified through some form of intuitive human thought process.

Knowledge management   The process of managing all that a company knows about its customers in an intelligent way so that some benefit is attained for both the customer and the service provider.

L

Lambda   A single wavelength on a multichannel DWDM system.

LAN (Local Area Network)   A small network that has the following characteristics: privately owned, high speed, low error rate, physically small.

LAN emulation (LANE)   In ATM, a service that defines the ability to provide bridging services between LANs across an ATM network.

Large core fiber   Fiber that characteristically has a core diameter of 200 microns or more.

Laser   An acronym for light amplification by the stimulated emission of radiation. Used in optical transmission systems because lasers produce coherent light that is almost purely monochromatic.

Laser diode (LD) A diode that produces coherent light when a forward biasing current is applied to it.

LATA (Local Access and Transport Area) The geographic area within which an ILEC is allowed to transport traffic. Beyond LATA boundaries the ILEC must hand traffic off to a long-distance carrier.

LEOS (Low Earth Orbit Satellite) A satellite that orbits pole to pole instead of above the equator and offers nearly instantaneous response time.

Liability Obligations a firm has against its own assets. Accounts payable, for example, represent funds that are owed to someone or to another company that is outside the corporation but that are balanced by some service or physical asset that has been provided to the company.

Light emitting diode (LED) A diode that emits incoherent light when a forward bias current is applied to it. Typically used in shorter-distance, lower-speed systems.

Lightguide A term used synonymously with optical fiber.

Line Overhead (LOH) In SONET, the overhead that is used to manage the network regions between multiplexers.

Line sharing A business relationship between an ILEC and a CLEC in which the CLEC provides logical DSL service over the ILEC's physical facilities.

Linewidth The spectrum of wavelengths that make up an optical signal.

Load coil A device that tunes the local loop to the voiceband.

Local loop The pair of wires (or digital channel) that runs between the customer's phone (or computer) and the switch in the local central office.

Long-term debt Debt that is typically due beyond the one-year maturity period of short-term debt.

Loose tube optical cable An optical cable assembly in which the fibers within the cable are loosely contained within tubes inside the sheath of the cable. The fibers are able to move within the tube, allowing them to adapt and move without damage as the cable is flexed and stretched.

Loss The reduction in signal strength that occurs over distance; usually expressed in decibels.

M

M13   A multiplexer that interfaces between DS-1 and DS-3 systems.

Mainframe   A large computer that offers support for very large databases and large numbers of simultaneous sessions.

MAN (Metropolitan Area Network)   A network, larger than an LAN, that provides high-speed services within a metropolitan area.

Manchester coding   A data transmission code in which data and clock signals are combined to form a self-synchronizing data stream in which each represented bit contains a transition at the midpoint of the bit period. The direction of transition determines whether the bit is a 0 or a 1.

Market cap(italization)   The current market value of all outstanding shares a company has. It is calculated by multiplying the total number of outstanding shares by the current share price.

Material dispersion   A dispersion effect caused by the fact that different wavelengths of light travel at different speeds through a medium.

MDF (Main Distribution Frame)   The large iron structure that provides physical support for cable pairs in a central office between the switch and the incoming and outgoing cables.

Message switching   An older technique that sends entire messages from point to point instead of breaking a message into packets.

Metasignaling virtual channel (MSVC)   In ATM, a signaling channel that is always on. Used for the establishment of temporary signaling channels as well as channels for voice and data transport.

Metropolitan Optical Network (MON)   An all-optical network deployed in a metro region.

Microbend   Changes in the physical structure of an optical fiber, caused by bending, which can result in light leakage from the fiber.

Midspan Meet   In SONET and SDH, the term used to describe interoperability. See also *interoperability*.

Modal dispersion   See *multimode dispersion*.

Mode   A single wave that propagates down a fiber. Multimode fiber allows multiple modes to travel, whereas single mode fiber allows only a single mode to be transmitted.

Modem   A term derived from the words *modulate* and *demodulate*. Its job is to make a computer appear to the network like a telephone.

Modulation   the process of changing or *modulating* a carrier wave to cause it to carry information.

MPEG (Moving Picture Experts Group)   A standards body tasked with crafting standards for motion pictures.

MPLS   A level 3 protocol designed to provide quality of service across IP networks without the need for ATM by assigning QoS "labels" to packets as they enter the network.

MTSO (Mobile Telephone Switching Office)   A central office with special responsibilities for handling cellular services and the interface between cellular users and the wireline network.

Multidwelling unit (MDU)   A building that houses multiple residence customers, such as an apartment building.

Multimode dispersion   Sometimes referred to as modal dispersion; caused by the fact that different modes take different amounts of time to move from the ingress point to the egress point of a fiber, resulting in modal spreading.

Multimode fiber   Fiber that has a core diameter of 62.5 microns or greater, wide enough to allow multiple modes of light to be transmitted simultaneously down the fiber.

Multiplexer   A device that has the ability to combine multiple inputs into a single output as a way to reduce the requirement for additional transmission facilities.

Multiprotocol over ATM (MPOA)   In ATM, a service that allows IP packets to be routed across an ATM network.

Multitenant unit (MTU)   A building that houses multiple enterprise customers, such as a high-rise office building.

Mutual inductance   The tendency of a change in the current of one coil to affect the current and voltage in a second coil. When voltage is produced because of a change in current in a coupled coil, the effect is mutual inductance. The voltage always opposes the change in the magnetic field produced by the coupled coil.

N

Near-end crosstalk (NEXT)   The problem that occurs when an optical signal is reflected back toward the input port from one or more output ports. This problem sometimes is referred to as isolation directivity.

Net income   A term for bottom-line profit.

Network Attached Storage (NAS)   An architecture in which a server accesses storage media via a LAN connection. The storage media are connected to another server.

Noise   An unpredictable impairment in networks. It cannot be anticipated; it can only be corrected after the fact.

Non-Dispersion Shifted Fiber (NDSF)   Fiber that is designed to operate at the low-dispersion second operational window (1310 nm).

Non-Zero Dispersion-Shifted Fiber (NZDSF)   A form of single mode fiber that is designed to operate just outside the 1550-nm window so that fiber nonlinearities, particularly FWM, are minimized.

Numerical aperture (NA)   A measure of the ability of a fiber to gather light; also a measure of the maximum angle at which a light source can be from the center axis of a fiber in order to collect light.

O

OAM&P (Operations, Administration, Maintenance, and Provisioning)   The four key areas in modern network management systems. The term was coined by the Bell System and is still in widespread use.

OC-n (Optical Carrier Level n)   A measure of bandwidth used in SONET systems. OC-1 is 51.84 Mbps; OC-n is n times 51.84 Mbps.

Operating expenses (OPEX)   Expenses that must be accounted for in the year in which they are incurred.

Optical amplifier   A device that amplifies an optical signal without first converting it to an electrical signal.

Optical burst switching (OBS)   A technique that uses a "one-way reservation" technique so that a burst of user data, such as a cluster of IP packets, can be sent without the need to establish a dedicated path before transmission. A control packet is sent first to reserve the wavelength, followed by the traffic burst. As a result, OBS avoids the protracted end-to-end setup delay and also improves the utilization of optical channels for variable-bit-rate services.

Optical Carrier Level n (OC-n)   In SONET, the transmission level at which an optical system is operating.

Optical isolator A device used to block specific wavelengths of light selectively.

Optical time domain reflectometer (OTDR) A device used to detect failures in an optical span by measuring the amount of light reflected back from the air-glass interface at the failure point.

OSS (Operations support system) Another term for OAM&P.

Outside plant Telephone equipment that is outside the central office.

Overhead The part of a transmission stream that the network uses to manage and direct the payload to its destination.

P

Packet A variable-size entity normally carried inside a frame or cell.

Packet switching The technique for transmitting packets across a wide area network.

Path overhead In SONET and SDH, that part of the overhead that is specific to the payload being transported.

Payload In SONET and SDH, the user data that is being transported.

Payload type identifier (PTI) In ATM, a cell header field that is used to identify network congestion and cell type. The first bit indicates whether the cell was generated by the user or by the network, and the second indicates the presence or absence of congestion in user-generated cells or flow-related operations, administration, and maintenance information in cells generated by the network. The third bit is used for service-specific, higher-layer functions in the user-to-network direction, such as to indicate that a cell is the last in a series of cells. From the network to the user, the third bit is used with the second bit to indicate whether the OA&M information refers to segment or end-to-end-related information flow.

PBX (Private Branch Exchange) A small telephone switch on a customerpremise. The PBX connects back to the service provider's central office via a collection of high-speed trunks.

PCM (Pulse Code Modulation) The encoding scheme used in North America for digitizing voice.

Phase modulation The process of causing an electromagnetic wave to carry information by changing or modulating the phase of the wave.

Photodetector   A device used to detect an incoming optical signal and convert it to an electrical output.

Photodiode   A semiconductor that converts light to electricity.

Photon   The fundamental unit of light; sometimes referred to as a quantum of electromagnetic energy.

Photonic   The optical equivalent of the term electronic.

Pipelining   The process of having multiple unacknowledged outstanding messages in a circuit between two communicating devices.

Pixel   A combination of the words picture and element. The tiny color elements that make up the screen on a computer monitor.

Planar waveguide   A waveguide fabricated from a flat material such as a sheet of glass into which are etched fine lines used to conduct optical signals.

Plenum   The air-handling space in buildings found inside walls, under floors, and above ceilings. The plenum spaces often are used as conduits for optical cables.

Plenum cable   Cable that passes fire-retardant tests so that it can be used legally in plenum installations.

Plesiochronous   In timing systems, a term that means "almost synchronized." It refers to the fact that in SONET and SDH systems, payload components frequently derive from different sources and therefore may have slightly different phase characteristics.

Pointer   In SONET and SDH, a field that is used to indicate the beginning of the transported payload.

Polarization   The process of modifying the direction of the magnetic field within a light wave.

Polarization mode dispersion (PMD)   The problem that occurs when light waves with different polarization planes in the same fiber travel at different velocities down the fiber.

Preform   The cylindrical mass of highly pure fused silica from which optical fiber is drawn during the manufacturing process. In the industry, the preform sometimes is referred to as a gob.

Private line   A dedicated point-to-point circuit.

Protocol   A set of rules that facilitates communications.

Proximity-coupling smart card   A card that is designed to be readable at a distance of approximately 4 to 10 inches from the reader. These devices often are used for sporting events and other large public gatherings that require access control across a large population of attendees.

Pulse spreading The widening or spreading out of an optical signal that occurs over distance in a fiber.

Pump laser The laser that provides the energy used to excite the dopant in an optical amplifier.

PVC (Permanent Virtual Circuit) A circuit provisioned in frame relay or ATM that does not change without service order activity by the service provider.

 Q

Q.931 The set of standards that define signaling packets in ISDN networks.

Quantize The process of assigning numeric values to the digitized samples created as part of the voice digitization process.

Quick ratio Calculated by dividing the sum of cash, short-term investments, and accounts receivable for a specific period by the current liabilities for that period. Measures the degree of a firm's liquidity.

Quiet zone The area on either side of the Universal Product Code (UPC) that has no printing.

R

RAM (Random-Access Memory) The volatile memory used in computers for short-term storage.

Rayleigh scattering A scattering effect that occurs in optical fiber as a result of fluctuations in silica density or chemical composition. Metal ions in the fiber often cause Rayleigh scattering.

RBOC Regional Bell Operating Company; today called an ILEC.

Refraction The change in direction that occurs in a light wave as it passes from one medium into another. The most common example is the "bending" that often is seen when a stick is inserted into water.

Refractive index A measure of the speed at which light travels through a medium; usually expressed as a ratio to the speed of the same light in a vacuum.

Regenerative repeater A device that reconstructs and regenerates a transmitted signal that has been weakened over distance.

Regenerator A device that recreates a degraded digital signal before transmitting it on to its final destination.

Remote terminal (RT) In loop carrier systems, the multiplexer located in the field. It communicates with the central office terminal (COT).

Repeater See *regenerator*.

Resilient packet ring (RPR) A ring architecture that includes multiple nodes that share access to a bidirectional ring. Nodes send data across the ring by using a specific MAC protocol created for RPR. The goal of the RPR topology is to interconnect multiple nodes ring architecture that is media-independent for efficiency purposes.

Retained earnings Represents the money a company has earned minus any dividends it has paid out. Does not necessarily equate to cash; more often than not it reflects the amount of money the corporation has reinvested in itself rather than paid out to shareholders as stock dividends.

Return on investment (ROI) The ratio of a company's profits to the amount of capital that has been invested in it. Measures the financial benefit of a particular business activity relative to the costs of engaging in that activity. The profits used in the calculation of ROI can be calculated before or after taxes and depreciation and can be defined either as the first year's profit or as the weighted average profit during the lifetime of the entire project. Invested capital, in contrast, typically is defined as the capital expenditure required for the project's first year of existence. Some companies may include maintenance or recurring costs as part of the invested capital figure, such as software updates. Because there are no hard and fast rules about the absolute meanings of profits and invested capital, using ROI as a comparison of companies can be risky because of the danger of comparing apples to tractors, as it were. Be sure that comparative ROI calculations use the same bases for comparison.

ROM (Read-Only Memory) Memory that cannot be erased; often used to store critical files or boot instructions.

S

Scattering   The "backsplash" or reflection of an optical signal that occurs when it is reflected by small inclusions or particles in the fiber.

SDH (Synchronous Digital Hierarchy)   The European equivalent of SONET.

Section Overhead (SOH)   In SONET systems, the overhead that is used to manage the network regions that occur between repeaters.

Sector   A quadrant on a disk drive to which data can be written. Used for locating information on the drive.

Securities and Exchange Commission (SEC)   The government agency responsible for regulation of the securities industry.

Selective retransmit   An error correction technique in which only the errored frames are retransmitted.

Self-phase modulation (SPM)   The refractive index of glass is directly related to the power of the transmitted signal. As the power fluctuates, so too does the index of refraction, causing waveform distortion.

Shareholder equity   Claims that shareholders have against a corporation's assets.

Sheath   One of the layers of protective coating in an optical fiber cable.

Signaling   The techniques used to set up, maintain, and tear down a call.

Signaling Virtual Channel (SVC)   In ATM, a temporary signaling channel used to establish paths for the transport of user traffic.

Simplex   One-way transmission only.

Single mode fiber (SMF)   The most popular form of fiber today; characterized by the fact that it allows only a single mode of light to propagate down the fiber.

Slotted ALOHA   A variation on ALOHA in which stations transmit at predetermined times to ensure maximum throughput and minimal numbers of collisions.

Soliton   A unique waveform that takes advantage of nonlinearities in the fiber medium; as a result, a signal suffers essentially no dispersion effects over long distances. Soliton transmission is an area of significant study at the moment because of the promise it holds for long-haul transmission systems.

SONET (Synchronous Optical Network) A multiplexing standard that begins at DS3 and provides standards-based multiplexing up to gigabit speeds. It is widely used in telephone company long-haul transmission systems, it was one of the first widely deployed optical transmission systems.

Source The emitter of light in an optical transmission system.

Spatial Reuse Protocol (SRP) A Layer Two protocol developed by Cisco for use in Resilient Packet Ring (RPR) architectures.

SS7 (Signaling System Seven) The current standard for telephony signaling worldwide.

Standards The published rules that govern an industry's activities.

Statement of cash flows Illustrates the manner in which a firm generated cash flows (the sources of funds) and the manner in which it employed them to support ongoing business operations.

Steganography A cryptographic technique in which encrypted information is embedded in the pixel patterns of graphical images. The technique is being examined as a way to enforce digital watermarking and digital signature capabilities.

Step index fiber Fiber that exhibits a continuous refractive index in the core that then "steps" at the core-cladding interface.

Stimulated Brillouin Scattering (SBS) A fiber nonlinearity that occurs when a light signal traveling down a fiber interacts with acoustic vibrations in the glass matrix (sometimes called photon-phonon interaction), causing light to be scattered or reflected back toward the source.

Stimulated Raman Scattering (SRS) A fiber nonlinearity that occurs when power from short-wavelength, high-power channels is bled into longer-wavelength, lower-power channels.

Storage area network (SAN) A dedicated storage network that provides access to stored content. In an SAN, multiple servers may have access to the same servers.

Store and forward The transmission technique in which data is transmitted to a switch, stored there, examined for errors, examined for address information, and forwarded to the final destination.

Strength member The strand within an optical cable that is used to provide tensile strength to the overall assembly. The member usually is composed of steel, fiberglass, or Aramid yarn.

Supply chain The process by which products move intelligently from the manufacturer to the end user, assigned through a variety of functional entities along the way.

Supply chain management The management methodologies involved in the supply chain management process.

Surface emitting diode A semiconductor that emits light from its surface, resulting in a low-power, broad-spectrum emission.

SVC A frame relay or ATM technique in which a customer can establish on-demand circuits as required.

Synchronous A term that means that both communicating devices derive their synchronization signal from the same source.

Synchronous Transmission Signal Level 1 (STS-1) In SONET systems, the lowest transmission level in the hierarchy; the electrical equivalent of OC.

T

T1 The 1.544-Mbps transmission standard in North America.

T-3 In the North American Digital Hierarchy, a 44.736-Mbps signal.

Tandem A switch that serves as an interface between other switches and typically does not host customers directly.

TDMA (Time Division Multiple Access) A digital technique for cellular access in which customers share access to a frequency on a round-robin, time division basis.

Telecommunications The science of transmitting sound over distance.

Terminal multiplexer In SONET and SDH systems, a device used to distribute payload to or receive payload from user devices at the end of an optical span.

Tight buffer cable An optical cable in which the fibers are tightly bound by the surrounding material.

Time-division multiplexing The process of assigning time slots to specific users.

Token ring An LAN technique, originally developed by IBM, that uses token passing to control access to the shared infrastructure.

Total internal reflection The phenomenon that occurs when light strikes a surface at such an angle that all the light is reflected back into the transporting medium. In optical fiber, it is achieved by keeping the light source and the fiber core oriented along the same axis so that the light that enters the core is reflected back into the core at the core-cladding interface.

Transceiver   A device that incorporates a transmitter and a receiver in the same housing, reducing the need for rack space.

Transponder   A device that incorporates a transmitter, a receiver, and a multiplexer on a single chassis. A device that receives and transmits radio signals at a predetermined frequency range. After receiving a signal, the transponder rebroadcasts it at a different frequency. Transponders are used in satellite communications and in location (RFID), identification, and navigation systems. In the case of RFID, the transponder is the tag that is affixed to the product.

Treasury stock   Stock that was sold to the public and later repurchased by the company on the open market. It is shown on the balance sheet as a negative number that reflects the cost of the repurchase of the shares rather than the actual market value of the shares. Treasury stock can be retired or resold later to improve earnings-per-share numbers if desired.

Twisted pair   The wire used to interconnect customers to the telephone network.

U

UPS (Uninterruptible Power Supply)   Part of the central office power plant that prevents power outages.

V

Venture capital (VC)   Money used to finance new companies or projects, especially those with high earning potential. Those companies often are characterized as being high-risk ventures.

Vertical cavity surface emitting laser (VCSEL)   A small, highly efficient laser that emits light vertically from the surface of the wafer on which it is made.

Vicinity-coupling smart card A card designed to operate at a read range of up to three or four feet.

Virtual Channel (VC) In ATM, a unidirectional channel between two communicating devices.

Virtual Channel Identifier (VCI) In ATM, the field that identifies a virtual channel.

Virtual Container In SDH, the technique used to transport subrate payloads.

Virtual Path (VP) In ATM, a combination of unidirectional virtual channels that make up a bidirectional channel.

Virtual Path Identifier (VPI) In ATM, the field that identifies a virtual path.

Virtual private network A network connection that provides privatelike services over a public network.

Virtual Tributary (VT) In SONET, the technique used to transport subrate payloads.

Voiceband The 300- to 3300-Hz band used for the transmission of voice traffic.

Voice/Telephony over ATM (VTOA) In ATM, a service used to transport telephony signals across an ATM network.

W

WAN (Wide Area Network) A network that provides connectivity over a large geographic area.

Waveguide A medium that is designed to conduct light within itself over a significant distance, such as optical fiber.

Waveguide dispersion A form of chromatic dispersion that occurs when some of the light traveling in the core escapes into the cladding, traveling there at a speed different from that of the light in the core.

Wavelength The distance between the same points on two consecutive waves in a chain, for example, from the peak of wave 1 to the peak of wave 2. Wavelength is related to frequency by the equation $\lambda = c/f$ where lambda (λ) is the wavelength, c is the speed of light, and f is the frequency of the transmitted signal.

Wavelength division multiplexing (WDM) The process of transmitting multiple wavelengths of light down a fiber.

Window A region within which optical signals are transmitted at specific wavelengths to take advantage of propagation characteristic that occur there, such as minimum loss and dispersion.

Window size A measure of the number of messages that can be outstanding at any time between two communicating entities.

X, Y, Z

Zero dispersion wavelength The wavelength at which material and waveguide dispersion cancel each other.

IMS-Related Standards and Specifications

3GPP IMS specifications can be downloaded from http://www.3gpp.org/specs/numbering.htm.

TS 21.905	Vocabulary for 3GPP Specifications
TS 22.066	Support of Mobile Number Portability (MNP); Stage 1
TS 22.101	Service Aspects; Service Principles
TS 22.141	Presence Service; Stage 1
TS 22.228	Service requirements for the IP multimedia core network subsystem; Stage 1
TS 22.250	IMS Group Management; Stage 1
TS 22.340	IMS Messaging; Stage 1
TS 22.800	IMS Subscription and access scenarios
TS 23.002	Network Architecture
TS 23.003	Numbering, Addressing and Identification
TS 23.008	Organization of Subscriber Data
TS 23.107	Quality of Service (QoS) principles
TS 23.125	Overall high-level functionality and architecture impacts of flow-based charging; Stage 2
TS 23.141	Presence Service; Architecture and Functional Description; Stage 2
TS 23.207	End-to-end QoS concept and architecture
TS 23.218	IMS session handling; IM call model; Stage 2
TS 23.221	Architectural Requirements
TS 23.228	IMS stage 2
TS 23.229	WLAN interworking
TS 23.271	Location Services (LCS); Functional description; Stage 2
TS 23.278	Customized Applications for Mobile network Enhanced Logic (CAMEL)–IMS interworking; Stage 2
TS 23.864	Commonality and interoperability between IMS core networks
TS 23.867	IMS emergency sessions
TS 23.917	Dynamic policy control enhancements for end-to-end QoS, feasibility study
TS 23.979	3GPP enablers for Push-to-Talk over Cellular (PoC) services; Stage 2

TR 23.981   Interworking aspects and migration scenarios for IPv4-based IMS implementations (early IMS)

TS 24.141   Presence Service using the IMS Core Network subsystem; Stage 3

TS 24.147   Conferencing using the IMS Core Network subsystem

TS 24.228   Signaling flows for the IMS call control based on SIP and SDP; Stage 3

TS 24.229   IMS call control protocol based on SIP and SDP; Stage 3

TS 24.247   Messaging using the IMS Core Network subsystem; Stage 3

TS 26.235   Packet-switched conversational multimedia applications; Default codes

TS 26.236   Packet-switched conversational multimedia applications; Transport protocols

TS 29.162   Interworking between the IMS and IP networks

TS 29.163   Interworking between the IMS and Circuit Switched (CS) networks

TS 29.198   Open Service Architecture (OSA)

TS 29.207   Policy control over Go interface

TS 29.208   End-to-end QoS signaling flows

TS 29.209   Policy control over Gq interface

TS 29.228   IMS Cx and Dx interfaces: signaling flows and message contents

TS 29.229   IMS Cx and Dx interfaces based on the Diameter protocol; Protocol details

TS 29.278   CAMEL Application Part (CAP) specification for IMS

TS 29.328   IMS Sh interface: signaling flows and message content

TS 29.329   IMS Sh interface based on the Diameter protocol; Protocol details

TS 29.962   Signaling interworking between the 3GPP SIP profile and non-3GPP SIP usage

TS 31.103   Characteristics of the IMS Identity Module (ISIM) application

TS 32.240   Telecommunications management; Charging management; Charging architecture and principles

TS 32.260   Telecommunications management; Charging management; IMS charging

TS 32.421   Telecommunications management; Subscriber and equipment trace: Trace concepts and requirements

TS 33.102   3G security; Security architecture

TS 33.108   3G security; Handover interface for Lawful Interception (LI)

TS 33.141   Presence service; security

TS 33.203   3G security; Access security for IP-based services

TS 33.210   3G security; Network Domain Security (NDS); IP network layer security

IETF Specifications

RFC 1889   Real-Time Transport Protocol (RTP)

RFC 2327   Session Description Protocol (SDP)

RFC 2748   Common Open Policy Server protocol (COPS)

RFC 2782   A DNS RR for specifying the location of services (SRV)

RFC 2806   URLs for telephone calls (TEL)

RFC 2915   The naming authority pointer DNS resource record (NAPTR)

RFC 2916   E.164 number and DNS

RFC 3261   Session Initiation Protocol (SIP)

RFC 3262   Reliability of provisional responses (PRACK)

RFC 3263   Locating SIP servers

RFC 3264   An offer/answer model with the Session Description Protocol

RFC 3310   HTTP Digest Authentication using Authentication and Key Agreement

RFC 3311   Update method

RFC 3312   Integration of resource management and SIP

RFC 3319   DHCPv6 options for SIP servers

RFC 3320   Signaling compression (SIGCOMP)

RFC 3323   A privacy mechanism for SIP

RFC 3324   Short-term requirements for network asserted identity

RFC 3325   Private extensions to SIP for asserted identity within trusted networks

RFC 3326   The reason header field

RFC 3327   Extension header field for registering nonadjacent contacts (path header)

RFC 3329   Security mechanism agreement

RFC 3455   Private header extensions for SIP

RFC 3485   SIP and SDP static dictionary for signaling compression

RFC 3574   Transition Scenarios for 3GPP Networks

RFC 3588   DIAMETER base protocol

RFC 3589   DIAMETER command codes for 3GPP release 5 (informational)

RFC 3608   Extension header field for service route discovery during registration

RFC 3680   SIP event package for registrations

RFC 3824   Using E164 numbers with SIP

▉ Information Resources

Telecom Resources

Telephony Magazine Online
http://www.telephonyonline.com

Telecom Daily Lead (daily insights from USTA)
http://www.dailylead.com/usta/

Today in Telecom

http://www.igigroup.com/news.html
Network World
http://www.subscribenw.com/nl2

Internet Telephony E-News
http://www.tmcnet.com/enews

Optical Resources

Light Reading (Optical Industry)
www.lightreading.com

Financial Resources

The Motley Fool (Investing Insights)
www.fool.com/community/freemail/

Forbes Online
www.forbes.com/membership/signup.jhtml

General Industry

McKinsey Quarterly
Subscribe to McKinsey Quarterly

CyberAtlas (online statistics)
www.cyberatlas.internet.com/

The Economist Online
www.economist.com/members/registration.cfm

Wainhouse Research Bulletin (videoconferencing industry)
www.wainhouse.com/bulletin

Information Week
www.informationweeksubscriptions.com

E-Marketer Newsletter
www.emarketer.com/news/newsletter.php

Darwin Observer
www2.darwinmag.com/connect/newsletters.cfm

CRM and Knowledge Management
www.crm-forum.com

Wireless Resources

CTIA News
www.wow-com.com/news/

Computer Industry Resources

ComputerWorld Magazine
www.cwrld.com/nl/sub.asp

Asia-Pac Resources

Telecom Asia
www.emarketer.com/news/newsletter.php

Asia Telecomm Newsletter
www.export.gov/infotech

CALA Resources

Latin America Telecom Newsletter
www.telecom.ita.doc.gov

EMEA Resources

EuroNet Newsletter
Subscribe to EuroNet

■ INDEX ■ ■ ■ ■

Note: Boldface numbers indicate illustrations; italic *t* indicates a table.

...nedia Subsystem (IMS) is a powerful, emerging technology that will
...vay we live, work, and communicate. Through convergence of fixed
...networks, IMS delivers seamless roaming to multimedia devices
...f location or access modality. This much-needed resource gives you
...nderstand overview of the development, evolving standards, and
...minent future of IMS.

...ur Understanding of IMS

...renowned professional author and educator with 25 years of
...the telecommunications industry, *IMS Crash Course* gives you a
...ective on why IMS evolved, how the technology works, its system
..., and potential regulatory issues—all in one convenient package.
...king to make sense of this breakthrough technology, its benefits,
...world implementations, read this book first.

Full coverage of IMS, including

- An early history of IMS
- Converging wireless and wireline
- Network, software, and signaling requirements
- IMS regulatory issues
- IMS's future

...E AUTHOR

...ard is the president of the Shepard Communications Group. He is the author of more than
...uding *Telecommunications Convergence*, *Telecom Crash Course*, and *VoIP Crash Course*.
...the Series Advisor for the McGraw-Hill Portable Consultant series.

...w·Hill *Companies*

...ill Education at:
...graw-hill.com

...hy Landi

...ng/
...cations

$39.95 U.S.A.
£21.99 UK
$51.95 CAN

ISBN 0-07-226306-7

5 3 9 9 5

9 780072 263060